ROCK OF THE MARNE

ALSO BY STEPHEN L. HARRIS

100 Golden Olympians

*Duty, Honor, Privilege: New York's Silk Stocking Regiment
and the Breaking of the Hindenburg Line*

*Harlem's Hell Fighters:
The African-American 369th Infantry in World War I*

*Duffy's War: Fr. Francis Duffy, Wild Bill Donovan
and the Irish Fighting 69th in World War I*

ROCK OF THE MARNE

THE AMERICAN SOLDIERS WHO TURNED THE TIDE · AGAINST THE KAISER IN WORLD WAR I ·

STEPHEN L. HARRIS

BERKLEY CALIBER, NEW YORK

BERKLEY
CALIBER

An imprint of Penguin Random House LLC
375 Hudson Street, New York, New York 10014

This book is an original publication of Penguin Random House LLC.

Library of Congress Cataloging-in-Publication Data
Harris, Stephen L.
Rock of the Marne : the American soldiers who turned the tide against the
Kaiser in World War I / Stephen L. Harris. — First edition.
p. cm.
Includes bibliographical references and index.
ISBN 978-0-425-27556-6 (alk. paper)
1. Marne, 2nd Battle of the, France, 1918.   2. United States. Army.
Infantry Division, 3rd—HistoryWorld War, 1914–1918.   3. World War,
1914–1918—Regimental histories—United States.   I. Title.
D545.M35H37 2015
940.4'34—dc23
2015012222

First edition: October 2015

PRINTED IN THE UNITED STATES OF AMERICA

10 9 8 7 6 5 4 3 2 1

Interior text design by Laura K. Corless.
Map on page 66 courtesy of United States Army in the World War, 1917–1919. Center for
Military History, Vol. 5. Maps on pages 98 and 137 courtesy of the National Archives
and Records Administration, Modern Military Records Branch.

Penguin
Random
House

To Sue once again, my soul mate since high school.

INTRODUCTION

The First World War (1914–1918) was the war that changed the world.

Empires were lost, monarchies overthrown, borders altered and new countries and new governments came into being. Horrific weapons of mass destruction were used for the first time—heavy artillery that fired from miles away, flattening towns and villages and even reaching into the heart of Paris; airplanes that dropped bombs from the sky; and poisonous gases that soaked the battlefield. Ten million people lost their lives. Millions more were hurt, either physically or mentally, soldiers and civilians alike. It was so ghastly it became known as the war to end all wars. And by the time it was over the United States had become a world power.

The cause of the war is still debated, but the assassination on June 28, 1914, of the heir to the Austria-Hungarian Empire, Archduke Franz Ferdinand, by Serb terrorists in Sarajevo, led to its start. His murder upset the balance of power between two groups—the Triple Alliance of Germany, Austria-Hungary and Italy, later known as the Central Powers, and the Triple Entente of France, Russia and Great Britain, later the Allies. Relying on German support, Austria declared war on Serbia. In response, Russia mobilized against Austria, causing Germany to declare war on Russia and two days later to declare war on France. Then, attacking on two fronts, the Germans checked the Russians on the Eastern Front and, in an effort to reach Paris, swung through neutral Belgium on the Western Front. Because the Germans had invaded Belgium, Great Britain declared war on Germany. This declaration drew Canada, Australia, New Zealand and India into the conflict. Italy tried to remain neutral but eventually sided with the Allies. Meanwhile, the crumbling Ottoman Empire joined forces with Germany and Austria-Hungary. Other nations also joined the fight, opening multiple fronts—including the Balkans, Egypt, Palestine and Arabia and even Persia. The United States, however, stayed out of the war.

On the Western Front, after the First Battle of the Marne, where the French stopped the Germans from reaching Paris, the war bogged down into trench warfare. Victories were measured in yards captured. The number of casualties was gruesome. The battles became legend: Belleau Wood, Château-Thierry, Caporetto, Gallipoli, Verdun, Vimy Ridge, the Somme, Passchendaele, Soissons, the Meuse-Argonne, the storming of the Hindenburg Line and, the turning point of the war and the subject of this book, the Second Battle of the Marne.

At sea, Great Britain strung a naval blockade around German ports. Germany responded with unrestricted submarine warfare. Its U-boats torpedoed merchant ships and then on May 7, 1915, without warning, sank the British luxury liner *Lusitania*. Among the 1,198 passengers and crew lost were 128 Americans. Reaction in the United States became so hostile against Germany that unlimited submarine warfare stopped.

The year 1917 finally brought the United States into the war. Germany not only resumed unrestricted submarine attacks, sinking more American ships, but also in secret negotiations tried to provoke Mexico into invading the United States if Mexico's neighbors to the north entered the war against the Central Powers. For the United States it was the last straw. On April 6, it went to war against Germany.

At the time, America was totally unprepared. It had a regular army of 127,588 soldiers and 76,713 National Guardsmen. When General John J. Pershing was put in command of the American Expeditionary Forces, he called for an army of over one million men. Building up that army, training it and then getting it to France in time to play a major role in the war was an extraordinary feat. It took almost a year before the United States had sufficient troops on the ground in Europe and elsewhere to make a difference in the outcome of the war.

In the spring of 1918 it made its presence known to the Germans at Cantigny, Soissons and Belleau Wood, and then, on July 15, Americans, fighting alongside the French, hurled back German armies attacking across the Marne River and in the Champagne region. With the Germans stopped, Ferdinand Foch, the supreme Allied commander, ordered a masterful counteroffensive that eventually drove the enemy back to the Hindenburg Line. There the Allies succeeded in storming the line.

On the eleventh hour of the eleventh day of the eleventh month, Germany capitulated and an armistice was signed. World War I was over.

WORLD WAR I TIMELINE

1914

June 28. Heir to the Austria-Hungarian Empire, Archduke Franz Ferdinand, assassinated in Sarajevo.

July 28. Austria-Hungarian Empire declares war on Serbia.

July 31. Russia, an ally of Serbia, mobilizes its military.

August 1. Germany declares war on Russia.

August 3. Germany declares war on France.

August 4. Germany declares war on neutral Belgium and invades the tiny country in a right-flanking move designed to defeat France. Because of the invasion, Great Britain declares war on Germany.

August 22. Battle of the Frontiers. In an offensive move near the German border France loses 27,000 men.

August 26–30. Battle of Tannenberg. On the Eastern Front the German army, led by Erich Ludendorff and Paul von Hindenburg, defeat the Russians.

September 5–10. First Battle of the Marne. French soldiers stop the Germans from reaching Paris.

1915

February 4. German submarines blockade Great Britain, warning that any ship on course toward England is a target.

April 25. The Allies open a failed nine-month campaign on the Gallipoli Peninsula, resulting in 200,000 men killed or wounded.

May 7. German U-boat sinks the *Lusitania*. 1,198 passengers, including 128 Americans, drown.

August 20. As anger grows in America, Germany halts unrestricted warfare against merchant ships.

December 19. General Sir Douglas Haig takes command of the British Expeditionary Force.

1916

February 21–December 18. Battle of Verdun. The longest battle of the war results in nearly one million casualties.

April 9. The Canadians win the Battle of Vimy Ridge.

May 31–June 1. Battle of Jutland. The navies of Great Britain and Germany fight to a draw in the war's only major engagement at sea.

July 1–November 18. Battle of the Somme. The British offensive against the Germans fails to make a breakthrough. Casualties reach more than one million.

November 7. Woodrow Wilson reelected president with the slogan "He kept us out of the war."

December 7. David Lloyd George is new prime minister of England.

1917

January 19. British uncover and translate German Foreign Secretary Arthur Zimmermann's telegram urging Mexico to invade the United States.

February 1. Germany resumes unrestricted submarine warfare.

March 15. Russian tsar Nicholas II abdicates.

April 6. The United States declares war on Germany.

April 16–29. Battle of Chemin des Dames. France makes little gain against the Germans, 250,000 casualties.

April 29–May 20. More than half-a-million French soldiers mutiny.

May 10. General John J. Pershing takes command of the American Expeditionary Forces.

May 18. The United States passes the Selective Service Act to draft able-bodied men for the armed services.

July 3. The first American soldiers land in France to a rousing welcome.

July 31–September 10. Third Battle of Ypres, also known as Passchendaele. Again no Allied breakthrough as the dead and wounded on both sides tally 700,000 men.

October 23. U.S. troops in combat for the first time.

November 7. Led by Lenin, the Bolsheviks overthrow the Russian government.

December 3. Russia's new government signs an armistice agreement with Germany.

1918

January 8. President Wilson sets forth his Fourteen Points for world peace.

March 21. The Somme Offensive, the first of five German offensives planned by Ludendorff before the Americans become a factor in the war, is launched against the British on a sixty-mile front.

April 3. Ferdinand Foch is named supreme Allied commander.

April 9. The Lys Offensive begins against the British, this time in Flanders.

April 12. General Haig galvanizes his armies by ordering them to fight "with their backs against the wall."

May 27. The Aisne Offensive, Ludendorff's third of the year, led by his First and Seventh Armies, crushes the French Sixth Army at Chemin des Dames.

May 28–29. Battle of Cantigny. General Pershing rushes his Second and Third divisions north to reinforce the French. The Second Division captures the village of Cantigny against veteran German forces, boosting the Allies' morale.

May 30–June 17. Battles of Belleau Wood and Château-Thierry. A U.S. Marine brigade attached to the Second Division and reinforced with elements of the Third Division stops the Germans at Belleau Wood while the Third's Seventh Machine Gun Battalion halts the enemy at Château-Thierry.

June 9–13. The Noyon-Montdidier Offensive, Ludendorff's fourth of the year, is stymied by the French under General Henri Pétain.

July 15. Ludendorff's fifth offensive, named *Friedensturm* ("Peace Assault"), opens in the Marne-Champagne sectors.

July 15–17. Second Battle of the Marne, the turning point of the Great War, is fought with Americans playing a key role.

July 16–17. The Bolsheviks murder Tsar Nicholas II and his family.

July 18. Field Marshal Foch opens French counteroffensive that starts to drive the German armies back toward the Hindenburg Line.

August 8. Allied counteroffensive on the Somme pushes the Germans into retreat.

September 26–November 11. The Meuse-Argonne offensive, including the storming of the Hindenburg Line, brings an end to the war.

November 11. At the eleventh hour on the eleventh day of the eleventh month the Allies and Germany sign an armistice agreement and after four years and thirty-seven million casualties peace comes to the Western Front.

1919

May 7–June 28. Treaty of Versailles.

PROLOGUE

//

"WE'RE HERE FOR BUSINESS"

On the morning of May 29, 1918, an urgent memorandum from General John J. Pershing's American Expeditionary Forces headquarters at Chaumont, France, carried an ominous warning to the Third U.S. Infantry Division, then in training nearby at Châteauvillain and its suburbs. "The 3d Division has been ordered to hold all units now in the divisional area in readiness to move this afternoon or tonight by motor truck or train to the north for the purpose of furnishing bridge guards for the bridge across the MARNE."

No destination was mentioned, but it was soon learned it was Château-Thierry, which had so far escaped much of the carnage of the First World War. The French there were in dire trouble as the Germans launched their fourth offensive of the year, termed "Operation Blücher," with the goal to defeat the British Expeditionary Force by forcing the French to move their reserves to the south, thus weakening the British army in Flanders and giving the Germans a tremendous advantage in manpower.

On May 27, a day after the start of Operation Blücher, one of the worst disasters struck the Allies. The French Sixth Army, under command of an arrogantly incompetent General Denis Duchêne, had blundered on the heights overlooking the Ailette River at Chemin des Dames. Ignoring orders from General Henri Pétain, his superior, to employ a defense in depth, known also as an elastic defense, against the German First and Seventh Armies, he bunched up seven divisions, three of them British, on the front line like sardines in a can. It left him no rear reserves and no chance to counterattack. The Germans hit Duchêne with a terrible artillery bombardment until his army was no more. According to supreme Allied commander Ferdinand Foch, the soldiers had simply "melted away as fast as they were flung into battle." Quickly taking advantage of Duchêne's blunder, the Germans drove his battered survivors back across the Aisne River for twelve miles and opened up a twenty-five-mile-wide breach in the Allied line. Three days later, the German Seventh Army reached the Marne River at Château-Thierry—Germany's deepest penetration into France since the start of the war. The German advance had extended the battle zone to the Marne, forming the "Marne Pocket"—an enormous triangular-shaped salient that was delineated by Château-Thierry as its apex and the city of Soissons to the northwest and the city of Rheims to the northeast. Each side of this triangular salient measured more than forty miles. The strategic military importance of Soissons and Rheims were their two key rail junctures; for a German army stretched too thin, capturing the railways in the Marne Pocket was a top priority. It would enable the rapid shifting of Germany's forces to critical areas.

After the battle of Chemin des Dames, the triumphant men of the German Fifth Grenadier Guards boasted to a captured lieutenant colonel of a beaten French infantry regiment, "Tomorrow we shall march to Paris." The proud lieutenant colonel, remembering the First Battle of the Marne, shot back, "No sir. To Paris? Never! Think of 1914! The Marne!" First Lieutenant Kurt Hesse of the Fifth Grenadiers, a regiment of picked storm troopers, remembered the officer's grave and dignified reply. "We respected his pride and—had a moment of reflection. Then, however, joy over the glorious success of the day prevailed. The Marne had been reached . . . from Chemin des Dames, across the Aisne and the Vesle, to the legendary stream. Scarcely any losses. The enemy, on the contrary, had suffered most serious damage. 'Let us advance on Paris!'"

Across the river, General Pétain wondered if his "feeble French units," as Foch now described them, could hold the Marne.

"No doubt," recalled Foch, "the [German] high command intended to open up the road to Paris at all costs."

The French capital was a tempting forty miles away.

In fact, the French government was preparing to flee to Bordeaux. A rumor reached the German high command that, according to a Seventh Army intelligence report, "large banks are sending all their valuable papers to cities in the west of France. Many people are leaving Paris with their belongings. The Paris, Orleans and Lyons railroad station [*sic*] decline to accept any more freight for transportation."

Foch immediately met with Pétain. They anxiously went over the dire situation facing the Allies. Foch made it clear that it was most crucial that the "enemy's advance on Paris must be stopped . . . especially in the region north of the Marne," even if it meant a "foot-by-foot defense of the territory." Orders, he said, must be drawn up "prescribing exactly what the troops must do, and see that these orders are strictly carried out by removing any commanding officer who shows signs of weakness."

North of the Marne, a confident General Erich Ludendorff— Germany's military mastermind since 1916—strongly believed another offensive offered a great opportunity to end the war. At a secret conference with Germany's imperial chancellor Georg von Hertling and field marshal Paul von Hindenburg, they agreed "our first step is to strike with all our might once more," and then the "depressed" Allies would certainly sue for peace. Hertling believed that by the first of September the Allies would be sending peace proposals to the German government.

No wonder Ludendorff named his next offensive *Friedensturm* ("Peace Assault").

After the disastrous battle of Chemin des Dames, a shaken French General Jean Marie Joseph Degoutte, who in a few weeks would be counted on by Foch to stop the Germans at the Marne River east of Château-Thierry, leaned over a table covered with a tattered map showing the enemy's threatening advances on the Western Front. He began to weep. Like many on the Allied side, Degoutte, soon to replace the disgraced Duchêne as commander of the demoralized French Sixth Army, had to wonder if, in fact, the Boche could ever be stopped. After all, back on December 15, 1917, Germany's armistice with Russia had freed up nearly fifty divisions for the Western Front. Now the enemy held a commanding numerical advantage over the Allies. There just weren't enough French and British troops to stem the tide, and the battle-worn veterans that were available had almost no strength left to go up one more time against the superior German army.

The Allies needed bodies! The fifty-two-year-old Degoutte knew it. Foch and Pétain knew it. And so did the British high command. To bolster his razor-thin ranks, Degoutte used soldiers from Africa—the Moroccans and the Senegalese. But what about the Americans? When it came to needed manpower, Degoutte had to wonder about them, as did almost every desperate French, Belgian and English citizen. More than a year had passed since the United States had declared war on Germany, and still, except for one division, the Americans seemed not ready to fight. Would they be ready before France had to sue for peace? A British soldier, watching from shore the ship carrying the Third Division into the great port of Le Havre, summed up the feelings of the Allies when he yelled up at the Americans leaning against the ship's railing. "Hit's 'igh time you fellas wuz gitten 'ere!" The rebuke stung the soldiers. Then one of them shot back in a Yankee drawl, "Say, if you guys over here had only amounted to somethin' on your job, we wouldn'ta had to come!"

The rejoinder set the officers from the Sixth Brigade howling with laughter. Mused the commander of the brigade, Brigadier General

Charles Crawford, "The heart of Europe had spoken to America and the heart of America had replied."

But the Germans were betting that the Americans were arriving too late and that their inexperience would make them easy prey when they reached the front lines. After striking quickly at the Rheims salient thirty-five miles east of Château-Thierry, followed by another strike on about August 1 against the British to the west in Flanders, code-named Operation Hagen, where they'd threaten the six main Channel ports, including Dunkirk, the Boche planned to turn toward Paris and end the war before the United States became a factor.

Although the number of U.S. soldiers on the Western Front was increasing by ten thousand a day, the AEF commander was not going to let them fill the gaps in the Allies' line willy-nilly—soldiers here, soldiers there. General Pershing's goal was to build his own army and have it fight under its own flag. That took time. Maybe by late fall his army would be ready, certainly by the spring of 1919.

After the Chemin des Dames debacle, he sent a sobering cable to Secretary of War Newton Baker. "The attitude of the Supreme War Council, which has been in session since Saturday, is one of depression. The prime ministers and General Foch appeal most urgently for trained or even untrained men. . . . It should be most fully realized at home that the time has come for us to take up the brunt of the war and that France and England are not going to be able to keep their armies at present strength very much longer."

As Pershing saw it, the time was soon coming when the Americans would be called upon to win the war. Thus, he would only allow fully manned and trained divisions to be attached to the French and English, and temporarily. He had offered that deal to the Allies in March, but for some reason they hadn't taken him up on it. Now, with the German armies preparing to cross the Marne at Château-Thierry, it was time to hold Pershing to that offer. General Pétain pleaded for at least two divisions to be sent north. The enemy had to be stopped at the river. Once across, Paris was in peril. With the government about to flee the capital,

Pershing knew that "at this moment the morale of the Allies required that American troops make their appearance in battle." Only two of his divisions were near enough to the Germans—the Second and Third.

Because the Third Division, at Châteauvillain, was closest to Château-Thierry, Pershing ordered it to leave at once for the Marne.

For the stout, bespectacled sixty-year-old commander of the Third Division, Major General Joseph T. Dickman, an ex–cavalry officer who spoke French, German and Spanish fluently, organizing and moving more than twenty-five thousand men by train or other means of transportation at a moment's notice was no easy task. It would take at least a day or two to locate enough trains at nearby rail yards and round up enough motor trucks and load them with troops and supplies and, as he put it, "all the paraphernalia of the panoply of war." The best the 1881 graduate of West Point could do in such a short time was to send his Seventh Motorized Machine Gun Battalion along with some troops from the Fourth Infantry on ahead. At the time, the machine-gun battalion was the AEF's only motorized battalion on the Western Front. He knew his decision meant that 24 officers and 353 of his men would have to make a stand against the entire German Seventh Army poised on the outskirts of Château-Thierry.

"The progress of events now became rapid," Dickman wrote. "The French were driven from the Chemin des Dames, and the Germans were headed for Paris. The 3d Division was destined for a quiet sector north of Toul, in conformity with the practice of giving the divisions some trench experience. My preliminary reconnaissance with a view of relieving the 26th Division took place at Boucq on May 28; but recall came by telephone and our destination was changed."

At 10:30 a.m. on May 30, Decoration Day, Dickman sent out his first field order of the war. To Major Edward G. Taylor, he wrote, "7th Machine Gun Battalion will proceed at once by road to CONDE-en-Brie." The rest of the division and artillery, and all but one detachment of the Sixth Engineers, would follow in a day or two.

The Third Division, barely three months in France and with hardly any training, even back at Camp Greene, North Carolina, where the brutal winter of 1917–1918 had curtailed much of its instruction, was off to the front. Of all the American divisions in France, the Third was least likely ready for combat. Warned a French staff officer, "They have had absolutely no front line experience and should therefore be used with judgment."

At 2:55 that afternoon, four hours after Major Taylor had received Dickman's field order, the convoy of the Seventh Machine Gun Battalion pulled out of Laferté-sur-Aube near Châteauvillain for its 110-mile journey to Condé-en-Brie, a small village on the confluence of the Surmelin and Dhuys Rivers. The convoy was comprised of seventeen squads, nine in A Company and eight in B Company, forty-eight half-ton Model T Ford motor trucks (each one overloaded by five hundred pounds), six other trucks, five touring cars (all built in England with steering wheels on the right side) and twenty-four Indian motorcycles (several equipped with sidecars). None of the machine gunners had seen or even driven any of the vehicles until May 24—six days before their departure. The battalion had to be canvassed for experienced drivers. Others had to be trained in a hurry.

If that wasn't worrisome enough, the equipment to be carried included thirty-two air-cooled French M1914 Hotchkiss machine guns, which the men had only started to learn how to operate four weeks earlier. Enough ammunition had to be found to keep the Germans at bay until the rest of the division arrived at Château-Thierry. Also, crammed aboard each truck were five-gallon cans of gasoline, supplies and rations for three days, and each soldier's backpack, some carrying personal belongings.

"By the dint of perseverance, by May 30th the train could be formed, started and stopped with occasional collisions," wrote B Company commander Captain John R. Mendenhall from Indiana, a West Pointer, as had been his father and grandfather before him. A fellow captain of Mendenhall's described him as a man with a "fine sense of humanity and sweetness" and a "brilliant young officer."

The route took the machine gunners, led by motorcycle patrols reconnoitering and marking the way, northeast along the Aube River, then past Mer-sur-Seine and the villages of Anglure, Sézanne, Montmort and Orbays, still untouched by the war. Homes were neat and trim. Flowers were in full bloom, strawberries there for the picking and orchards filled with apples. Wheat grew in the fields alongside the road, ready to be harvested. It looked as if that part of the world was at peace.

At first the convoy's speed was kept at twenty miles per hour, which turned out to be too fast. Many of the trucks could not keep up. Because of the overloading, springs squashed atop axles, tires blew out, and then the convoy began to separate, opening mile-long gaps between the vehicles. A slower pace of twelve miles per hour was agreed on. The steep hills were the worst. In some cases, the men had to climb out of their trucks and walk to the top of the hills, oftentimes pushing their vehicles.

"Delays were frequent," Captain Mendenhall remembered. "Motorcycles proved invaluable in guiding and carrying spare parts to broken-down trucks."

Lieutenant Paul T. Funkhouser from Evansville, Indiana, a twenty-three-year-old lawyer yet to practice his trade, led the way aboard his motorcycle. He kept riding back and forth to let the drivers know where to go, and then dashing off to the head of the column. Another motorcyclist was Private C. L. Stewart, who stayed in the saddle for twenty-four straight hours, even after he had suffered shrapnel wounds in the neck, back and both legs as the battalion closed in on Château-Thierry.

It was 9 p.m. by the time the convoy neared Sézanne. It had traveled almost one hundred miles in seven hours. Here it refueled, vehicles that needed it were overhauled, and the men took a well-deserved rest. Condé-en-Brie was not too far up the road. With any luck they'd be there by morning.

After the break, the journey started up again. Although it was the dead of night, no lights were allowed. Traveling became harder. The convoy again got stretched out. At daybreak, it began to run into thousands of refugees fleeing from the towns along the Marne. They came trudging toward the Americans, most of them with tears streaking their faces, carrying everything of value they could take with them. Oxen pulled hay wagons piled high with furniture, bedding, birdcages and chicken coops. Children walked next to their mothers, clutching their skirts. Men and women without animals to be hitched to their carts had strapped themselves in harnesses and now struggled mightily to pull their load along the dusty road. The stream of refugees was endless. The road was jammed with them, slowing the convoy to even more of a crawl.

Looking down from his truck, First Lieutenant Luther W. Cobbey from Cleveland, Ohio, saw "French women and old men leading cows and sheep; some with a few belongings loaded on one-horse wagons. Some pushing hand carts and moving in every conceivable way. Some carried bundles on their backs. These refugees took up most of the road. It was very hard for us to get our Company past."

Recalled Mendenhall, "The expressions on the faces of the refugees were most pitiful and we began for the first time to realize something of the real meaning of war."

He remembered, too, how they still managed to "smile and wave encouragement to 'les Américains,' who alone were moving north against the current of fear and depression."

Mixed in with the refugees were retreating French and British soldiers, thoroughly demoralized and discouraged. Behind them came horse-drawn artillery. Up on the hills beside the road, light artillery batteries were being set up and the French fired at the unseen enemy somewhere up ahead. As the convoy drove on, the Americans heard the distant roar of incoming artillery.

At half-past noon on May 31, after being on the road for twenty-two hours with no sleep and covering 110 miles, the convoy entered Condé-en-Brie with radiators steaming and gasoline low. The village was under artillery attack. Amid the shelling, Major Taylor met with a French colonel who ordered his battalion to continue on to Château-Thierry and report to General Jean-Baptiste Marchand, commander of the 10th Colonial Division. Once again, the convoy was on the move, heading toward the Marne. As the shelling continued, the men loaded their machine guns—just in case.

But where was Château-Thierry? Since leaving Condé-en-Brie, Taylor and his men had been driving for more than three hours. On their journey, they had been lost several times and they didn't want to get lost again now that they were so close to the fighting. Still driving past the endless stream of refugees, Taylor and his officers were surprised to see several American war correspondents in the company of the retreating soldiers. The reporters were equally surprised to see American soldiers.

An officer hollered to them, "Where's Château-Thierry?"

"Just up ahead," one of the reporters answered. "Are you here for pleasure or for fighting?"

"We're here for business!"

One hour later, the exhausted men of the Seventh Machine Gun Battalion finally reached their destination. It was 3:30 in the afternoon.

Château-Thierry, a small city of gray-stone buildings and red-tiled roofs, straddles the Marne. As the river cuts through Château-Thierry, a canal paralleling it forms a big city island of crisscrossing streets of shops, restaurants, residences and a park. The largest portion of the city is on the north side, where the French and Germans were now fighting street-to-street, house-to-house. A bluff dominates the north side, with an ancient, fortified castle built in 720 by Charles Martel, considered one of France's greatest heroes and the grandfather of Charlemagne. From the top of the castle, the Germans had a sweeping command of the entire city and surrounding countryside. When the Germans first reached the outskirts of Château-Thierry, Lieutenant Kurt Hesse thought the "ground before us looked like a paradise. The sun shone brightly, and a cool breeze was blowing through the valley. This was a different atmosphere—not war, but peace." A park guarded by two towers led up to the ancient castle.

Dominating the south side of Château-Thierry, which was level ground, was an extensive system of rail yards. The tracks of the Paris-Metz railroad passed through this area. Two bridges crossed the Marne and a third crossed the canal. There were no other bridges for five miles in either direction, making Château-Thierry the key location for crossing the river. The bridges over the Marne were named for their location: West Bridge, East Bridge. On the north bank, the West Bridge exited into a large square. Beyond the square stood the park and then the bluff and ancient castle. The East Bridge, on the right, was about four hundred yards distant, near a police station and sugar refinery. On the other side of the bridge, from east to west, ran a river road with green, waist-high wheat fields between it and the river. Where it flowed past Château-Thierry, the Marne was about fifty feet wide and too deep to ford. To stop the Germans from overrunning the city, the bridges had to be defended.

One mile south of Château-Thierry at a cantonment in the village of Nesles, two of Major Taylor's company commanders, Mendenhall and Captain Charles Houghton, reported to General Marchand, a legendary French officer, while the rest of the strung-out convoy arrived in bits and pieces. A dashing figure with a resplendent beard, the fifty-four-year-old Marchand had fought in Africa in the 1880s, had been part of the conquest of Senegal and had stayed on to explore sources of the Niger and Nile Rivers. In Africa, he had faced down the great British soldier, Lord Kitchener in a territorial dispute in eastern Africa, almost starting a war with England. The general explained that he was in total command of the defense of Château-Thierry and directed Mendenhall and Houghton to bring up their guns immediately, "to occupy positions on the south bank of the Marne, to cover the approaches to the bridges and to protect the withdrawal of the French to the south shore, after which these bridges, now being mined, would be destroyed."

At 6 p.m., the convoy "rushed" into Château-Thierry, wrote Lieutenant Cobbey, "going under shell fire for the first time." When it reached Rue Carnot, the city's main street that ran straight as an arrow toward the West Bridge, the Americans grabbed their Hotchkiss machine guns, ammunition strips and rations, everything but their backpacks, and leaped from the trucks. Rifle fire crackled in the distance as the Germans forced the French back across the Marne. Joining a contingent of Senegalese soldiers from Marchand's 10th Colonial Division, the men of the Seventh Machine Gun Battalion dashed to their assigned positions in the besieged city as artillery shells fell around them, blowing holes in buildings and littering the streets with rubble and, in time, wounding fourteen Americans.

Taylor had divided Château-Thierry into two sectors. A Company, Houghton commanding, was assigned the West Bridge sector, where it took up positions in houses, yards and a warehouse along the riverbank and at both ends of the island. Mendenhall's B Company had charge of the East Bridge sector. One platoon of fourteen men and two machine guns from A Company, led by First Lieutenant John Ter Bush Bissell, a Pittsburgh native and 1917 graduate of West Point, and Sergeant Harley Phillips, crossed the West Bridge to the north side of the river to cover the withdrawal of a French Senegalese unit as ordered by Marchand. Bissell, who had a quiet demeanor, had studied at Hamilton College before entering West Point. He came from an old New York Dutch family on his mother's side. A great-great-uncle had graduated from West Point in 1821 and had been killed in action at Monterrey during the Mexican War. Another uncle lost his life at the Battle of Cold Harbor in the Civil War. As Bissell's team ran over the bridge and set up one machine gun by a tower near the entrance to the park, it received only scattered gunfire from snipers. The other machine gun was held in reserve until a better spot was found where it could be used with deadly force. If attacked, Bissell was to fight a delaying action, pass information to the rest of the battalion over on the south bank as to what was happening and, if forced, fall back across the river.

Six other machine-gun squads were posted along the south bank, at the edge of the island and to the right of the West Bridge.

B Company covered the East Bridge to protect the battalion's flank in case the Germans tried to cross there. Cobbey moved two machine-gun squads into a two-story brick house at the edge of the river. He placed one gun by a first-floor window, covering the bridge, manned by thirty-year-old Sergeant Ezra M. Muse, a cashier and paymaster at Richland Mills back in his hometown of West Columbia, South Carolina. The second gun Cobbey put into a shed attached to the house.

Lieutenant Charles Montgomery slipped into a sunken garden south of the bridge and set up his guns. Funkhouser, commanding three machine guns, positioned them in a wooded peninsula east of the bridge on the Crézancy Road. The other machine-gun squads were holed up in the sugar refinery.

The remainder of the battalion stayed in reserve at Rue Carnot, up the street about a quarter of a mile from the West Bridge.

"Orders were issued to remain concealed and fire only on orders of the officer," recalled Mendenhall. Night fell, utterly dark, and the Seventh Machine Gun Battalion, now without sleep for almost forty-eight hours and without enough food to quiet growling stomachs, waited for the dawn.

On June 1, the first light of morning came at 3:44. A mist covered the river, nearly obscuring a battalion of Germans marching in a column west along the river road toward the East Bridge. Their spirits had to be soaring. To the northwest, the Germans were about to drive the French into Belleau Wood and to the west move into the village of Vaux. Next they planned to capture Hill 204. Château-Thierry would then be completely cut off. As they marched along, the Germans were unaware that they were in danger. When they were five hundred yards away, the Americans fired on them. The surprised soldiers broke and ran, taking shelter in the wheat fields.

"They were screened from view, but not from fire," noted Mendenhall.

The Germans, in short leaps and bounds, worked their way toward the East Bridge. Because of their positions, Cobbey and Funkhouser and their squads were the only machine gunners in the entire battalion that could stop them.

"The Dutchmen made nine attempts to effect a crossing," Cobbey reported. "They would come up and be driven back by the machine gun fire from the four guns that Paul and I had. We accounted for a good many Dutchmen during this attack."

But the German firepower increased, including an artillery bombardment that eventually killed First Lieutenant Thomas W. Goddard, the first officer in the Third Division to lose his life in battle, and three enlisted men, while they were unloading ammunition. Gas bombs hit the Americans. Command posts were driven into cellars where wet-blanket partitions were strung up to avoid the use of gas masks. The intense shellfire worked the machine gunners "into a high state of nervous tension," wrote Mendenhall. "This was evidenced by sharp commands, impatience bordering on intolerance and an inability to grasp new situations quickly." And for some reason, Major Taylor failed to command.

Meanwhile, as Lieutenant Bissell and his platoon on the north bank of the river were aiding the withdrawal of French troops, word reached Taylor that the German Seventh Army, impatient to get across the Marne, planned a major attack on Château-Thierry. Artillery fire increased and heavy-caliber cannons were used for the first time. Americans and French on the south bank regrouped. All reserve weapons were brought up to the river and the men were placed in new positions.

Under heavy artillery fire and with buildings aflame, the main German force massed in front of the mined West Bridge, packing the square and the streets leading into it. On the bridge itself, French and Germans were locked in frightful hand-to-hand combat. On the south bank, the men of A Company had to hold their fire until the bridge was cleared of French soldiers. But General Marchand could not wait for his men to get safely over the bridge. He had it blown up. "With a deafening explosion," wrote Mendenhall, "the bridge flew into the air, carrying both French and Germans with it." Hundreds of soldiers who were not killed by the explosion drowned.

The moment the bridge was destroyed, the Americans fired into the jammed square. "The Germans . . . waiting to rush the bridge instead melted into the dark," Mendenhall recounted, "leaving many mute witnesses to American marksmanship."

Not realizing the bridge was gone, other Germans kept charging into the square, only to get mowed down. "Twice again the Germans massed in the square, their higher commanders either not realizing that the bridge was gone or believing that it could still be crossed on the wreckage. Each time by the light of burning buildings they dispersed with great losses."

To General Marchand, the blowing up of the bridge was the turning point in the defense of Château-Thierry. "At the moment when the Germans arrived on the large bridge and believed themselves to be in possession of the same, a terrific explosion destroyed the entire central portion and threw into space some Boche corpses. The American machine guns held the south bank. They formed a protection for the withdrawal of the troops retiring from the northern section. The courage of the Americans was beyond all praise."

At nine-thirty in the evening and with his wires cut, Mendenhall sent runners with oral messages to his platoon commanders in the East Bridge sector, ordering them to move where they could cover his company's right flank. His messages were misinterpreted. Believing he had called for a withdrawal along the riverbanks, the platoons pulled back.

The runner reaching Cobbey told the lieutenant to "retreat with all possible speed; that the Germans had crossed the river and were on our side." Cobbey followed the instructions "given which were nothing less than to 'beat it.'" He pulled his platoon back several kilometers outside of Château-Thierry and took a position on a hill that overlooked the Marne. Here he found Funkhouser with his platoon. They put their guns into position and awaited the German attack. With the river in their sector left unguarded, Cobbey and Funkhouser knew the Germans had a great opportunity to cross the Marne and take Château-Thierry. But luck was on their side. By 1 a.m. the Germans had yet to take advantage of the American withdrawal.

Funkhouser looked at Cobbey. "Don't you think we had better go back into Château-Thierry and find out whether the Germans are actually in the town?"

The two lieutenants and a runner then slipped back to the bridge and discovered that no Germans had crossed. They went straight to the battalion command post to find out why they'd been ordered to retreat. Cobbey was stunned to find Taylor so disengaged with the battle. "The major denied any knowledge of our retreat, and showed no interest in the matter," Cobbey later wrote. "He didn't seem to give a darn what we had done or might do." Taylor's superior officer, Lieutenant Colonel Fred L. Davidson, in a special operations report sent to General Dickman two weeks later, noted that there "seems to have been a lack of positive orders issued by the battalion commander, the companies being left too much to their own initiative." Taylor's adjutant, First Lieutenant Erskine J. Hoover, according to Davidson, was "obliged, in many instances, to personally issue orders in the name of the battalion commander in order to get action of some sort." Afterward, Taylor was removed from command, never to be seen again. Major Roland F. Walsh replaced him.

Acting on their own, Cobbey and Funkhouser brought their platoons back into town and repositioned their machine guns, protecting the East Bridge sector.

It wasn't long before the Germans charged the bridge.

From inside the sugar refinery, the machine gunners cut them down. Several times the Germans rushed the bridge and each time they were repulsed. They got close enough so that the Americans not manning machine guns shot them dead with pistols. Harold E. Marble from Brockton, Massachusetts, was stunned when their French machine guns got so hot they had to cease firing until the weapons cooled down. "I was never so scared for a while in my life," he confessed years later. "I'll admit it, but soon I got used to watching those smoking, overheated guns turn from a vivid red to a dull, ashy gray."

In Funkhouser's new position he stopped a German attempt to cross the river on a pontoon bridge. "By machine fire he chased some of the Dutchmen away who were half dressed and who had stripped in order to get into the river to place the bridge," Cobbey commented. "The attempt to cross the river stopped about seven o'clock that evening."

Stranded on the north bank were Bissell, his men and a number of French soldiers. In the inferno of flames, machine-gun bullets ripping into bodies and ricocheting off buildings and zinging across cobblestone streets, with Bissell leading them, they fought their way east, trying to get to the other bridge that was protected by Cobbey's two machine-gun squads. If they couldn't cross the bridge, then they'd have to swim for it.

Cobbey, peering into the night, spotted men trying to cross the East Bridge. It was too black to make out who they were. Behind the men he heard the rattle of machine guns. Thinking they were Germans, he had his men open fire.

Over the noise someone called out, "Cease fire!"

Fearing it might be an enemy ruse, Cobbey did not want to take a chance and stop firing. He told his men to keep shooting while in the darkness he slipped away to the edge of the bridge. He yelled across to determine who was there. He discovered to his surprise that it was Bissell and the remnants of his platoon and many Frenchmen ready to swim the river. He hurried back to his squad, picked out a few men and took them back across the bridge. They carried Bissell's wounded and dead to the south bank of the Marne.

"Going back to the guns we were able to open up fire in time to stop a crossing by the Germans who had been pressing Lieut. Bissell from the north side," recalled Cobbey. "Their attempt lasted an hour."

Mendenhall later wrote, "Lieutenant Cobbey unhesitatingly crossed the bridge in the face of the enemy fire, found Lieutenant Bissell with his men preparing to swim the river and dissuading them led them back over the bridge to safety. This act of heroism was characteristic of all our men."

Bissell brought some bad news with him. A French officer north of the Marne had told him that two enemy divisions had crossed the river and annihilated A Company. If true, that put Cobbey's B Company in extreme danger. Mendenhall ordered B Company to withdraw, almost leaving the East Bridge unguarded. In the house by the bridge, Sergeant Muse remained at his post by the window. He refused to leave because he had a clear view of the bridge and could stop any Germans trying to cross. As he wrote later to his father, "Don't worry for I am tough and can stand it if anyone can." Mendenhall then reported to Major Taylor, who informed him that Bissell's report was "erroneous." The Germans had not crossed the West Bridge because it had been blown up. He ordered Mendenhall to get his men back to the river and to take up their old positions.

The battle continued into the next day. The men still had no sleep, or at best caught only naps when they could. Their support came from the Colonials, Senegalese sharpshooters the Americans found strangely fascinating. "These men scarcely removed from their savage state . . . have remarkable eyesight," described Mendenhall. "With faces scarred in fantastic patterns and polished ivory ornaments in their ears and noses, they took keen delight in exhibiting strings of shriveled brown human ears from their German victims and worn on a string around their necks." They were an uncomfortable crew to have around, he admitted, "for one was never sure just what they intended to do."

Robert Dinsmore from Gulfport, Mississippi, temporarily attached to the machine gunners as an interpreter, wrote to his hometown newspaper, maybe with some embellishment, "Well, I'm a southerner and always will be, but I stood side by side with these black Senegalese French negroes and laughed when they cut the Germans' heads off with their sugar cane knives."

The machine gunners out in the open had to find cover under railroad cars whenever German airplanes flew over, directing its artillery where to drop their shells.

Try as they might, the Germans could not breach the American's stout defense, supported by the Colonials. Two of the heroes were privates from New Jersey, James Punco and Charles Gallagher. When the French were unable to shore up a breach in the defense because they were getting killed, Punco, saying it "don't look good to me," scooped up the tools and with bullets flying past him, rushed to the break. Gallagher followed him. They repaired the wire entanglements. Punco received a wound in the leg and Gallagher was shot six times. Both men survived, but Punco later had his leg amputated. The French gave him the *Médaille Militaire* and Gallagher the *Croix de Guerre*.

In the early morning of June 4, the East Bridge was finally blown up. For remaining at his post, Sergeant Muse received the American Distinguished Service Cross. A few hours before the explosion, one company from Third Division's Ninth Machine Gun Battalion and two French machine gun companies arrived at Château-Thierry. They then relieved the Seventh Machine Gun Battalion, which had been in a constant battle since May 31.

Wrote Mendenhall, "The relief, late in arriving, was barely completed by dawn. There had been no let-down in the fireworks and some guns, too hot to dismount, were left behind. Finally, in Liberty three-ton trucks instead of Fords, the battalion rumbled past the southern edge of the city, made a dash down the dangerous Rue Carnot and, in short order reached the woods of Nesles. Just as we entered the woods we heard a dull detonation to the north. The east bridge had been destroyed. The Marne was barred!"

When the machine gun battalion had returned to their trucks they found to their dismay that the Senegalese had looted their backpacks; they'd been cleaned out by the very French Colonials they'd put their lives in jeopardy to help. And adding more insult to the Americans, later while they paraded by Marchand their entire dinners were stolen.

In his special operations report to Dickman, Lieutenant Colonel Davidson, the division's top machine-gun officer, wrote, "It is believed that the 7th Machine Gun Battalion was to a great degree responsible for the final check of the late German drive." He did not mention the looted backpacks.

From his headquarters, General Marchand had high praise for the battalion, from the day it arrived to the day it was relieved. He penned, "Immediately the Americans reinforced the entire defense, especially at the approaches of the bridge. Their courage and skill as marksmen evoked the admiration of all.

"Crushed by our fire, the enemy hesitated and, as a result of counter attacks, vigorously supported by the American Machine Guns, they were thrown beyond the edges of the town.

"CHATEAU-THIERRY remained entirely in our hands."

He went on to proudly state, "The episode of CHATEAU-THIERRY will remain one of the very fine deeds of this war. It is a pleasure for all of us to certify that our valiant allies with us participated in this event—our bonds of affection and of confidences will be strengthened by the same pride which we share in common."

Although back in the United States, it wasn't the Seventh Machine Gun Battalion getting credit for its heroic stand, but the Marines. One major newspaper trumpeted, "With the help of God and a few Marines we stopped the Germans at Château-Thierry." Although it was at Belleau Wood where this action actually took place, northwest of Château-Thierry, and the Marines did it with the help of the Second Division as well as the Third Division's Seventh Infantry

N ow that the men of the Third Division had proven themselves to one French general, could they do it again to another before German military mastermind General Ludendorff could bring the Allies to their knees? This time the French general the Americans had to prove themselves to was none other than Jean Marie Joseph Degoutte of the newly refitted Sixth Army, one of the generals who Field Marshal Foch was counting on to stop the Germans and save Paris.

Could the doughboys of the Third Division do it once again?

CHAPTER 1

"THEY MAY KILL US, BUT THEY CANNOT WHIP US"

On the brisk morning of May 31, 1918, the nearly twenty-seven thousand troops of the Third U.S. Infantry Division, as inexperienced in the art of war as babes in the woods, rolled out of their training camps around Châteauvillain, on the Aujon River a dozen or so miles east of Chaumont, where General Pershing, able to play only a limited role in the coming battle, was fretting in his AEF headquarters about how his men would do in the coming days fighting under French flags and not Old Glory. If he'd heard a remark attributed to one of the division's soldiers from the 38th Infantry, he'd have felt better.

"We was never sent to no trenches to learn fightin'. No, siree, no dugout warfare for this little old outfit. They didn't have to bury us in a quiet sector in Alsace before turning us loose on the Boche. In May General Foch says to General Pershing, he says I need a classy regiment up on the Marne. So up we went."

The Americans had been attached to the 38th French Army Corps, commanded by a general with the impressive name of Jean Frédéric Lucien Piarron de Mondesir, but who simply went by Piarron de Mondesir.

The 38th Army Corps had been folded into Duchêne's Sixth Army, following its disaster at Chemin des Dames, and sent to take over a defensive position south of the Marne around Château-Thierry. Duchêne had not yet been replaced by General Degoutte. The green doughboys were to help stem the German advance across the Marne River between Château-Thierry and the Surmelin Valley to as far east as Varennes. Their orders the moment they reached the Marne were simple enough— defend the passages over the river. On May 31, the newly promoted corps commander, General de Mondesir, wrote under the heading "Distribution of Elements of the 3d Division": "The mission of the troops of the 38th Army Corps, namely: To defend the terrain with the utmost energy, no matter how great the violence of the enemy's effort."

Before Pershing's order sending the Third Division north to the Marne, it had been learning from the French how to use their Chauchat automatic rifles—cheaply made weapons that oftentimes jammed when fired—and the proper way to toss hand grenades. From the English, they learned how to handle the bayonet. Smirked an American lieutenant, the English believed only the bayonet would win the war. "Our own officers, however, continued to stress rifle marksmanship." The division had been marked for a three-week stay in a quiet sector north of Toul where it was to relieve the 26th U.S. Division and gain three weeks' experience in trench warfare. But then that destination was changed and the division was to go to another location on May 31, this time to the Vosges Mountains in eastern France, near the border with Germany. A day before it was to leave for the Vosges, the new, most urgent order, to embark for the Marne was issued.

For many of the division's soldiers, leaving the training area was a sad day because they had made friends with the French villagers, most of them women, old men or young children, some of the children orphaned by the war. A number of the officers, General Joseph Dickman included, when they weren't training, were having a grand time hunting wild boar in the forests around Châteauvillain, and dining on sumptuous hunt breakfasts at some farmhouse or hunting lodge.

Fitchburg, Massachusetts, native Private Andrew McCabe, from the 38th Infantry's B Company, liked his billets, except for the roosters. "Thirteen fellows besides myself are living in two large rooms and we have a large fireplace, a table, chairs and a real bunk," he informed his family. "You can believe me, you have to travel some here to get a better place than that and besides we have one fellow who can talk French and you can not imagine how convenient that is for us. There is no chance of getting extra fatigue for missing reveille as the roosters wake you up before the bugle call every morning."

He added, "I have seen very few persons but children, old men and women, but it seems that no one is too old to work and you see them doing all the farming and other work around."

In the Thirty-Eighth's K Company, Private Leroy D. Goodgion of Kingston, New York, described how the "people here seem to enjoy our presence and show their admiration by doing what they can. They are very courteous to us all, and in return for their good meaning we forward our courtesies the best we know how. Occasionally, we can understand a word or phrase when conversing, but generally avoid a conversation with the village belles, fearing we might accidentally use an improper phrase. Safety first!"

In a postscript, he wrote, "I think you may form a conclusion that I am on an excursion instead of serious affairs, namely 'Fighting to free democracy from the hated autocracy.'"

Leaving was especially difficult for George W. Ridout, a chaplain from the Young Men's Christian Association assigned to the 38th Infantry Regiment's Third Battalion. Ridout, a handsome man approaching fifty years of age with dark, graying hair, thick eyebrows and long eyelashes, was dubbed "Holy Joe" by the troops. A Methodist minister who before the war had been a professor of theology at Taylor University, an evangelical college in Upland, Indiana, Ridout urged his followers in the battalion to always carry a copy of the New Testament in their left breast pocket, over their heart, because he believed that the holy book would protect them from harm. In the small village of Montribourg, where he lived during the division's time of training, the residents there called him "Uncle George."

Nearly all the villagers came out to see the troops off. Many of the women were softly crying. An American captain thought that "our leaving had served to remind them of the days when their own boys had hastily been called away years before. They recalled their many sorrows of the war." The captain asked a French officer to find out why a certain women was crying. Her reply was, "It makes me sad to know that many of these American boys will soon have died for France."

There were only a few incidents that upset the civilians. One was the theft of some wine, another a rude officer, and the third was when the men bathed in a little stream near a château that had been turned into a hospital to care for wounded French soldiers. It was run by a handful of Englishwomen who had to look out at the Americans frolicking in the water like otters.

In the village, Ridout had befriended a five-year-old girl, Louise, whose father had been killed in the war. "She was very shy and at first would not come near a soldier," Ridout remembered, "but eventually I won her over and she would come to me and we would take walks in the flower-bedecked fields, and those two months I was in that little village little Louise helped me greatly to overcome homesickness. That little child seemed to feed my hungry heart."

Louise was Catholic, as were most of the villagers. At night when she said the rosary she prayed for "Uncle George."

"The day we marched out of that little village was a memorable one in more sense than one," he wrote in his memoirs. "The village people hated to see us go; they said 'au revoir' to us with tears in their eyes, and the children cried too. . . . My little Louise clung to my neck and kissed me through her tears. We said 'au revoir' and departed and went from that little village where peace and quiet and contentment reigned, to be ushered upon another scene within a few days where the air was filled with booming guns, where war in reality was being waged, where there was hurry and confusion and congestion and the voices of the Captains giving orders, the whirling of the heavy wheels carrying supplies and guns and ammunition to the front."

Dickman later recalled in his memoirs, "It is certain that we left behind us an enduring and favorable impression of the young American soldier from beyond the seas." To his brother, Clem, he wrote on August 15, 1918, "You can set it down that the American solider is the best in Europe and that when it comes to the essential elements of discipline, such as respect for property and regards for women and children, sanitation and hygiene, he discounts any European troops I have seen. The French people are very glad to have the American soldiers occupy their premises, for they then feel safe and know that their property, what is left of it, will be cared for."

Now the division, minus the Sixth Engineers and its Third Field Artillery Brigade, comprised of three regiments and trench mortar batteries, was on the way, headed north toward the crowded railhead at Montmiral, a key town ten miles from the Marne. The artillery brigade would not head out until almost a month later because it needed nearly one thousand horses to pull its guns, and rounding up that many horses took time. As it was, it was an odd caravan, if one could call it a caravan: quickly assembled troop trains, horse-drawn wagons, motorized trucks, motorcycles and, for the division's top brass, a fleet of green Cadillac Type 57 motorcars. The Cadillac was the vehicle chosen by the AEF as its official car because its endurance proved better than any other similar motorcar. General Motors sent more than two thousand Cadillacs to France for military use.

All parts of the caravan traveled at different times and at different speeds. The division's first units to board the lead train were the 38th Infantry's K Company and two companies of the Ninth Machine Gun Battalion. They boarded the train at midnight after spending an unusually cold evening in bivouac, shaking and shivering and trying to keep warm. When Corporal William G. Fitzgerald of Ballston Spa, in upstate New York, and his fellow men in the 30th Infantry marched seven miles to reach the train, it was during the day and the temperature had climbed.

"Many fell out, and also fainted from the heat," he put in his diary. Standing only five feet, five inches tall, Fitzgerald added, "Packs weighed 125 pounds. All our equipment was carried, besides ammunition and extra shoes." He'd had to leave his personal belongings with a Frenchwoman who lived in the house next to where he'd been billeted. The woman had befriended him, and when he had suffered from a sore throat when he first arrived at the training camp and couldn't eat, she had "heated me some milk and I drank it." His regiment rode in side-door Pullman cars.

O n the road, in the lead Cadillac, scrunched among gas masks, steel helmets, pistols and maps, sat the division commander, who in the months to come would earn the affectionate nickname among his men of "Daddy Dickman." He was almost sixty-one years old, and as he wrote to his wife, "My health is very good and I feel confident that I will be able to last until the end is over. There are very few officers of my age who are engaged in active campaigning."

A native of Dayton, Ohio, he was the son of a Civil War captain in the 58th Ohio Volunteer Infantry. The 58th saw action at Shiloh and the Siege of Vicksburg. After Dickman had graduated from West Point, he served on the western frontier, chasing Geronimo and, allied with Mexico's federal soldiers under the dictatorship of Porfirio Díaz and troops of Texas Rangers, helping put down a Mexican insurgency led by Catarino Garza and his bandits. He also fought in Cuba during the Spanish American War on the staff of General Joseph Wheeler, where he had been cited for gallantry, and then in 1900 during the Boxer Rebellion, as part of the Peking Relief Expedition and in the Battle of Pa-Ta-Chao. Dickman had been described by those who knew him well as aggressive, daring, positive, firm, modest and unassuming. An ex-Marine said the portly cavalryman had "a painter's eye for landscapes, a gourmet's taste for wines" and, when he got to the Marne and first walked the sector assigned to his division, "a soldier's eye for the ground."

Riding with him in the Cadillac was his chief of staff, Lieutenant

Colonel Raymond Sheldon and several other members of his staff. Sheldon was a native of Princeton, New Jersey, and a graduate of England's Oxford University. He had joined the army during the Spanish American War as a second lieutenant. He later went to the Philippines and then China. He was described as a "bright, active, well instructed soldier" and a "tireless worker, supervising every detail he could handle." By the end of June, however, he'd be replaced by the self-assured Colonel Robert H. C. Kelton from Pershing's own staff. Behind Dickman and Sheldon, in the other Cadillacs, came the division's brigade commanders and several of its regimental commanders, including the scholarly Brigadier General Charles Crawford of the Sixth Brigade. Crawford was raised on the plains of Kansas, and a West Point classmate described him as coming from "a vigorous Irish family that gave him an inheritance of a strong body, a keen and active mind, and courage for living life in the full measure of pioneer tradition."

When America broke off diplomatic relations with Germany on January 31, 1917, more than two months before it declared war, General Crawford, then a major and an 1889 graduate of West Point, had been stationed in the Panama Canal Zone with the 10th Infantry as inspector of troops guarding the canal's vital points. He constantly checked all the locks in case of sabotage. The fear was that German sailors—there were eight German commercial vessels in the canal at the time, with crews totaling more than 150 men—might slip out of the jungle at night and blow up the machinery that ran the locks. The Americans quickly commandeered the vessels and imprisoned all German citizens, as well as Germans who had settled in the Canal Zone years ago and had married native women. At the time Crawford felt the imprisonment was a rash step. A month after the United States declared war, the 10th Infantry was transferred from the Canal Zone to Fort Benjamin Harrison, outside of Indianapolis. The First Officers' Training Camp was organized, and Crawford's job was to determine which noncommissioned officers of his regiment should be given commissions as officers. He was soon promoted to colonel and sent to a camp at Gettysburg,

Pennsylvania, assigned to the 60th Infantry. When the War Department almost doubled the size of a U.S. regiment, the 60th then became part of the 7th Infantry, and Crawford moved on to Camp Greene, North Carolina, and was tapped to command and train the Third Division's Sixth Brigade. He'd already had experience training raw recruits. In New Mexico during the 1890s he had enlisted and organized a company of Apache scouts, and later was an instructor at the army's Infantry and Cavalry School at Fort Leavenworth, Kansas.

One of the things Crawford, who had been cited for his fearlessness under fire at the Battle of San Juan Hill during the Spanish American War, stressed during training at Camp Greene was the soldier's spirit. "The morale of a soldier," he reasoned, "depends on his confidence that he can kill his enemy when his foeman comes within range of his rifle and that the closer he gets the more sure he is of killing."

E ver since the division had been organized at Camp Greene, on November 23, 1917, Dickman had had plenty of time—almost a half year—to get to know his senior officers well, Crawford among them, their strengths and their weaknesses.

All except one, a Johnny-come-lately to his division who had already led a regiment in combat, who admitted that his blood was flowing a little faster as the division pushed northward toward the enemy, a soldier destined to carry the nom de guerre "Rock of the Marne."

Colonel Ulysses Grant McAlexander, commanding officer of the Sixth Brigade's 38th Infantry Regiment, riding on one of the trains with his troops, had been with the division barely two weeks. All the general knew about him was negative, that he'd been relieved as commander of the First Division's 18th Infantry Regiment for supposedly sleeping at his post in a combat zone. Before the charge, McAlexander's regiment was the first in the American Expeditionary Forces to plant the American flag on the front line. Even so, he was "branded . . . unfit for command of a front-line regiment." As punishment, he'd been sent to the rear for a desk job at the Port of St. Nazaire. Certainly a career-killing move for any infantry officer. But six months later Pershing gave him a reprieve and reassigned him to lead the 38th. Even so, Pershing's inspector general, Colonel André W. Brewster, a Medal of Honor recipient during the Boxer Rebellion, had told Dickman that although McAlexander was a fellow graduate of West Point, he needed to keep an eye on him because he was still "under a cloud."

The cantankerous McAlexander had chosen to ride on one of the trains with his troops as it rattled north toward Montmiral—and not in a Cadillac—because he wanted them to get to know their colonel. "My greatest concern," he once revealed, "was how the enlisted men felt. Did they have the implicit faith and confidence in their officers? Especially how did they feel towards their colonel, who, of necessity, must control their very existence."

While he rode north among his troops, he had two furies burning inside him. The first, which he kept to himself, was the "great injustice" done to him by the top officers of the First Division, as well as General Pershing, by declaring him unfit to command an infantry regiment when, in fact, he'd been in a forward position with his men on the front line. Uppermost in his mind was to carry out an old Scottish threat: "I'll fecht ye till I dee!" He figured the best way to do that, now that he had been given a second chance, was to mold the 38th into the best regiment on the Western Front and show them all "what asses they [had] made of themselves by sending me to the rear."

The second fury that burned in his heart was to avenge dozens of women and children killed during a German long-range artillery assault on Good Friday that had leveled a Parisian church. The parishioners were buried under heaps of stone and rubble. Among the dead were three prominent American women as well as three Americans from the family of Mary Grinnell, sister of former New York governor

Levi Morton. The shock was so great that Mrs. Grinnell died a few days later. In New York City, a solemn high mass in memory of the slain was held at St. Patrick's Cathedral and a memorial service took place at the Cathedral of St. John the Divine.

"I made those women and children mine," McAlexander bitterly declared. "My mother, my sister, my daughter, my children were being destroyed by mad savages! From that moment I devoted every energy, mental and physical, to devising ways and means of killing everything in a German uniform."

The writer Laurence Stallings, a Marine who would lose a leg at Belleau Wood, labeled him "a pugnacious colonel." John S. D. Eisenhower, the son of the President, later said that he was a "warrior in every sense" and "if he had a weakness as a commander it was his habit of exposing himself too rashly to enemy fire."

A native Minnesotan of Scottish descent, raised on a Kansas farm, and a West Pointer, Class of 1887, McAlexander, "Ulie" to family and friends, came from a clan that took pride in naming their kin after war heroes. His father, a first lieutenant in the Sixth Regiment Minnesota Infantry Volunteers during the Civil War, had been named Commodore Perry McAlexander. In choosing Ulysses Grant for his only son, he'd put pressure on him to live up to that name. McAlexander read everything about the Civil War. His heroes were Grant, of course, William Tecumseh Sherman and Philip Sheridan. Before he got into West Point, the young Ulysses went first to the University of Kansas in the fall of 1882. But the following spring a frightening smallpox epidemic had swept through the campus, and students, McAlexander one of them, fled Lawrence for the safety of their homes. When he arrived home, he found out that he'd been offered an appointment to West Point. That fall, when he showed up at the military academy, he was walking across the Plain in front of the superintendent's quarters when he noticed walking toward him a tall soldier with a short, grizzled beard and "the skin of his face looked like old sunburned rawhide." It turned out to be General Sherman, one of his heroes. "I wondered then how anyone could become so great." As it turned out, a monument to Colonel Sylvanus Thayer, the "Father of West Point," was being unveiled that day. General Grant was delivering the address. Afterward, McAlexander thought, "I had just seen two of my heroes." Four years later, at his graduation at West Point, McAlexander marched up to receive his diploma from his third hero, General Sheridan. Reading his name, Sheridan held the diploma for a moment and stated, "Ulysses Grant! Young man, I hope that you may add an additional luster to that glorious name!" He then handed the new lieutenant his diploma.

Now fifty-three years old, bald, bowlegged, sporting a thick but trim mustache and still a colonel, "Old Mac," as one of his officers called him, had fought in the Indian Wars, the Spanish American War, where he'd received the American Distinguished Service Cross for gallantry at San Juan Hill, and in the Philippines.

While out west, he was once nearly captured by a renegade band of Indians that had swept down from Canada into Montana in the summer of 1889, raided a Flathead reservation, swiping ponies, killing buffalo and some people, and then headed for the railroad station at Ravalli. A cavalry troop rode out of Fort Missoula to end the renegades' reign of terror. McAlexander was then a twenty-four-year-old second lieutenant. He was sent on a scouting mission to see if any Indians were roaming the countryside. He found none and returned to his unit, which had just pitched camp. With evening coming, he asked permission to go fishing for trout in a nearby stream. As he worked the stream, he moved a mile away from the encampment. Casting into a pool, he felt he was in danger. He saw one of the renegades one hundred yards away, mounted on a pony. He kept fishing as if he had not a care in the world. Another renegade appeared forty yards away. He continued to fish, casting his line into the stream when a third renegade eased his pony into the stream a few yards away from McAlexander. The renegades then circled around him. "Here I was in a predicament of my own making, resulting from my own stupidity. I, a graduate of the U.S. Military Academy, isolated from our troops, was reflecting no glory on West Point. I was simply a military ass." Instead of turning back toward the camp, he walked deliberately away from his own troops, into the underbrush, and then bolted for the railroad tracks with pistol in hand. The renegades did not follow, and a humbled McAlexander walked quickly back to camp with no trout to show for his harrowing experience.

West Point classmate Major General Mark L. Hersey, who commanded the Fourth Division during the war, called McAlexander "the stubbornest creature that ever drew the breath of life." At San Juan Hill, McAlexander, a hard man to impress, had witnessed Lieutenant Colonel Teddy Roosevelt's famous charge. Roosevelt had "splendid courage," he commented, "but unfortunately was not a soldier. He made an *opéra bouffe* of the soldier business and 'got away with it.'" Because he was a West Point graduate, he added, with a little ridicule, that the Rough Riders had been commanded by a doctor of medicine, Leonard Wood, and "their Lieutenant Colonel [was] a civilian with political ambitions who capitalized handsomely on his uniform."

Just before McAlexander had been sacked and dispatched to St. Nazaire, his First Division brigade commander, Brigadier General George B. Duncan, an admirer of the colonel, wrote to the division's commander recommending that he, McAlexander, be promoted to brigadier general. In doing so, he described him as having an "aggressive disposition, but loyal and subordinate to superior authority." He was an officer who "is dependable and conscientious, does not spare himself and in open warfare maneuvers handles his command with rapidity and discretion." Yet the moment McAlexander had been relieved of command of the 18th Regiment, he became "a maniac in his hatred of the Commander of the First Brigade [Duncan himself], the Commander of the First Division and the Commander-in-Chief of the A.E.F."

He had been only two weeks in command of his new regiment, a regiment that, although hardly a year old, he thought was pretty good. It had been organized in Syracuse, New York, in August 1917 and trained "splendidly," McAlexander believed, by Colonel Joseph Compton Castner. A graduate of Rutgers University with a civil engineering degree, Castner, as a twenty-nine-year-old lieutenant in 1898, had explored much of Alaska for the United States government. Ten years later, he built the famous Schofield Barracks on Hawaii's island of Oahu. The barracks were then called "Castner Village." In May 1918, after his promotion to brigadier general, he was transferred from the 38th to the Fifth Division and put in charge of its Ninth Infantry Brigade.

However, when McAlexander took over for Castner, he still felt that the 38th Infantry was not quite ready for any upcoming battle. He worried if he had enough time to instill in his men the "McAlexander spirit." The way he put it: "You may be killed, but you can't be licked—no man is licked until he wills to be licked!" He had to be certain his men would never be licked, even if they had to die where they stood to prove it.

His second in command, Lieutenant Colonel Frank H. Adams, from Vincennes, Indiana, recalled that McAlexander's "oft repeated words, 'They may kill us, but they cannot whip us,' was the slogan that carried the regiment to victory."

The 38th's regimental adjutant, Captain Parley D. Parkinson, three years out of West Point, who had been part of Pershing's Punitive Expedition into Mexico in 1916, had summed up his commander's leadership philosophy. "Do you wish an invincible, unconquerable regiment? Then organize it, train it and fight it along invincible, unconquerable lines. Imbue it with pride that scoffs at danger, inspire it with a soul of intrepidity and honor and make it know that its defeat is impossible; that it may be killed, but it cannot be beaten. Such an organization is the 38th U.S. Infantry."

One of the first things McAlexander noticed when he took control of the regiment was that the men were sluggish. They lacked the "snap and ginger in their movements" that he wanted. "Reactions must be instantaneous and intelligent. Commands must be automatically obeyed." One of the problems he faced with his new regiment was that hundreds of his men were immigrants or had grown up in immigrant neighborhoods back in America and therefore did not speak English. Another large percentage of them were illiterate. When the regiment was at training camp in North Carolina, one of the regiment's officers had uttered, "My God, what can I do with them!" At least, the officer admitted, "every man knew how to shoot."

More than anything, because he so despised the Germans, McAlexander wanted to "cultivate in each man an eager desire to close with the enemy, to get so near that his own rifle would soon put an end to opposition. I wanted each man to be sure to kill at least one of the Germans. I told them that each German wounded would cause more trouble than if dead, but to never stop shooting until there was nothing left to shoot at."

Wrote McAlexander, "I pounded into the heads of my officers and men that we were still Americans and that American methods of combat were still the best in existence for us; that the infantryman's rifle was the most accurate and death-dealing of all weapons, that it was the equivalent of a bayonet that could stab at half a mile. . . . I wanted every soldier to be able to put absolute confidence in his rifle and his own ability to use it."

One of his front-line officers stated, "McAlexander studied the regiment with that rare understanding of a gifted leader. His work was clear. It was his job to *teach us to fight!*"

Riding in one of the Cadillacs, not traveling by train with his own men, was McAlexander's counterpart in the 30th Infantry, Colonel Edmund Luther Butts, one of the youngest regimental commanders in the AEF. Better known among his friends as Billy, Butts, whose regiment was destined to fight alongside McAlexander's as part of the Sixth Brigade, had no furies bottled up inside. If there were, he kept them to himself. But as we'll see, his rage came later, after the Second Battle of the Marne. According to his boss, General Crawford, Butts was a favorite of Dickman's.

Like McAlexander, he was a native of Minnesota. He was the son of an influential Washington County probate judge who, in the Civil War, had fought at Bull Run, Fredericksburg, Chancellorsville and Gettysburg with the "Irish Rifles" of the 37th New York Volunteers. Butts, an 1890 graduate of West Point, had made quite a name for himself on the banks of the Hudson as a boxer and proponent of physical fitness. A few years after graduating, he devised a system of physical training that was then adopted throughout the army as the model to mold its soldiers into shape. Ironically, Butts, who stood a compact five-nine, got into West Point as an alternate after a year at the state's university, when Minnesota's first choice to fill the Washington County slot failed to pass the academy's physical fitness test. Butts's physique, recalled a classmate, was "straight and trim and powerfully muscled." Butts also wrote "Butts' Musical Rifle Drill," a cadence system that is used in close order drills.

Back at Camp Greene, when the division was being organized, Brigadier General Crawford observed that Butts had put more time into athletics, close order drill and physical fitness because he did not appreciate field training. Pamphlets with instructions teaching men maneuvers he tossed in the wastebasket. The Sixth Brigade commander thought it unfortunate and did not approve. And that disapproval stayed with him on the banks of the Marne. "Colonel Butts . . . wanted his men to march to the step of the band," he later pointed out. He feared that when in battle Butts would toss away orders given him. But in fairness to Butts, he was following the old army custom where a commander was judged on how his troops maneuvered on the parade ground and not so much on battle efficiency. Crawford remarked, "Under the circumstances of 1917–1918, the mummery of parade and calisthenics should have been almost entirely omitted as Colonel Castner had done with the 38th

Regiment. The physique of the men cannot be materially changed by athletics in the time allowed."

Butts, now at age fifty, a veteran of the Sioux Indian Wars, the Spanish American War and the Philippine Insurrection, and for a few years professor of military tactics at the University of Minnesota, knew, as did almost all the officers in the Third Division, that how well they and the troops under their command performed on the banks of the Marne could very well define their careers. Would their legacy as leaders be won or lost in the days and weeks and months ahead?

CHAPTER 2

//

"GOIN' TO HELL"

As the caravan pushed north, every soldier in the division, from General Dickman on down to the lowest private, was "keyed up to a high degree," noted Captain Harold W. James of the 38th, "not knowing what was to come." Also from the 38th, Dayton, Ohio, resident Second Lieutenant Elmer Focke, who before leaving Châteauvillain had written a "farewell letter" to his mother and then made out his last will and testament, had one objective before the war was over. Back at the training camp he'd gotten to know a French lieutenant who had received three *Croix de Guerres*. To Focke's astonishment, the officer wore a ring with a German officer's tooth in its setting. In a letter to his father, Focke bragged, "That's what I want & I'm going to have it before I get back."

When one of the trains slowly rolled past a station, an American soldier from the Sixth Infantry, standing on the platform with his men awaiting orders, yelled up, "Hey, Jack, where are you going?"

The Third Division soldiers yelled back, "Goin' to Hell, don't you want to go along?"

As the Americans pushed north, all of them were jarred by the spectacle of war that now spread across the French countryside like a black plague. Graves everywhere. And refugees pouring south as "if Attila, the Scourge of God, himself were on their trail."

Thirty-year-old supply officer Captain Fred Walker, with the fabulous middle name of Livingood, found himself filled with an uneasiness that he and his fellow soldiers would be unable to make good because of their lack of training and experience. From his train window he "saw along the railroad tracks and in the fields on both sides the graves of those who fell in 1914 in the great first battle of the Marne. Each grave wore a circular disk upon which the tricolor of France was painted. For miles and miles we could see them as we passed. Sometimes there would be groups of two or three, but they were nearly all single in the very middle of cultivated fields, in the woods, on the very edge of the railroad track, by the side of the roads. Wherever the hero fell there he was buried. Around each was a little lattice fence and on the reverse side of the disk in French were the words, 'For glory of his country.'"

Looking at the graves, Walker probably thought of Captain Paul Paschal's remark two months earlier when the division had shipped out of New York harbor aboard the *Aquitania* and was passing by the Statue of Liberty. "I wonder how many of us will ever see that old girl again." As the train rolled on, Walker, not yet a major, but soon to command the 30th's First Battalion, knew there was a good possibility that he and many of his comrades in arms would never return. "We had visions of those dear to us being widows and orphans," he wrote in his memoirs. "But even so they would never know the sufferings we bore nor the manner in which we were to die."

Chaplain George Ridout, riding through the same piece of country, saw the same "graves of French and German dead [that] were on both sides of the road, sad reminders of the bloody struggle" and what was yet to come.

The division passed trains going the other way and trains halted on sidings. Some were loaded with French soldiers, others crammed full of German prisoners. The gaunt faces of the prisoners stared out from open doors and windows. "They looked tired and were very young," Walker recounted. He was surprised at their small bodies. He'd always thought Germans were big, husky and brutal fellows. "These boys were undersized and frail."

From Walker's train one of his soldiers sang out, "Well, if that is the best the Boche can trot out, lead me to them!"

Crawford noted the refugees trudging along the road and thought, "Men, women and children with the doleful countenance of despair plodded south in confusion. There was little doubt in the minds of these country folk that the war was lost."

Lieutenant Focke told his parents back in Ohio, "It was not a very pleasant feeling to see French soldiers retreating to the rear in small groups. To make matters worse, on one of our rest periods, I looked to the side of the road and there lay an empty Greene and Greene cracker box from Dayton, Ohio. Talk about home sick!"

Looking at the French soldiers through his pince-nez glasses, Captain Jesse W. Wooldridge from the 38th's G Company, who three days earlier had turned thirty-three, saw them as "Just sweet children they were, and weary. God, how weary!"

Yet, for three hours on the afternoon of June 2 a solid column of trucks loaded with those weary French soldiers passed through Montmiral headed northwest on its way to the front. The French field artillery followed, and it wasn't until midnight that it had finally passed through the village.

To McAlexander, "The sight of the French refugee women and children is enough to make a stone cry out in pity. When I think of the German 'Kulture,' it simply means slavery and I am willing and anxious to kill it by every means and any means."

First Lieutenant Clarence E. "Ike" Lovejoy, in McAlexander's K Company, a newspaper reporter in civilian life who would later be the founding editor of *Lovejoy's College Guide*, wrote the nearer the caravan got to

Montmiral, and with the sound of German artillery shells exploding a few miles to the north in the town of Condé-en-Brie, the worse the rumors of a French defeat spread. The train he rode in "stopped and shunted at about every station" on the route, and here at these stations the men heard the rumors. The Germans had already crossed the river it was said. "Strange and ominous were the reports that came from French officers en route. It was the mightiest day of the German offensive. . . . We knew that and appreciated the urgent need of Americans on the Marne. But we didn't realize the Boche had reached that river and were crossing until the excited Frenchmen thrust maps under our eyes and pointed to positions." It wasn't just at Château-Thierry that the Germans had crossed the Marne, but also at Dormans and Fossoy, two villages the division would later defend. "And they're still coming," cried the French officers.

These French officers even beseeched General Dickman to turn back, saying "it was useless to try to stop the Germans."

When sections of the caravan reached Montmiral, every road and highway leading into or out of this major railhead on the Paris-to-Metz line was swamped with fleeing civilians, the rail yards jammed with crowded eastbound boxcars. Women and children wept while the men, too old to fight, their faces drawn, tried to look brave. "At intervals French army cannons could be seen on the roads bound northward, but their progress was slow," Lieutenant Lovejoy stated. "Carts, wagons, old-time phaetons and two-wheeled chaises—every possible kind of horse drawn vehicle were heaped high with personal possessions while the men and women clubbed the horses for more speed. On top of even huge loads of clothing and bundles often rode a crippled grandmother holding a few-months-old baby."

Inside and outside the railroad station and in the baggage and freight sheds every inch of ground was covered with wounded soldiers waiting to be placed aboard hospital trains. Ambulances kept pulling up to the station and unloading litters of patients. Many were horribly mutilated.

Lovejoy was astonished that "never a cry or a moan was to be heard from those soldiers," French, English and a few Americans from the Seventh Machine Gun Battalion that was still holding off the Germans at Château-Thierry. And the walking wounded, on the road for hours to reach a dressing station, came limping into Montmiral from the north.

"The wounded were lying about the vicinity of the depot everywhere," Captain Walker, an Ohioan, recollected. "The platforms and waiting rooms were full of them and the front yards of nearby houses held their share. Doctors and nurses were flying about."

Walker later saw an officer from the Seventh Machine Gun Battalion driving a truck into Montmiral. Walker recognized the officer and asked him where he was going. He said he was taking some men who'd been killed back to headquarters. As the truck passed, Walker looked in and "saw three corpses. That was my first view of American dead."

The dead were everywhere, according to William F. Freehoff, a captain in the 38th. "Hundreds of bodies yet to be disposed of by burial," he wrote. "The sight was a ghastly one."

Working among the wounded, helping the doctors and nurses, were American Red Cross volunteers. Again, Lovejoy was overcome because a "half dozen of the prettiest American girls ever created" were doing all the work. "Perhaps it was our love and respect for them, perhaps their beauty was real, yet in our eyes they were angels. But, oh, how tired they were! Several had not slept for four days, but had moved rearward with the troops as the German rush continued."

Among the Red Cross volunteers that Lovejoy found so pretty was Miss Mary Withers of Kansas City. She'd gone to France to work for the Fund for French Wounded and then joined the Red Cross. She had been with the French and British soldiers in their retreat after the battle at Chemin des Dames. At Château-Thierry she and her colleagues set up their canteen to feed the soldiers when they reached the city. "All the refugees coming in, all the stragglers from the armies, British and French, all lost from their units. They had not had food for days. Some wounded, some sick and bloody. It was ghastly," she wrote her mother. From

Château-Thierry the Red Cross volunteers moved to Montmiral, slept in cold and damp caves and placed their canteen at the railroad station. "The Americans came through by the thousands just in time to see the retreat," she continued. "And yet they went off singing."

When Dickman reached Montmiral, it was lunchtime and he was starved. He ordered his driver to find a restaurant. Shops and stores were closed and barricaded, but his driver located a café that had managed to stay open. When he entered the café, he was surprised to see three women wearing Red Cross uniforms. He was even more surprised when one of them turned out to be an old friend, Hattie Squiers. The widow of diplomat Herbert G. Squiers, Hattie had known the major general at the turn of the century when her husband was secretary of the American Legation in China and Dickman was with China Relief Expedition. She was in charge of running Montmiral's small Hospice de St. Vincent de Paul, a hospital already overflowing with soldiers. The other women were also socially prominent and beautiful: Mary Hoyt "Hoytie" Wiborg, from New York and Paris, and Lady Abinger, well known in Parisian circles as the mistress of the late French president Felix Faure, who, it was rumored, had died in her arms. As Dickman found out, these women were the "only ones left to care for two hundred wounded who had been abandoned in the general panic."

Indeed, the hospital's surgeon, along with Hattie's maid, had fled. "I was left alone with Hoytie Wiborg, Lady Abinger, my English friend, and the two little Mlles, all of whom did the most glorious work," she'd written to her sister. She described how the "refugees would simply break your heart. Three big motor trucks arrived here filled with old men and women, some of them 90 years old. They had been in their cellars for five days and had to be carried out by force. Some brought their rabbits and chickens in bags, dead, of course, when they reached here. One old woman took her poor old husband to the pump under my windows, and tried to wash him and clean him up. He was weeping like a child, so I went down to aid and comfort them. It was heartbreaking to hear him tell of leaving their little farms and homes, where they had always lived and with no future, nothing to look forward to. It made my heart ache."

New York Times war correspondent Edwin L. James reported, "Hundreds of French wounded probably owe their lives to the pluck and bravery of two American women, Mrs. Herbert G. Squiers and Mary Hoyt Wyborg [*sic*] of New York. Alone and unaided except by two nuns, they cared for 600 French wounded for twenty-four hours in a little town by the Marne."

The Third Division poured into Montmiral, either by car, wagon, truck or train, or on foot. The railroad that ran through the village was on a single track and not sufficient to handle the thousands of soldiers pouring in, and the regiments and battalions had to detrain at different points along the way and then march to their destination. "Dumped from their box cars far south of their detraining point," according to First Lieutenant Arthur T. Brice, Jr., a twenty-five-year-old adjutant in the 7th Infantry's Third Battalion. His battalion then had to march through Montmiral to its assigned encampment somewhere near the Marne—a hike that was over twenty miles and took two days to complete.

For the rest of the division, minus its artillery and engineers, getting to their assigned positions was equally frustrating. The various units knew where they had to go—they just didn't know how to get there. The French had offered no guides. The Americans had to march at night, sometimes wandering around in the dark until they were lucky enough to find their places.

Crawford complained that there'd been trouble bringing up supplies by truck and medical supplies had been left behind. He saw to it that those medical supplies were on their way.

Chaplain Ridout, marching with the 38th's Third Battalion, heard the roar of distant artillery and he saw the far-off hills "covered with the smoke of bursting shells and burning villages and towns." The battalion bedded down in the woods around an old château and all that night slept to the sound of artillery miles away. In the morning "all was hurry and congestion," the chaplain wrote. He and another YMCA volunteer, William H. Danforth of St. Louis, Missouri, using a fence railing as a table, ate a quick breakfast of "bacon and hard tack and drank our coffee with relish." (During the war, Danforth, who had founded the livestock and poultry feed company Ralston Purina, grew to like the army word for food, "chow." When he got back from the war, he added the word chow to all the feeds that his company manufactured. "Purina Chows" became world famous.)

As the Third Battalion, commanded by Major Maxon Lough, who would go on to become a brigadier general in World War II and wind up a prisoner of the Japanese and a survivor of the Bataan Death March, and the rest of the Third Division marched toward the front along hot, dusty roads, they were sometimes met by Frenchwomen who had stayed at their farmhouses, fearless of the German threat. At one farmhouse, a woman came out with a big pail of water and two glasses for the thirsty, sweat-caked soldiers. Here they were able to refill their drained canteens.

The soldiers were soon back on the trail, when one of them fell out of line with a "bursting headache." Ridout went to him, shouldered the boy's pack, which weighed about seventy-five pounds, and carried it, along with his own, for the next five miles.

When the troops paused for a brief rest during this long march, Ridout, earning the nickname of "Holy Joe," would gather some of the more devout of them and hold a prayer service in some field, where nearby were the graves of the fallen French and Germans who had been killed during the First Battle of the Marne.

McAlexander, writing later about the march to the front, pointed out, "It was unknown ground to us, with no chance to explore it before moving into position. The French gave us no guides and we were up against the problem of finding our own places on a dark night, with officers and men dog tired after so grilling a march."

Later, when the division's artillery units moved up to the Marne, they, too, kept getting lost. The 76th Field Artillery, temporarily assigned to Crawford's Sixth Brigade, had been ordered north at "utmost speed." The horses pulling their wagons were green and trudged along. Time and again, they "strayed in the darkness" and "wandered on and on" until they found a familiar landmark.

Captain Percy Gamble Black, West Point, Class of 1917, twenty-three years old and son of Major General William M. Black, who at the time was the AEF's chief of engineers, said he'd never forget his regiment's night march. He feared they might be lost and marching blindly into German lines. "The road which stretched out ahead, between rows of poplar trees gleamed white in the moonlight," he wrote. "Before us the whole horizon was lit by the flash of guns, and everywhere along it rockets rose or star shells burst, while now and then the deeper red of a Bengal flare could be seen above the hills. Always the distant rumble of the cannon grew louder as we approached the battle-line. We bumped along over the cobbled streets of silent villages. Not a light showed in the houses. No one stirred. The cannoneers walking behind their pieces were singing 'Pack Up Your Troubles in Your Old Kit Bag' as they marched. A feeling of intense excitement was in the air."

Lieutenant Colonel Parker Hitt, a member of the AEF Signal Corps who'd been attached to the Third Division as the liaison officer and who later became known as the father of modern American military cryptology, observed the troops as they marched into place. In a June 1 operation report, he wrote, "I saw a good deal of the division in motion. The march discipline in spite of four days' rations carried by the men and the heat and dry conditions of the road, was excellent and shows most careful previous training."

As night fell, the Third Division marched on through the darkness. Ahead of the Americans flashes from artillery shells lit up the sky. "They grew greater and brighter," Walker wrote. "We began to hear the far away

Boom! Boom! Boom! . . . Now and then we could see red, white or green rockets ascend into the heavens and return to earth. There was no doubt there was a battle in progress ahead of us and we were headed straight towards it." The thought thrilled Walker that here he was, as he put it, "fortunate enough to take part in actual battle in one of the world's greatest wars."

Eventually the Fifth and Sixth brigades bivouacked between Château-Thierry and the Surmelin River that flowed north into the Marne. The Fifth Brigade, commanded by West Pointer Brigadier General Fred W. Sladen, was ordered to encamp at or near the following towns: the 4th Infantry in the area around Viels-Maisons; the 7th Infantry headquarters at Monthurel, while the rest of the regiment was posted around Connigis, each about two thousand yards from the Marne; and the Eighth Machine Gun Battalion in the towns of Saint-Agnan and La Grange-aux-Bois. Crawford's Sixth Brigade was sent to the following areas: Butts's 30th Infantry went to Viels-Maisons to await further orders; McAlexander's 38th Infantry was spread out in the towns of Saint-Eugène, Nesles, Bois de Nogentel and Courboin as well as Bochage Farm; and the Ninth Machine Gun Battalion at Coufremaux. Each of these towns was a mile from the Marne River.

Dickman's divisional headquarters was in the town of Viels-Maisons, where General de Mondesir already had his command post. The American general moved into a deserted house owned by one M. Boyer who, when the German offensive began, had wisely taken a vacation in the south of France. Dickman noticed that Boyer "had been thoughtful enough to leave his safe unlocked so as to save the clumsy German soldiers the trouble of opening it with dynamite."

When the division finally arrived at its desitination, Dickman reported that his troops were bivouacked south of the Marne. Their health was "good," morale "excellent." He noted that they were "tired and weary, but intensely earnest and anxious to participate in the actual fight. Many guns have been passing, also cargo and ammunition trucks, all going east. Firing heavy and continuous tonight."

Now that the division, mixed in with exhausted French troops, had taken up defensive positions within a mile of the Marne, it was time for the Americans to get to know their foreign comrades-in-arms, dig in and get used to the daily dosage of enemy artillery and machine-gun fire and the airplanes that dominated the skies, while preparing for the German onslaught.

CHAPTER 3

"BAD MILITARY ETHICS"

The sector given the division to defend, wedged between sectors of the French 125th Division on the right and the French 39th Division on the left, extended for about seven miles along the south bank of the Marne, from the eastern suburbs of Château-Thierry past the small farming villages of Etampes-sur-Marne, Blesmes, Fossoy, Mézy and, halfway up Hill 231, Moulins, to a point about six hundred yards west of Varennes. Crézancy, a larger village with a regional hospital and an agricultural college, stood nearly two miles from the Marne, directly south of Mézy. In the American sector the Marne was fifty feet wide. It was a deep river with a fast current, and for an advancing army, crossing it would not be an easy task. There were four small islands in the river, opposite the enemy-held villages of Chartèves, Mont-Saint-Pére, Gland and Brasles on the north bank and a sluice dam west of Mézy. Several bridges spanned the river, two in front of the Third Division, at Mont-Saint-Pére and the village of Jaulgonne. Seven miles east of Château-Thierry the Marne made a wide loop north at a place called the Jaulgonne Bend before turning south and east again, forming a natural salient that on the eve of the battle jutted two miles into German-held territory—offering the enemy the great advantage for enfilade and reverse fire. On the north side the banks were steep and wooded, with lines of willow trees and thick underbrush—a perfect spot for concealing a large force. On the division's side of the river, the banks were less imposing, mostly flat, but gently rising to a height of five hundred feet—an open plateau of fertile farmland, covered with wheat fields and clumps of woods known as the Bois d'Aigremont. Colonel Edmund "Billy" Butts thought the Bois d'Aigremont was "advantageously situated for defense" because it offered areas of concealment for a complete regiment, machine gun battalions and artillery.

On the eastern edge of the division's sector, a hilly, forested region, the little Surmelin River, as McAlexander called it, entered the Marne from the south. Describing the Surmelin River, Ike Lovejoy called it a "so-called river [because], probably, the French have no word for creek." The Surmelin Valley, a "wide rich plain, plentifully dotted from the Marne as far south as Montmiral with tiny farming towns and prosperous cultivated fields," cut a natural corridor toward Paris. The sides of the valley were steep and wooded and thick with foliage. Rising on the eastern slope was the Moulins Ridge, also referred to as Moulins Ruiné and militarily named Hill 231. The Paris-to-Nancy railroad, with its ten-foot-high embankment, along with a major wagon road, paralleled the Marne's south bank until the railroad came to the Surmelin River, where it curved southward and followed the Surmelin to the major railhead at Montmiral and then on to the French capital.

After studying the lay of the land, General Dickman observed: "As there were no other railroads and highways between Château-Thierry and Dormans towards the south, the Surmelin Valley formed a sort of gateway of high strategical importance to an invading force from the north, aiming at Paris. The general situation, therefore, presented favorable conditions for an offensive operation on the part of the enemy, excepting the obstacle of the river. But, it was thought that no defenders could remain on its banks under a concentrated fire of artillery, machine guns and minenwerfer."

A study done by the U.S. Army Chemical Corps in 1959 agreed with Dickman's assessment. "The strategic feature of the sector occupied by the Third Division was the Surmelin Valley, a natural gateway to the south." Major Walter C. Short, who had fought with the First Division during the war and later made a study of the Champagne-Marne Defensive, described the Surmelin as the "best inroad to the south between Château-Thierry and Rheims, from both a tactical or strategical point of view." Thus the valley became "the main vantage point to be desired by the enemy."

From the moment the division reached the Marne Valley on the first days of June, even before it got settled in, the Germans concealed in the woods across the river sniped at the Americans and from miles back fired long-range artillery shells that landed in their midst. It was unsettling for the soldiers, especially for those who had never been in combat. During one of the early encounters with enemy artillery a shell exploded in the 7th Infantry's subsector west of the 30th Infantry. Two French soldiers and two horses were killed and one American officer and eight of his men were wounded.

The 30th Infantry's Captain Fred Walker, then a seven-year veteran, who had enlisted as a private in the Ohio Cavalry after graduating from Ohio State University, remembered his first encounter with incoming shells. He had just sat down to a supper of beans with B Company of the First Battalion when he heard a "rushing, screeching sound as if some huge planet or meteor was approaching." The spooky sound grew louder and someone yelled "Shell!" Everyone at the table ducked. The shell exploded twenty-five yards from them, chewing up the ground and sending dirt and sticks flying. The soldiers had gone to inspect the shell hole when they heard a pop from far across the river. Another shell was on its way.

"As it came on screaming louder and louder I felt helpless as a child,"

Walker recounted. "I did not know what I should do. I was completely surprised, in fact, I was scared."

Walker, who'd soon be promoted to major and take command of the First Battalion, spotted a stone fence. As the Germans fired a third shell, he leaped behind it and "dived for cover." The shell hit some distance away. Walker looked up and there "stood Sgt. Major [Raymond] Dougherty looking at me with a grin on his face as cool and calm as a cucumber." Walker was suddenly angry with himself. He went back to the table to finish his plate of beans, but was too upset to eat. Shells kept coming. This time he stood his ground. "I decided I was not going to let my legs run off with me again and they never did."

Daily the Germans sent artillery shells flying over the river, a harassing fire that was more an annoyance than a continuous bombardment.

Walker remarked that the enemy was "alert and his observation . . . keen," and the thoughtless and careless American—"and there were many of them in our ranks—was sure to receive a projectile from some German gunner. As a rule these sniping shots, sometimes from artillery, sometimes from machine guns, accomplished little more than to frighten the fool who had endangered his fellows as well as himself. Those who were near always took delight in the discomfort or fright on the part of the dunce."

First Lieutenant Robinson Murray in the 38th's F Company, a Harvard graduate and an advertising executive back in Boston before the war, wrote on June 10 to Margaret "Peggy" Piersol, a Vassar College alumna and now a Red Cross nurse in Paris, who was beginning to win his heart, "The shells go screaming along overhead like huge skyrockets. You can hear them coming and going and it seems each time as they could be seen perfectly easily, but never are."

George Ridout, the YMCA chaplain, wrote about learning the knack of dodging incoming shells. "When the [shells] come along, and thank heaven, as a general thing you can hear the whistle of the thing a few seconds before it hits the ground, and this gives you a chance, if you are quick, to jump into a dug-out or behind a rock or tree, or throw yourself prone on the ground, and yet this does not always ensure safety."

Ridout was standing next to an officer one day when the German artillery was pestering the American line. Shells were landing on one of the villages. One shell hit the edge of a church tower, but did not destroy the structure. The officer said, "When under shell fire keep away from the church because the Huns get their range on the town from the church."

In his diary of June 4, nineteen-year-old upstate New Yorker Corporal Billy Fitzgerald, scribbled, "Big bombardment on all morning. Shells whizzing over head—getting near the firing line. Oh boy!"

To his Ohio family, Lieutenant Focke, who had studied at Notre Dame and Georgetown University Law School, described what he felt when experiencing his first artillery attack. It was a nightmare, he wrote. "My body quivered to such an extent that I thought my flesh was dropping from the bones of my body." When he got used to the artillery, he wrote, "Weeee, there goes another one but we shouldn't worry, for the one you hear will never hit you & the one that hits you you will never hear, so there you are." After writing to his parents, Focke, who to be on the safe side carried a little prayer in his pocket that his sister had given him, added, "Mean old Ferdinand came near landing one of those whiz bangs pretty close. We are having a lot of sport and enjoy the experience very much."

A captain in McAlexander's regiment, Jesse Walton Wooldridge, a Kentuckian now living in California, looked at it differently. "We simply laid down and hoped in a maudlin, disconnected way one of the shells the Germans welcomed us with would make a direct hit and end it all."

For Sergeant Angelo Pappas of Ipswich, Massachusetts, and Private Henry Tellone of Newark, New Jersey, both in the 38th Infantry, the shelling on June 4 ended it all. They were the first men of Colonel McAlexander's regiment to be killed in action. A week later the death toll had risen. A little cemetery for the 38th, fenced in by a high stone wall, was then established in the village of Courboin, about five miles from the

Marne. Chaplain John B. Peters marked each grave with a wooden cross bearing the words "Killed in Action."

On another occasion there were no bodies for the 38th to bury. On an evening just before sundown, a wagon filled with hand grenades squeaked along a road near Courboin where men of the Sixth Engineers were at work. The heavily laden wagon, pulled by a team of horses, had three soldiers on board. For no known reason the hand grenades exploded. "An enormous hole was torn in the ground," an engineer remembered of the explosion, "and nothing was left of the men and horses but a few scattered pieces which the Engineers picked up on their shovels." Three engineers suffered wounds.

"Blood of one's own friends, his buddy, perhaps his tent-mate, had been shed," Ike Lovejoy lamented. "It was saddening," he went on, in the same vein as his colonel's hatred toward the Germans, "but it was also a spur to fight, to tear, to kill those enemies of mankind who had brought on this world struggle."

McAlexander's maxim about soldiers lost in combat: "Salute them, then Forward!"

Although the deaths bothered McAlexander, the shelling seemed not to. He had been in combat out west, in Cuba and in the Philippines. The first time a German shell roared toward him, he and a sergeant were down with their men. They heard the shell clearly as it headed their way. It crashed through the top of a tree and struck "so close that for the first and only time during the war did I 'hit the dirt.' The shell had missed our heads by a few feet only and plunged into the earth not five yards away." He raised his head to see where the shell had struck, and as he did so the "panic-stricken" sergeant tried to crawl under the colonel's body. Laughing, McAlexander called out, "Sergeant, what in Hell are you trying to do?"

Another time, when McAlexander was out inspecting the troops, the Germans commenced a brisk firing of 77-caliber shells. The soldiers dashed for the dugout, pushing and shoving to get inside. One soldier hollered, "Where's the colonel?" When they peered out, they saw McAlexander "cussing out a man for being slow in getting to shelter, although he was running as fast as his legs could carry him."

Although the artillery was a dangerous nuisance, McAlexander was more upset with the French. It began on his first night at the front, after making sure his regiment was in place and bedded down. Exhausted, he wrapped himself up in a blanket and rolled under a wagon to wait for daylight. At around one in the morning an excited courier ran up to him, calling that he had a message from the French commander. The Germans were crossing the Marne and attacking his regiment's outposts. McAlexander bolted out from under the wagon with his heart pounding, wondering why he hadn't heard any rifle fire or exploding hand grenades. What was happening to his men? They had never faced an enemy, and he wasn't there to lead them. After six months in exile at St. Nazaire, he'd just got command of a combat regiment. Two weeks! His stomach churned. He started to throw up. He had to sit on a log, gather his thoughts. And then everything went black and he pitched forward in a dead faint! He wasn't out for long. Filled with shame and humiliation, he raced toward his men.

"That ghastly fear as to what was probably happening to my front line battalion, with no communication except by runners over a strange road and in darkness, simply overwhelmed me and I had gone under," he later confessed. The report had been false. The Germans had not crossed the river and attacked his men. "It left me in a frame of mind that distrusted every French report until its truth could be verified."

First, the French had not provided guides to lead his men through the dark to their front-line position. Second, a French commander had raised a false alarm. What next? General Jean-Baptiste Marchand of the 10th Colonial Division, who had been at Château-Thierry, showed up with his Senegalese soldiers. He mixed them in with McAlexander's regiment. The American colonel explained to the French general that fifteen hundred of his troops were from the American South and most of them did not like blacks, even if they were Senegalese. He then asked for his own section but was denied. He next asked for at least a continuous line for his men, a line without the Senegalese mingled in. He and Marchand argued, and the general, who only a few days earlier had praised the division's Seventh Machine Gun Battalion for its courage and skillful marksmanship at Château-Thierry, snapped that "Americans are very new at the game of war, that the Germans are full of ruses, and that it was for the purpose of stabilizing the American line, that the Senegalese battalions are placed on the same front, between the American battalions."

McAlexander was livid, but held his tongue. He prayed there'd be no problems between his Southern troops and the Senegalese.

Wooldridge found the French patronizing and that their method of teaching American soldiers how to fight on the Western Front had "the general effect of inducing a timidity and lack of aggressiveness for fear of making errors. Colonel McAlexander did not share in these hallucinations and was one of the infantry officers who knew the war would be won by infantry fire."

On the first night the Americans were in position, the language barrier between them and the French had deadly consequences. A front-line sentinel with the Ninth Machine Gun Battalion challenged an oncoming French soldier. The soldier did not halt. Using his pistol, the sentinel shot the French soldier through the stomach.

To avoid such confrontations or confusion, General de Mondesir had early on attached liaison officers to each regiment of the Third Division as well as to General Dickman's headquarters. Four were attached to the 30th Infantry and three to the 38th. Each colonel had his own liaison officer assigned directly to him.

While McAlexander had built up a distrust of the French officers he'd been in contact with, the 30th's Colonel Billy Butts, on the other hand, implicitly trusted a dashing young officer assigned to him. Lieutenant Leon Marchand, no relation to General Marchand, had witnessed in 1916 the slaughter at Verdun. A Protestant minister, he had come over from the

French 202nd Regiment to serve with the Americans. According to Butts, he was a "high type man." The colonel's entire staff "had great confidence in his judgment." It was Marchand, a man of God, who accompanied Butts on a personal reconnaissance of his subsector, advising him on how to set up his defenses.

Walker found the French officers he dealt with to be congenial and very courteous. "I grew to be very fond of them because they took a great deal of interest in us and gave us many valuable pointers about concealment." He said they liked American cigarettes and candy and "in exchange for them they would give us good wine. They always laughed at us and our habits of drinking wine." To the French officers, wine was for meals only. According to Walker they had a certain grade of wine at the beginning of each meal, another grade during the meal and a liqueur to add the finishing touches. "We, in true America style, drank wine at any and all hours of the day or night and we did not care a great deal about its grade just so it was good."

I n spite of the liaison officers, Dickman was still having problems with French commanders, including the corps's chief of staff, "a cross-grained little Frenchman, known to his comrades as L'Ours, or the Bear." During the first two weeks of June, the positions of the division's regiments, on a front that meandered for twelve miles, were shifted about as if de Mondesir and the infamous "Bear" were using them as peas in a never-ending shell game. The Bear, Dickman complained, made "life a burden" to the American soldier. The 4th Infantry had five position changes and the 7th four. A battalion of the 30th Infantry had been sent to Hill 204 and Vaux to support units of the Second Division. Then the 7th, with soldiers so green when it came to any combat experience, was pulled out of the line, along with a detachment of the Sixth Engineers, and sent to fight with the Second Division northwest of Château-Thierry. The 7th's First Battalion, led by Lieutenant Colonel Frank H. Adams before his transfer to McAlexander's 38th Infantry, relieved two battalions of U.S. Marines at Belleau Woods. The Second Battalion relieved more Marines between Bois de Belleau and Bouresches, and the Third Battalion was placed in a position south of the village of Torcy. In their first battle, the 7th lost 51 killed, 265 wounded and 34 missing, most of them from the First Battalion. In fact, none of the 7th's battalions got much credit for their role at Belleau Wood—for the U.S. Marines their shining moment of the war. But a number of men from the Third Division felt the Marines were their own best press agents. A second lieutenant in the 38th Infantry wrote to his brother, "The Third Division has not had much in the way of a press agent as have the Marines." General Dickman was still miffed that the Marines got most of the credit for stopping the Germans at Château-Thierry and not his Seventh Machine Gun Battalion. McAlexander went so far as to state that when the time comes for Marines to write about the Marne it was his guess that "it will be all about the Marines at Chateau-Thierry as they are the big 'braggarts' of this war."

With one of his battalions already in action around Vaux and Hill 204, Butts, much to his dismay, had two more companies, led by Captain W. Sterling Maxwell, later his adjutant, sent west of Château-Thierry to guard bridges on the Marne between Charly and La Ferté-sous-Jouarre, an eleven-mile stretch of the river. Even though Maxwell was attached to the French 10th Regiment of Mounted Chasseurs, he had no French liaison officer assigned to him when he marched his troops off to their new post. His messengers had neither motorcycles nor bicycles, and no telephone. They had to commandeer their surgeon's horse to get messages back to French headquarters. Maxwell's instructions were even incomplete. He and his men, each carrying a heavy load of gear, including four days' food rations, and marching through the night from 6 p.m. to 5 a.m., wound up lost several times. But they made their trek and fulfilled their assignment so well that Major A. Nadaud of the 10th Mounted Chasseurs wrote to his general, de Mondesir, "I have the honor to report that the detachment of the American army placed at my disposal June 4, 5 and 6, for the defense of the bridges of the MARNE, from Charly to La Ferte-sous-Jouarre, has given me entire satisfaction." He went on to state, "The men as well as the officers were imbued with the finest spirit, and all did their best to understand and fulfill the missions confided in them."

T o make matters worse for General Dickman, his division head-quarters was moved to three different locations in ten days.

"Rather to the discouragement of the unit commanders and staffs of the 3rd Division, the French higher authorities saw fit to divide brigades and even split regiments of the battalions," wrote Lieutenant Lovejoy. "This was the period when the 7th Infantry was sent across the Marne west of Château-Thierry to cooperate with the Marines."

It was also the time when McAlexander's Third Battalion was pulled out of the front and sent twelve miles west of Château-Thierry to relieve a squadron of Sixth Chasseurs of the French 4th Cavalry Division.

In a lengthy memo to Pershing's assistant chief of staff, Colonel Fox Conner, from the new chief of staff for the Third Division, Colonel Robert H. C. Kelton, complained that there was too much shifting about. Kelton, who had spent the early part of his military career in the coast artillery, had been on Pershing's staff before his transfer to serve under Dickman replacing Lieutenant Colonel Raymond Sheldon. Kelton felt he had a special connection to Fox Conner, a highly influential member of Pershing's inner circle. Kelton and Conner and other officers at Pershing's headquarters were all friends or at least acquaintances, and Kelton and Conner had worked together at Chaumont. In his memos to Conner, the opinionated Kelton always presented himself in a positive manner, while oftentimes putting down his fellow officers in the Third Division, including his own boss, Dickman. General Crawford had no use for Kelton. He said he "had the self confidence of the theorist who had never handled the real tools of the trade." On the other hand, Dickman found Kelton a highly efficient officer and a forceful character. But Kelton also had a quick temper, and he once got into a personal spat with de Mondesir's own chief of staff, the Bear, that left a bad feeling between the French and the Americans.

A native of San Francisco, Kelton hailed from a long line of military officers—his late father, a general and Civil War veteran, had graduated from West Point in 1851. Kelton had earned his commission as a graduate of the Army Artillery School and the Army and Navy War Colleges. In 1910 he married Edith Russell Wills, considered the most beautiful woman of Newburyport, Massachusetts, and a descendant of a *Mayflower* pilgrim. The wedding had made news throughout the northeast because Edith had been engaged to Captain Nathan Appleton, a man forty years her senior who was still married but seeking a divorce from a wife he hadn't lived with in twenty-one years. When the divorce finally came through, Appleton was on his deathbed. Edith was at his side when he died. Four years later she married Kelton.

In his memo of complaint to Conner, Kelton wrote, "As a result of these shifts and changes, coupled with the necessary relief of the front line battalions, which cannot move in the daytime at all, many of the men had not had their shoes off . . . and we're beginning to get reports of trench feet." He added that there were no nearby bathing facilities and not enough water to cook with, "excepting the battalions of McAlexander's regiment, on the right sector, which are down in the SURMELIN Valley."

Crawford believed that the nervousness of the commander of the 38th Army Corps approached hysteria—the reason the division had been shifted about like musical chairs. "This was exhibited in the fussy way in which he was constantly rearranging the troops in his sector." He explained that the sixty-year-old Piarron de Mondesir, whom he called "this lovable French general" and a man of "delightful character," would "put a battalion in position and before it got acquainted with its surroundings, or started to organize the ground with trenches they would be moved and an entire rearrangement made." He added that the "French had no confidence in their own troops and less in the Americans." Operating with the French, he proclaimed, was a severe trial.

To Dickman, Crawford reported that hardly a day passed without a change of position in front of the enemy, whose menace made such changes a delicate and dangerous operation. The troops in his brigade, he wrote, "were somewhat tired out and perhaps irritated by this shifting of positions which had to be carried out at night."

Lieutenant Colonel Parker Hitt of the Signal Corps noted that the "constant changes in the location of troops is complicating the supply question to a certain extent," but added "on the whole things are moving smoothly."

The relationship between the French and American officers, according to Dickman, who spoke fluent French, "required constant watching on my part and conversations with the corps commander to mitigate annoyances and keep peace in the family."

In the meantime, a detachment of the division's Sixth Engineers were easily outperforming their French counterparts in cutting stakes from standing timber to be used in barbed-wire entanglements. It took the French a day to cut one thousand stakes. In the same amount of time, the Americans cut four thousand.

Looking back on the days when the Third Division served under the French, Major General Robert L. Howze, a Congressional Medal of Honor recipient in the Indian Wars who would later replace Dickman as the division's commander, wrote a "frank statement" to General Pershing's headquarters: "Man for man our troops first equaled, then surpassed the French in efficiency, and they have been continuing the surpassing process with increasing rapidity. Quicker to think, resourceful, philosophical, of excellent physique, and above all, practical."

A nother issue: the engineers, as well as soldiers in the division's other units, were not fond of the food the French served.

First, there was never enough of it to fill the enormous appetite the Americans had, forcing foraging parties to scour the countryside. Cattle, chicken and hogs roamed the fields and woods, left behind by the farmers who had fled south. Vegetable gardens were ripe for the picking—radishes, lettuce and asparagus.

Lieutenant Lovejoy explained, "Many a fat hog was reported to the company commander as killed by shell fire and straightaway turned over to the mess sergeant. Yet, strangely enough, there was invariably a hole in its head just about the size a bullet from an automatic service pistol could make." One of the engineers wrote, "Almost every night details went out with wagons and returned before daylight with offerings for the cooks, ranging from half-grown chickens to sixteen-hundred-pound beeves."

One night, according to the historian of the Sixth Engineers, Bob Graham of E Company slipped into a barn not far from the Marne and discovered a sow, some pigs and a few chickens. He and several other engineers from his company "made short work of the pigs and chickens, but the sow, being full grown, was not so easily disposed of." A wagon was commandeered and backed up to the barn door. But the sow broke loose and, with Graham holding on to her tail for dear life, bolted into a thick stand of woods. "A rapid search found both of them near the edge of the river, in what was considered No-Man's Land. The sow was hastily tied up and carried away by the escort without drawing the fire of the enemy. Perhaps Fritz had been hungry himself and took pity on the salvagers. Who can say?"

First Lieutenant Craig P. Cochrane of the Ninth Machine Gun Battalion described the pigs in a letter to his parents in Rochester, New York. "We have a collection of pigs now, for the company mess. Five of them all about a foot and a half long with very curly tails and very long snouts, considering the size. . . . We did have some rabbits and a cow, but they have gone the way of everything good to eat."

The men bartered with the few German farmers who had stayed in their homes and not fled. In exchange for two bags of Bull Durham a soldier could get a yearling calf. Four bags and the soldier brought back a healthy cow that could be milked daily. According to Lovejoy, a detail from the regiment's intelligence section returned with four cows and three calves.

Meanwhile, the French "hobnailed hardtack" and canned beef was so bad that the Americans called it "monkey meat." One soldier described its taste as being like "it had been preserved in gasoline, soap or some unedible compound and the men refused to eat it unless they were famished."

Second Lieutenant Elmer Focke recalled a squad of French soldiers that had been assigned to his company to teach the Americans about trench warfare. "Our kitchens were in a so-called barnyard with a stone wall," he wrote. "The first morning, some French soldiers (nicknamed 'frogs') came for breakfast. They urinated against the stone wall near the kitchens and the American soldiers raised hell!"

While the men were hatching plots to get more food to their liking, they were introduced to the Colt automatic pistol. In the woods north of the village of Courboin they familiarized themselves with the weapon that General Crawford boasted was of "outstanding superiority." But within a week of learning how to shoot the pistol, three soldiers were killed while at target practice. Once they got the hang of it and later, after the Marne battle, Crawford said, "A man carrying two [Colt pistols] was a familiar sight."

The disruption of the 3d Division and scattering of its units over a wide area, under foreign supervisors, while carrying out the policy of the French high command, afforded neither instruction or profitable experience," Dickman reasoned. "It was bad military ethics and was bound to leave sore spots. It placed the regiments at a disadvantage among strangers, retarded the development of the division, delayed the construction of defensive works, and reflected on the regimental and higher commanders and staff. . . . Nothing could be gained by protest or controversy. We could only bide our time."

At 5 p. m. on June 5, from his headquarters at Viels-Maisons, General de Mondesir sent the following order stating that the zone of the 38th Army Corps would be organized immediately. The Corps's mission: (A) "On the south bank of the Marne to prevent the enemy from establishing passages and from crossing the river. To throw back immediately all enemy forces gaining a foothold on his bank." (B) "On the north bank, to prevent at any cost the advance of the enemy through the valley of the MARNE."

The next day, on June 6, the Third Division was at last given its own sector to defend so there'd be no more shifting about. The hard work of "organizing the ground"—digging in, constructing trenches, hollowing out foxholes, laying out barbed-wire entanglements and building artillery-proof command posts to carry out the Corps's mission "commenced in earnest."

CHAPTER 4

///

"THE FIRST AND PRINCIPAL DUTY . . . IS SECRECY"

A cross the Marne River the Germans were indeed preparing for their attack. The high command reasoned that what had worked at Chemin des Dames ought to work when the armies of Crown Prince Wilhelm struck across the Marne east of Château-Thierry and attacked the Rheims salient, striking as far east as Verdun, then driving south and southeast toward Epernay and Châlons-sur-Marne.

"The mission of the attack," wrote the crown prince's chief of staff, "is to cause the fall of the hostile positions on the Reims [*sic*] plateau by taking the crossing at Epernay."

If the offensive worked as planned, the Germans would roll up the French armies at Rheims and Verdun and those two cities would fall. To the southwest of Rheims the French Fifth and Sixth Armies would be split, allowing the Germans to march down the Marne valley toward Paris.

The key to the attack's success was artillery, and tons of it.

At Chemin des Dames, nearly a thousand guns of different calibers had rolled up to the Ailette River on railroad cars and then been positioned where the French Sixth Army couldn't see them or hit them with their own artillery. General Duchêne was unaware of the magnitude of artillery that had been hauled into place. One reason, as strange as it sounds, was that the croaking of thousands of frogs living in the Ailette River had created such a din that it drowned out the noise made by the emplacement of the artillery. When the Germans opened with their massive bombardment, the French were totally surprised. Their front lines, packed tightly together, were decimated. Dugouts and trenches were ripped up. Railheads miles back were destroyed. A rolling barrage followed the main artillery thrust, and the infantry stormed the shattered remnants of Duchêne's army. The easy victory lifted the hopes of the Germans that the Allies could be brought to their knees with one more major blow, and certainly their morale would hit an all-time low.

On the Marne and at the Rheims salient, Ludendorff wanted a repeat of Chemin des Dames: surprise, heavy bombardment on both front-line and reserve troops with high explosive shells and canisters of gas, followed by a rolling barrage and elite storm troopers armed with mobile weapons wiping out the survivors. He was a believer in artillery. In a lengthy memorandum to his generals, he wrote that a larger artillery force must break the more determined resistance of the enemy.

"An attack fulfills its purpose as soon as the losses inflicted upon the enemy become greater than our own," he went on, as if the number of his own casualties meant nothing. "This is always the case in a successful surprise attack. It is, therefore, a question of hurling the troops upon the enemy without being influenced by fear of losses and without losing sight of assistance and preparation by artillery fire."

Ludendorff reminded them that in Germany's previous offensives of 1918, like Operation Blücher at Chemin des Dames, the "use of gases, short violent preparatory fire and the use of a slow moving rolling barrage are methods which have again proved their value."

He closed, "If we take all opportunities for work according to the Orders of the High Command we shall maintain the tactical superiority in maneuver which we have acquired, and we shall advance to new and great successes."

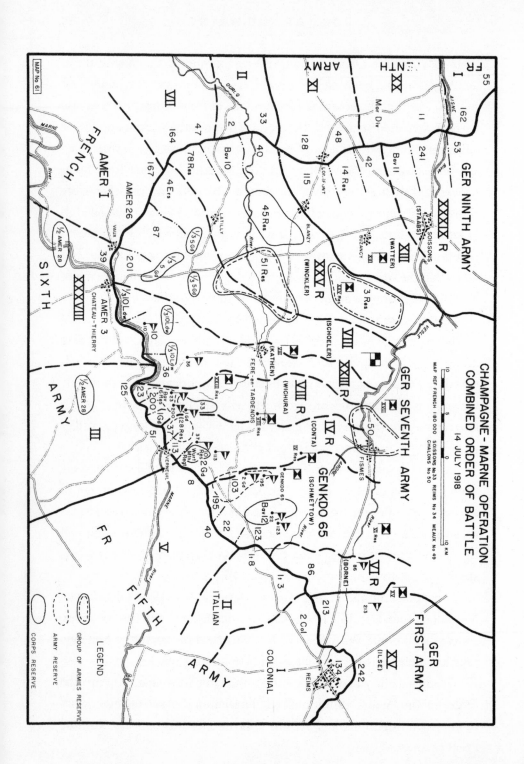

CHAMPAGNE - MARNE OPERATION
COMBINED ORDER OF BATTLE
14 JULY 1918

MAP No. 61

MAP REF FRENCH 1:80 000 SOISSONS No.33 REIMS No.34 MEAUX No.49
CHALONS No.50

10   5   0   10 KM

LEGEND

GROUP OF ARMIES RESERVE

ARMY RESERVE

CORPS RESERVE

T he Army Group of the Crown Prince, the First, Third, Seventh and Ninth Armies, had been moving up from Château-Thierry to beyond Rheims. For the Germans, Rheims was the key. If they captured the Rheims salient, then they would control the rail center there and its many trains would help solve the major logistical problem of hauling supplies to the Crown Prince's armies that were now stretched very thin, outdistancing themselves from needed food and vital weapons of war. With severe shortages of gasoline, most supplies now had to be brought forward by horse-drawn vehicles and not motorized trucks. The taking of the Marne salient would also give the Germans more railroad lines, especially the Paris-to-Metz railroad.

The First and Third Armies drew the assignment of taking Rheims. To the west, between Château-Thierry and Dormans, opposite the Third U.S. Division, Ludendorff placed the largest of his armies, the Seventh, commanded by a Prussian, sixty-eight-year-old *Generaloberst* Max von Boehn, fresh from his stunning victory at Chemin des Dames. Boehn ordered his 23rd Corps to take over the "Marne Defense." Heading the corps was another Prussian, General Hugo von Kathen, sixty-two years old, with a sweeping handlebar mustache. Kathen had been in command of the corps for more than a year, and on the Eastern Front in the summer of 1917 he had led it during the successful Galician offensives against the Russians. He'd earned a reputation as a master of open warfare. Captain Edward Herlihy in McAlexander's regiment, who obviously had never met the general, derisively described him as "a stupid ass, an aristocratic slob like the Crown Prince, probably a relative of the Kaiser." Corps Kathen, as it was named, was eventually composed of the 10th and 36th Infantry Divisions, including the 47th, 128th, 175th and 398th infantry regiments and the elite Fifth and Sixth Grenadier Guards. Also part of Corps Kathen was the 10th Landwehr Division, held in reserve.

It was a mighty foe north of the Marne that was building itself up and getting ready for the *new and great success* Ludendorff had promised—this time against the Americans.

The plan was for von Boehn's Seventh Army to cross the Marne east of Château-Thierry, spearheaded by Corps Kathen, and advance southeast, through Dickman's division and the French 125th Division, in the direction of Epernay, twenty miles from the Surmelin River. At the same time the Crown Prince's First and Third Armies were to attack from the east in the Rheims salient. They would march through the well-defended Forêt de la Montagne de Rheims and join up with the Seventh Army at Epernay. The three armies would then continue east toward their target, Châlons-sur-Marne, with the Seventh Army then swinging on to Paris. Because of the great success at Chemin des Dames, Ludendorff counted on the drive to be done in forty-eight hours.

"The attack," he later noted, "was to be made chiefly by those divisions that had carried the advance across the Chemin des Dames."

If successful, Ludendorff planned in the days ahead for the Group of Armies of the Bavarian Crown Prince Rupprecht to march against the British in Flanders in the west, a double offensive that would open a wedge between the Allies.

The immediate plan for the Seventh Army focused on taking out General Degoutte's Sixth Army and that, of course, meant General Dickman's Third Division.

The Fifth Grenadier Regiment was to cross the Marne just to the east of the Surmelin River and at points near the village of Jaulgonne, where the Surmelin flowed into the Marne. Moving on a narrow front, the regiment was to head south over the crest of Hill 231, between Moulins and the Moulins Ruiné, capture the village of Paroy and then move in a southwesterly direction across the valley of the Surmelin and attack the Bois d'Aigremont.

The 175th Infantry Regiment, meanwhile, was to cross to the east of the Fifth Grenadiers. It was to pass to the west of Moulin Ruiné and from there go straight south, cleaning up the villages of Launay and Connigis and reaching its first day's objective line in the vicinity of Coufromaux.

The 128th Infantry Regiment was to follow the Fifth Grenadiers and the 175th Regiment, if necessary, and push forward the attack.

The Sixth Grenadier Regiment's assignment was to cross at several points north of the village of Mézy. The crossing was to be made by pontoons, boats and ferries and later by bridges. The town of Mézy was to be captured. The troops were to form for an attack to the east and west of Mézy, along the railroad line, and then move directly south and occupy a line running through Grèves Farm, Le Denjen Farm and Longourds. An outpost line about one mile in advance of the regiment was to be set up.

The 398th Infantry Regiment was to cross to the west of the subsector assigned to Colonel McAlexander's 38th Infantry.

The 47th Infantry Regiment was to cross just north of Mézy as soon as the pontoon bridge was completed. It was to support the Sixth Grenadiers and the 398th Infantry. After crossing, the 47th was to take up a support position in the woods north of the village of Crézancy, and later, as the attack progressed through the Bois d'Aigremont, defended by Butts's 30th Infantry, it was to move to another support position one thousand yards west of Saint-Eugène. When the assaulting regiments had reached their first day's objectives, the 47th was to move into the front line and take over a sector between the Sixth Grenadiers and the 398th Infantry.

The assaulting echelons of all regiments were to form under cover of the railroad embankment and move south under the protection of a rolling barrage, which was to start at 3:50 a.m. Engineer companies were assigned to each regimental crossing with instructions to prepare the crossing and the approaches to the river and to further assist in the embarkation of the assaulting troops.

The passage of the river was to be made under cover of darkness and dense clouds of smoke that were to be released from the northern bank. The smoke was expected to cover the river and prevent all observation by the Americans. The infantry and machine-gun companies were to cross the Marne on pontoons and, later, on ferries, and the

artillery and vehicles were to follow on bridges, which were to be
thrown across early in the morning.

The 10th Landwehr Division was to assist in the preparations for
the attack and hold the northern bank of the Marne.

The artillery bombardment was to start at 12:10 a.m. (1:10 a.m. German time). The bombardment was to cover the entire area of the first
day's advance. The shelling was to lift from the strip of ground 350 yards
south of the river at 2:40 a.m. in order to enable the infantry to cross. The
barrage followed by the infantry was to start from the railroad line at
3:50 a.m. Two batteries of escort artillery were assigned to each of the
grenadier regiments.

B ut success depended on surprise. The high command demanded
total secrecy. It didn't want the enemy to find out which armies
were where and when they meant to strike.

In a memorandum entitled "Secrecy," sent to all commanding officers
of Army Group German Crown Prince now north of the Marne and north
of the Vesle, General Bruno von Mudra, whose First Army, in tandem
with the Third Army, had the honor of taking Rheims, stressed that
during the period of preparation for the attack "the first and principal
duty . . . is secrecy." He was worried that the "greatest danger of secrecy
lies in apparent innocent talks among officers. Partly through carelessness
and inattention, and partly through an effort to be 'newsy' and 'knowing
it all,' the men have often given rise to 'rumors' among the troops and even
among the population."

Mudra was adamant that artillery orders and maps had to be "kept
under lock and key in quarters in the rear and must never be carried
along on reconnaissances into the front lines, nor to observation positions,
nor into far advanced artillery positions."

He ordered commanding officers to "instruct their officers and men on
the importance of secrecy." He warned that anyone disobeying such orders
would be disciplined with the "utmost severity." Letters and correspondence

sent to Germany would be read carefully and censored, if necessary. Soldiers on furlough "must keep absolute secrecy when questioned by people." Large columns of men could only march during the day if conditions were foggy; otherwise, he wrote, movement was to take place at night. Occupied villages were to be kept absolutely dark. Bivouac fires were forbidden.

"Even during the very last hours of the preparations, the day the attack is supposed to take place and the assignment of targets for the artillery preparation must not be made known to non-commissioned officers and men, even not to those of the artillery and trench mortars."

The utmost secrecy, then, was the first order of the day, every day.

On June 8, General Mudra, from his First Army headquarters, sent a secret message to Army Group German Crown Prince, an outline of the attack across the Marne to capture the strategic village of Epernay. "The center of gravity of the attack," he stated, "should be in the direction of Epernay." The attack would move in a southeasterly direction. The key to success was to keep a straight line, and that meant that the right flank, crossing into territory defended by the American Third Division and the French 125th Division's 131st Infantry Regiment, had to keep up. "It appears absolutely necessary," Mudra wrote, "to take possession of the terrain west of the Surmelin River at least to the line, Gland-St. Eugene."

Guarding the Surmelin Valley, from the west bank as far as the villages of Mézy and Fossoy, was the Third Division's Sixth Brigade—the 30th and 38th Infantries, the Ninth Machine Gun Battalion and the 10th Field Artillery. Straddling the Surmelin River were troops of Colonel McAlexander's 38th. Mudra's target, Saint-Eugène, was on the Surmelin, three and a half miles south of the Marne. To succeed, Crown Prince Wilhelm had to count on the Seventh Army to do its part and crash through the defense of Brigadier General Crawford's Sixth Brigade along the Surmelin Valley.

The Germans planned to use four groups comprised of divisions to reach Epernay. Group A, led by two divisions, with another division in reserve readiness, was to cross at the village of Chartèves, where the Sur-melin flowed into the Marne—the heart of McAlexander's subsector. Group B, with three divisions in the line and another in reserve, was to cross the Marne at Tréloup, a village two to three miles east of the Surmelin—the sector held by the French division, soon to be strength-ened by four companies of Pennsylvania National Guardsmen from the 28th U.S. Division. Mudra wanted to cross at Dormans, but there the river was too difficult to get over. He then selected Tréloup. Group C, with three divisions in the line and one in reserve, had as its main task to advance on Epernay. Two divisions were to cross at Vincelles. A third division was to attack Venteuil, a village north of the Marne, and drive the French defending it back over the river toward Epernay. Two miles to the north of Venteuil, Group D, with three divisions leading the way and three more on standby, was to dominate the hills and valleys west of Fleury. The French had its armies east and northeast of Fleury, in the forests south of Rheims. Mudra then warned the Crown Prince that he must count on a stubborn defense by the enemy northeast of the Marne because they had already prepared for the attack.

"It is estimated," Mudra pointed out, "that all [my] reinforcing troops will be brought up by marching and that the standard gauge railroad will bring up four trains daily, the narrow gauge road seven trains; loaded with ammunition. Therefore, the ammunition can be in readiness at the railhead by the end of June. As it is brought up, it will be sent to the firing positions. . . . In addition much work will be required to prepare the woods and forest so that the artillery and ammunition trains can cross them. Therefore, we will have to allow for an additional 12 days' time from July 1."

That meant that the earliest the attack could be launched was mid-July, sometime around Bastille Day.

Mudra believed that "if surprise succeeds—and this is the prerequi-site for the attack—then the center of the army will encounter relatively little resistance."

But could the Germans keep their surprise attack a secret?

CHAPTER 5

GERMAN PREPARATIONS

Across the Marne, the Germans still believed they could operate in total secrecy, keep the French and the Americans unaware that tons of artillery, from guns to shells of all calibers, were being hauled closer to the Marne River to be within range of the enemy's front-line troops and reserve troops and supply lines miles to the rear. Back in May, at Chemin des Dames, they'd been able to secretly wheel in their artillery and bring up tens of thousands of infantrymen, but then they'd had the strange ally of those frogs croaking by the thousands, a chorus so loud it drowned out the creak and rumble of an army on the move. There were no frogs in the Marne, or if there were, the mating season had been over for months and a silence now hung like a shroud over the river.

Unable to rely on frogs, the Germans had to find other ways to keep their movements hidden.

Considering the amount of artillery that had to be brought into position and the emplacements that had to be constructed, it would prove a formidable undertaking to get the work done without the enemy knowing. In front of the Third Division, eighty-four batteries were to be placed where their big guns could pound the foe with high-explosive shells and several types of deadly gas, especially striking those troops dug in along the Surmelin Valley. The Germans had been known to fire shells of mustard gas eight to nine miles behind the lines.

For every French and American battery, the Germans planned to have two of their own, when possible. Each battery, whether long-range guns or shorter-range guns, had a task—the "neutralization of the hostile positions," to fire on the enemy's own artillery, to level "villages [as far back as Montmiral], camps, command posts, wireless stations, routes of approach, balloons, etc.; enfilading hostile positions." Batteries closer to the river were to take on the enemy's front lines, flatten the flanks and spread gas through their ranks.

To terrify the enemy, the Germans relied on three types of gas. The most prevalent was mustard gas. A systemic poison, mustard gas attacks the lungs when inhaled and blisters the skin, while its vapor can cause blindness. Private Lewis S. Dowdy of the Third Battalion Headquarters Company suffered a dose of mustard gas and phosgene gas. "Mustard gas is different," the native of Clinton, Indiana, explained. "It is very disagreeable. Smells like crushed mustard seeds or horse radish, and burns like fire." He also got a taste of phosgene gas. "In a couple of days I had pains in my chest with fever and chills." It had been estimated that the German Seventh Army had close to 500,000 gas shells ready to fall on the Third Division.

Without a doubt, mustard gas killed many soldiers who after the war suffered long, torturous deaths, and in most cases, their deaths went unrecorded as wartime casualties. Among the most famous Americans to die this way was the great New York Giants baseball pitcher Christy Mathewson, who languished in a Saranac Lake sanitarium in New York's Adirondack Mountains until his death on October 7, 1925—ironically the day of the opening game of that year's World Series. Mathewson had gone to France after the 1918 season with future baseball Hall of Famers Ty Cobb, George Sisler and Branch Rickey, all of them serving as instructors in chemical warfare.

At the training center near Chaumont, an accident with mustard gas struck about eighty recruits as well as Cobb when they were trapped in a dark, airtight chamber. In a panic, the soldiers tried frantically to push their way out. Cobb was "damn lucky" to get out. "I fell outside," he later recalled. "Most of the poor bastards were trapped inside. When it was over there were sixteen bodies stretched out on the ground. Eight men died within hours of lung damage. In a few days others were crippled."

Cobb wound up with a hacking cough. A colorless discharge drained from his lungs for weeks. Mathewson, who had not been in the chamber, but outside, inhaled enough gas residue to infect his lungs. He told Cobb, "Ty, I got a good dose of the stuff. I feel terrible."

When he died seven years later, his cause of death was listed as tuberculosis of both lungs. He was forty-five. Cobb went to Mathewson's funeral. "Big Six," he said, "looked peaceful in his coffin. That damned gas got him, the doctors said. Almost got me."

The other gases were blue cross and green cross gases, so named because of the color of the mark on their shell casings. Both were respiratory irritants, principally affecting the lungs. The gas masks issued to the Third Division were British small-box respirators. They were molded facemasks with goggles and either self-contained canisters or canisters in haversacks connected to the masks by flexible pipes designed to filter out or neutralize the gas. All of the Third Division's battery positions as well as any billets within four miles of the front line had also been ordered to carry ample supplies of chloride lime for decontamination of the ground and bicarbonate of soda for decontamination of the eyes and skin.

To stealthily move an army over rail and rough roads south to the Marne, where it would take up positions in the woods and villages and the bluffs overlooking the river, called for some ingenious trickery.

First, all artillery movements to the south had to be made at night. On moonlit nights, caissons lugging equipment toward the front and troops accompanying them had to be stretched out over long distances so as not to be easily detected by airplane or balloon observation. They had to hug the side of the road, keeping within the shadow of the trees. "Transportation to and near battery positions far to the front," one order read, "must be absolutely without noise."

To avoid such rattle and clatter, the iron rims on the wheels of all vehicles had to be wrapped in cushions made of old carpet, curtains or rags to deaden the noise. When there was not enough of these materials, willow branches were to be used in their place. Cushions of pine branches and grass rope were to be avoided because they fell apart too quickly. Leather washers replaced metal washers to silence the creaking of axles. Horses' hooves also had to be wrapped in rags. In fact, anything that clattered or rattled had to be wrapped. Artillery guns had to be hidden in villages or clumps of woods "even if that should cause crowding of batteries."

When enemy planes flew overhead, all vehicles and men were to get off the road and take cover in the shelter of the forest. Campfires were forbidden at night, and during the day only smokeless fires were allowed.

However, in trying to get its artillery and infantry placed where they'd be most effective without the French or the Americans knowing created a weakness in the German position. There was to be no construction of bombproof shelters for men and ammunition. The Germans feared that construction of any type, except for camouflage, would attract the attention of the enemy.

Ironically, the code words for the attack, approved by General von Boehn of the Seventh Army, were "Road Construction."

If the Germans thought the French and the Americans, who were waiting, watching and listening on the other side of the river, had no clue that something was afoot, they were mistaken. Observers from the Third Division, hidden on the riverbank, heard noises that meant construction of some kind was being done—against the specific orders that General von Boehn had issued.

Captain Edward Herlihy of the 38th Infantry reported, "Increased aerial activity, reduced enemy artillery firing, and the noise of wheeled transportation near the north bank of the river at night left no doubt in the minds of the men of the 2d Battalion as to the German intention to attack."

What was going on could only be guessed. Major Fred Walker, now the new commander of the 30th Infantry's First Battalion, went to the forward positions every night to check on his men. He asked them what they saw, and it was always "nothing." But they told him they frequently heard voices from the other side and music and "sounds of moving transportation and pounding noises during the night."

Other soldiers by the river swore they'd heard the chop of swinging axes and the felling of trees. As was later found out, the enemy was piling up timber to be used for bridging across the Marne and for boats to ferry soldiers to the south bank.

The Germans were getting ready. It was time for the Americans to take prisoners to find out what was actually going on.

CHAPTER 6

"PRISONERS ARE URGENTLY NEEDED"

On June 8, Dickman issued Operations Order No. 6. The mission of the 38th Army Corps, he reminded his top officers, was to constantly take the initiative over the enemy. One of the ways to do that was "to know exactly, from day to day, what is going on in advance of the front, in order to discover the enemy's intentions." To achieve this goal "reconnaissance should be made by patrols of sufficient strength to obtain information desired. It is not the intent of this Division to remain passively on the defensive. Prisoners are urgently needed for the purpose of identification."

No one knew for certain what German forces were across the river, what their strengths were and when they planned to make their attack. But it was certain that they were building up their forces and, when sufficient, would attack the war-weary French and the greenhorn Americans. Another Chemin des Dames.

"No Man's Land in this area," Ike Lovejoy quipped, "was a strip of water."

The division beefed up patrols along the river to make certain no

German raiding parties slipped over to capture prisoners of their own. Sentinels were grouped in pairs or more to make sure they had enough firepower to halt any enemy found sneaking up on the south bank of the Marne.

The night after receiving Operations Order No. 6, Colonel McAlexander, anxious to show that his regiment was the best, planned the first raid into German-held territory. He wanted to go on the patrol with his troops into no-man's-land, as he had done when commanding the 18th Infantry, but General Crawford had given him a direct personal order that he was not to accompany his men across the river. So McAlexander tapped First Lieutenant Joseph R. Busk and five hand-picked enlisted men from the First Battalion's B Company for the job. Before they left, his hate for Germans still a burning fury, he told them, "Don't let anything alive show itself on the other side except those you go over and get for information!"

Busk was a twenty-three-year-old native New Yorker who'd spent much of his childhood roaming the woods near his parents' farm in Litchfield, Connecticut, as well as camping up in Maine. He had left Harvard before graduating to join the military.

The patrol was set to cross the Marne at midnight. Busk thought the best way to cross the river was by swimming. He'd heard that a few days earlier a lieutenant in the 7th Infantry, Walter Flannery from Pittsburgh, seeing a wounded French soldier hiding in the bushes on the north bank, had swum across the river and brought him safely back. Busk and his men, armed with automatic pistols, trench knives and rope, slipped into the cold river. The strong current quickly carried them downstream. As he struggled to get back to shore, Busk was certain the enemy had seen the patrol. He aborted the operation and reported to his superior officer. He told him the river could be crossed successfully, but there needed to be more preparation, a thorough reconnaissance of the riverbank and a dark night. A powerful swimmer could swim the river with a rope. The rope could then be tied to a raft and the raft pulled across.

Another patrol to be sent into enemy territory was not attempted until June 14, five days after Busk's try. It wasn't from McAlexander's regiment. The mission was given to Butts's 30th Infantry. First Lieutenant Raymond B. Jauss of Headquarters Company led it. A civil engineer and graduate of Columbia University, the twenty-four-year-old Jauss had married Miss Harriet James before heading off to the Plattsburg Officers' Training Camp, where, in 1917, he was commissioned a second lieutenant. He and his wife were residents of New York City's Gramercy Park.

Jauss picked six enlisted men for his patrol. They were to reconnoiter several islands that were separated from the south bank by a marsh. Crawling onto the island nearest the other side, they heard voices coming from the north bank about twenty-five yards away. As they inched closer, the voices they heard were distinctly German and the Germans were singing. Jauss returned and reported that the area opposite the island was "very lightly held and affords opportunity for a safe crossing by a friendly patrol."

Still, two patrols by the division and no prisoners taken. Several other patrols also failed. The Germans knew Americans were on the south side of the river, and when the patrols failed, they taunted them in English.

An operation's report from Dickman's chief of staff summed up the problem. "Last night our patrols succeeded in crossing the river in two different places. No enemy encountered. . . . The enemy is no where to be found on the northern bank of the MARNE. He is further back occupying certain sections of the towns and small farms at the edge of the woods. Lack of material (boats, rafts, etc.) preventing patrolling parties in force from getting across the MARNE. Tonight larger patrols are being sent across the MARNE for identifications of enemy."

Brigade commander Crawford added, "It was an extremely difficult operation to handle. The banks were high, the stream was deep and the water almost ice cold."

The next night, June 15, at 1 a.m., McAlexander ordered another raid. He called it a small expedition. This time, his raiding party had a boat. That was because the rest of the Sixth Engineers had joined the division three days before, on June 12th.

The engineers had arrived bloody, battered and unbowed. In late March they'd been constructing heavy steel bridges for the British Fifth Army on the Somme River east of Amiens. On March 21, the Germans had launched their first great offensive of 1918, striking the British Third and Fifth Armies on a sixty-mile front. Joining the British and Canadian troops in an improvised unit known as "Carey's Force," after Major General George G. S. Carey of the Fifth Army's 20th Division, the Americans dug trenches and then on the 25th traded in their picks and shovels and other implements of bridge construction for rifles. The orders were to hold the Amiens line to the last. The Somme Offensive lasted until the end of March. In a hard-fought battle, the Sixth Engineers had suffered twenty-nine killed and fifty-six wounded. A month later, still in the Amiens sector, they had come under fire again. The casualties were lighter, but still deadly: three killed, seven wounded and sixteen gassed.

Now back with the Third Division, they immediately made their presence felt. Locating a sawmill in one of the villages, they constructed boats and fashioned oars and paddles.

Now the raiding parties did not have to swim to cross the river.

For the raid on the 15th, McAlexander selected Major Robert E. Adams to lead the patrol because, according to the colonel, he was the "best officer on boat-handling in this regiment." A U.S. Marine, Adams had been with the 38th for only a few weeks after being transferred from the Sixth Marines, where he'd been in combat at Belleau Woods. He now commanded the Third Battalion. Handing a wire secured to a boat to one of his men, he ordered him to swim across the river. As the swimmer neared the other side he "lost control of his nerve and began screaming." Adams had him yanked back and sent another swimmer into the river, clutching the wire. This time the wire snapped. The raid was abandoned.

Another aborted attempt. No prisoners. Dickman had to be miffed.

McAlexander, also miffed, ordered a patrol for the next night, on June 16. One officer, two corporals and three privates crossed the Marne at 1 a.m. Near the Brasles-Gland Road, they slipped into the woods, setting up an ambush. They stayed there until 2 a.m. When no Germans were seen, the patrol returned, again empty-handed.

But the day before, on the 15th, the Germans had snared an enemy soldier of their own. An evening memorandum from the Seventh Army, not mentioning whether the captured soldier was French or American, reported, "A prisoner brought in this morning, confirms the presence of the American 3d Division."

The Germans had also interrogated other prisoners on the 15th and 16th and intercepted wireless messages and learned that "General Duchens [*sic*], the commander of the French Sixth Army against which our attack was directed on May 27, has been relieved of command."

The Germans had been successful where the Americans had so far failed. The Germans kept a steady airplane attack. On June 15, six planes, swooping low over the villages along the river, fired into the streets with machine guns. French antiaircraft guns drove them back.

Then, on the night of June 16–17, Lieutenant Busk got a second chance to cross the river, near the village of Gland, and to finally capture some Germans. His patrol was bolstered by Second Lieutenant Charles Frizzell, a fellow New Yorker, and five enlisted men, armed with automatic pistols, two automatic rifles, trench knives and hand grenades. At 1 a.m. the men paddled their boat across the Marne to the north bank. Corporal Pensher and Private Maul were left to guard the boat with the automatic rifles while the others crawled along a path through the woods that paralleled the river. Busk decided to stay hidden in the woods and wait for more light before proceeding.

At 3 a.m., with sunrise less than an hour away, the patrol moved forward toward Gland. Moments later they flushed from the woods a German who dashed for the village. The patrol tossed grenades at him. Standing behind bushes and trees about thirty feet away from the patrol, ten Germans opened up with automatic fire. Busk took a hit and fell. His men returned fire with their pistols. Realizing Busk had been shot, the men ceased firing. For some reason the Germans also stopped. Frizzell and Sergeant Charter brought Busk back into the woods by the river. Acting fast, Charter dove into the Marne and swam to the south bank to get the artillery to bombard Gland. The rest of the patrol, carrying Busk, retreated to the boat and recrossed the river. Busk's wounds were such that he remained in a hospital for several months, and never rejoined his regiment until after the last battle had been fought.

The next night, still without having captured a German, another patrol set off, determined to bring back a prisoner. The patrol was from Colonel Butts's regiment, led by Captain Francis M. Lasseigne of D Company. The son of a West Pointer, Armand Isidore Lasseigne, who had fought against Chief Sitting Bull in the Indian Wars and in the World War was colonel of the 14th Infantry, "Jud" Lasseigne had not gone to West Point like his father, but had earned his commission at the Plattsburg Officers' Training Camp. He had already led one patrol, on June 13. He'd gotten over the river, but returned without success.

Butts did not want any foul-ups this time. He put together a twenty-four-man patrol, selecting soldiers from the First Battalion. Among the men were three cooks, two mechanics, a machine gunner and a musician, twenty-year-old Julius Zawadzki, a Polish immigrant now living in Newark, New Jersey. Second in command was First Sergeant Richard Smith from the 30th's Headquarters Company. Another sergeant was Earl W. Heite from the machine-gun company, carrying a small American flag given to him by the Red Cross.

With rain falling, the large patrol crossed over from Mézy at 11 p.m. in two rowboats. As it reached the north side, the moon came out from behind the bank of rain clouds, lighting up the countryside so brightly that the men had to hunker down in the wet woods and bushes so they wouldn't be discovered. Finally, at midnight, more clouds moved in to blot out the moon. Captain Lasseigne, Sergeant Smith and Sergeant Joseph Narazny of Hamtramck, Michigan, quickly formed the patrol into attack formation and moved it up to the main road heading toward the town of Chartèves, where they were sure to find the enemy. They slipped inside the town, and as they passed one of the houses they heard snoring from within. They snuck into the house, and down in the basement were five Germans fast asleep. They were in their uniforms, but their feet were wrapped in old sacks. Lasseigne and his men rousted the startled Germans out of their beds, secured them and, using their trench knives to prod them along, marched them to the river's edge. When the patrol, with prisoners in tow, had left the house, Sergeant Heite took out his small American flag and stuck it over the front doorway—a perfect calling card.

Because there were now thirty men counting the prisoners, not all of the party could fit in the two boats. Several men, including Heite, stayed on the north bank while the rest paddled across. On the way to the south bank one of the rowboats sprung a leak and had to be abandoned. The other rowboat made it without a hitch. Alone, Sergeant Narazny then recrossed the river to get Heite and the others. After they had pushed off into the waters of the Marne, a German patrol reached the bank, machine guns and rifles ablaze. The rowboat was riddled with holes, took on water and sank.

Luckily no one was wounded, but the Americans had to swim for it with bullets zinging past them—all but Heite, who couldn't swim. Narazny grabbed Heite, pulled him through the swift current and dragged him up on shore, saving his life.

Finally, a raid had been successful. General Dickman was elated. He sent off a report to Pershing about the successful operation, praising Lasseigne. To Lasseigne and the others in the patrol, he wrote his "appreciation and thanks for the very gallant conduct on this occasion. The results accomplished were of the utmost importance."

The story of the raid was covered by war correspondents and ran in newspapers across the country. In the June 19 edition of the New York *Evening World*, the headline read, "DARING EXPLOIT OF AMERICAN PATROL IN CROSS MARNE, Bring Back Prisoners, Then Rescue Americans Whose Boat Had Capsized." The headline a day later in the *New York Times* was more subdued: "AMERICAN PATROLS CROSS THE MARNE. Two Parties Go Over in Small Boats and Clash with the Enemy."

Not to be outdone, McAlexander launched two patrols the next night, June 18. This time, however, McAlexander, who had been ordered not to accompany any patrol across the river, had to get involved. He thought it a splendid chance to show his men, from lieutenants down to privates, that "I was as interested in the operation as any of them could possibly be, and wanted to contribute my share in the actual labor." He helped shoulder the large boat with his men as they carried it down to the crossing point at the river's edge. "Eagles and chevrons and privates mixed in that operation," he proudly recalled.

The patrol, under the command of First Lieutenant V. N. Taylor and Second Lieutenant William H. Haynes from C Company, with twenty men, was sent into Gland, where a "big Yankee sergeant grabbed [a sentry] by the neck and threw him across the road." The patrol was then engaged in a pistol fight against thirteen soldiers, killing all but one—an eighteen-year-old soldier who readily surrendered because he wanted to be captured. He said he had wanted to go to America before he was conscripted into the army, but he couldn't leave his country. He was taken to McAlexander. "He was brought to me," the colonel wrote to his wife the next day, "and wanted to follow me around as playfully as a dog. I was a bit sorry for his comrades, but as they all began to fight there was but one thing to do and it was all over in twenty seconds."

One of the souvenirs brought back from the raid was a belt buckle stamped *"Gott mit uns"* ("God with us"). "Well, old man," McAlexander mused, "if you were with them, you got a devil of a licking that time."

The other patrol was led by A Company's First Lieutenant Robert Crandall of Stamford, Connecticut, who, along with H Company's Second

Lieutenant R. W. Edwards, Sergeant Patrick Farrell, Corporal Martin Anderson and four others, was to penetrate the east end of the town of Brasles. All the men had been chosen because they claimed to be good swimmers. If they failed to capture any Germans, then Edwards, Farrell and Private Antonius Nederpelt, who spoke German, were to remain on the north bank of the Marne until daylight and then return if they were still unable to nab a prisoner. The men darkened their faces with burnt cork, put on soft slippers and wore caps, not helmets, with no insignia.

Twenty-eight-year-old Crandall, another graduate of the Plattsburg Officers' Training Camp, married with two children, was born to be in the military. He had joined the United States Coast Artillery when he was seventeen and was stationed seven years in Key West, Florida. There he'd become an expert gunner. Then a few years before the war he had organized a volunteer company of seventy-five men at Bedford Hills, New York. A nighttime raid against an entrenched enemy offered Crandall a great chance to prove his leadership skills to his tough taskmaster, McAlexander.

At 11:15 p.m. Crandall's patrol paddled to the north bank. They hid there for fifteen minutes and then Edwards and three men crawled more than one hundred yards to the main road to Brasles. Ten minutes later, Crandall and the rest of the patrol crawled up to them. They waited next to the road facedown. They were in luck. Eight Germans came along. They stopped opposite Crandall and his men. The lieutenant wanted to surround the enemy and try to take them all prisoner. But Sergeant Farrell was too eager. He hurled a grenade at the Germans. A firefight ensued. The racket brought more Germans running from Brasles. Six members of Crandall's patrol broke for the river, firing as they ran. Crandall and Nederpelt stood their ground until forced back.

When they got to the river, the rest of the patrol, in a panic, had already jumped into the water and were swimming to the other side.

Crandall called out: "How many men have got across?" He received no answer.

Four of them were swept downstream and drowned, including Lieutenant Edwards and Corporal Anderson, whose body was never found.

He was later reported as missing in action. Only Farrell and a Sergeant Cuff had made it safely to the other side.

On the north bank, in enemy territory, Crandall and Nederpelt knelt by the boat. They knew if they shoved off from the bank they'd be easy targets for the Germans. Then Crandall figured that maybe the Germans thought the entire patrol had tried to swim across and was no longer a threat. He ordered Nederpelt to stay by the boat and he'd go back to where the firefight had taken place. Maybe there'd be a wounded German. He crawled the hundred yards. A wounded soldier was on the ground. No other Germans were around. Crandall dragged the wounded soldier back to the boat. He and Nederpelt lifted their prisoner into the boat, got in themselves and paddled back to friendly territory. After dressing the German's wounds, Crandall brought him to McAlexander's command post.

Now he had to find the missing men from his patrol. He vainly searched the banks of the river. He thought that they might still be in the woods on the other side, hiding. He was tempted to get in the boat and go back, but it was getting too light. Instead, he took his binoculars and for almost two hours, until 4:50 a.m., scanned the edge of the north bank and saw nothing. He went to his own command post and filed his report.

On the next raid, the Germans were ready. Butts sent troops from the Third Battalion under First Lieutenant Alden C. Purrington from Haydenville, Massachusetts. Before they could get all the way across the river, German machine gunners hiding in the bushes ripped into them. Their boat was sunk. The men made it back to their side of the river, drenched and shivering.

Before yet another raid could be launched across the river, a German fell into the Third Division's lap. Ernest Hoeher, a twenty-nine-year-old soldier in the Fifth Company, Second Battalion, 377th Regiment of the 10th Landwehr Division, had experienced enough of the war. A waiter in civilian life, Hoeher had served on the Eastern Front, fighting the Russians. When Germany and Russia stopped battling each other, the 10th Landwehr Division, along with dozens of other divisions, rolled west and into France. It was now entrenched somewhere on the north bank of the Marne between Brasles and the Jaulgonne Bend. Hoeher had made up his mind to swim the river and surrender to the Americans.

On the night of June 21, he walked out of Gland, slipped into the Marne and was about halfway over when a German sentinel saw him. A machine gun was put into action, spraying the water with bullets. He ducked under and kept his head barely above the water so he could breathe. When the shooting stopped, he started to swim again. He reached the south bank and called out as he pulled himself ashore. He ran away from the river, still calling out, and then dropped to the ground face-first, afraid he might get shot by the Americans. Moments later he was captured.

Hoeher had plenty to tell. He named the commanding officer of the 10th Landwehr Division and the regimental and company commanders. He swore he saw Jaeger regiments massing behind Fismes, a village twenty miles northeast of Château-Thierry and a few miles northwest of Rheims. When his regiment came close to the Marne, the roads were filled with soldiers. He saw French and American prisoners; a number of the French were black Colonial soldiers. His Fifth Company was entrenched northwest of Gland. Other companies in the regiment were spread out west of them. The fighting strength of his company was 100 men, although the size of a German company was 150. The ages of most of the men were between eighteen and twenty-two. The command post for his regiment was five or six kilometers north of Gland. There were also two other regiments in the area, the 372nd and 378th. He told how many machine guns were in his company, how many artillery guns he had seen—as many as thirty-seven of different calibers—and these were about to be shifted to new locations.

But then he said the Germans had no intention of attacking. Instead, they were taking up defensive positions. Trenches were to be dug, but so far none had been started. And he had seen no bridges or pontoons—a sure sign that the enemy planned to attack across the river.

That piece of information had to be a surprise to the French, who expected a German attack at any moment. What the Allies couldn't know, of course, and neither could Hoeher, was that Seventh Army commander General Boehn, to cover the fact that Ludendorff was in the midst of planning another offensive, had given strict orders to his officers: "The troops must be informed that preparations are merely a measure of defense to one of Foch's counter attacks." If one of the troops was either captured or, like Hoeher, deserted to the other side, then the story he'd tell, because he believed it, would be one of defense, not offense.

The Allies didn't buy it. All along the Marne River and farther east past Rheims, a front of more than sixty-five miles, they knew the Germans had to be preparing to strike. They believed Ludendorff was aiming at Paris. After his great success at Chemin des Dames, the French capital was too tempting a target not to go after. Following the enemy's four offensives already in 1918, a fifth had to be in the offing. Supreme Allied commander Ferdinand Foch refused to believe the enemy would now switch to the defensive. If it did, then Foch, itching to go on the offensive, would counterattack.

CHAPTER 7

///

"The Marne Must Be Defended with One Foot in the Water"

At Chemin des Dames, General Duchêne had blown it. Ignoring Pétain's orders for a defense in depth or elastic defense, he had jammed his troops into the front line, using a rigid defense, and then watched in horror as they were destroyed. Now the Allies, readying for the Germans, planned to use the elastic defense on the Marne and in the Champagne sector.

And this time Pétain's orders would not be ignored.

The elastic defense, called by the Germans "giving way," employed as many as five parallel trench lines. A token force, armed mostly with rifles and machine guns, held the front line to give the impression that it was heavily defended. When the attack came, the role of the token force was to slow the German's rolling barrage and then withdraw. The Germans, believing they had routed the enemy because they had found little or no resistance when they crossed no-man's-land, would be sitting ducks for a strong counterattack by the Allies' main force holding the second line a mile or so back of the front line—out of range of German artillery. Allied artillery units manned the third and fourth lines—smaller-caliber artillery in the third line and the larger guns in the fourth line. After the Allies dropped high-explosive shells on the front line just vacated by their own men, but now crawling with Germans, the troops in the second line would countercharge. The enemy attack would be stopped in its tracks. That was the theory. Let the Germans hit the front-line trenches, and then, believing they had their enemy on the run, they'd sweep into the open and there the counterattack would annihilate them.

A smart strategy, possibly, especially when there was no river standing in the way. That was true in the Champagne Sector, held by the French Fourth Army under the command of the charismatic one-armed Henri Gouraud, the Lion of Africa and at forty-six the youngest general in the French army. There the terrain was ideal for the elastic defense—flat and open. There it ought to work like a charm. But if there were a single crack anywhere in the Allies' defense that would allow for a breakthrough, then the advantage could swing back to the Germans. Thus the Allies had to hold every inch of this defensive line that since the start of the war had formed a protective arc around the beleaguered French capital.

General Dickman got his first look at the elastic defense planned for his sector on July 11 when the new commander of the French Sixth Army, General Jean Degoutte, who had replaced General Duchêne, visited him at his headquarters in the Château la Doultre. Degoutte, who had, like Gouraud and Marchand, earned his military reputation in Africa, and then in 1917 led a division of Moroccans against the Germans in the Champagne, laid out the plans to Dickman. With his corps commander, de Mondesir, present, Degoutte explained that the front line should be occupied only lightly and that the main defense should be made farther back, after the enemy had committed to his attack. "The Marne," he said, "must be defended with one foot in the water." He warned the American general that if he dared place a heavy concentration of men by the riverbank, German "batteries delivering a concentrated enfilading and reverse fire from the hills on the north bank" would destroy them all.

Degoutte had made it clear to him that he was worried about the ability of the inexperienced Americans to fight well. He had kept pestering Dickman about whether they could "stand the gaff, would remain in their positions under heavy artillery fire," pointing out that when the "German barrage comes it will be formidable."

Dickman glanced uneasily at de Mondesir. He saw that he, too, was uneasy about the plan, but still deferred to his boss.

Five days earlier, de Mondesir had sent out a memorandum entitled "Instructions Concerning Defense of the Marne." It put in writing verbal orders that had been given to Dickman and the commanding general of the French 125th Division on July 5—orders that went against the defense of elasticity. "It is on the Marne itself that we shall have the least difficulty in stopping the enemy," de Mondesir stated, "because he can cross it only by small groups in boats or by columns over footbridges. Consequently, he will inevitably be disorganized when he reaches the bank.

"Our outposts on the Marne, therefore, must stand fast, without thought of withdrawing. Their own reserves must carry on the fight right up to the bank of the MARNE. Companies of the same battalion will not be divided between the outpost line and the main line of resistance.

"In the position of resistance depth must be sacrificed in order to provide density in the front line."

Now the commander of the Sixth Army, who had seen firsthand the debacle at Chemin des Dames and certainly did not want to witness a similar disaster, had changed the strategy from de Mondesir's call for the troops to hold fast to the river to the defense of elasticity.

To Dickman, however, the new plan was a "violation of fundamental principles and utterly erroneous." The idea that ten thousand Germans would cross the Marne, reach the railroad embankment unmolested and then be destroyed by Americans yet to taste battle was ludicrous. But he grudgingly accepted the plan. If it worked, then it would "let 10,000 Germans come across to the railroad unmolested, [and] so confident were we of our ability to destroy them on the plain long before they could reach our main line on the crest of the plateau." He had confidence that his troops could pull it off if they had to, and he was also grateful that after the meeting Degoutte had not left him with written orders. And that, he believed, offered him some leeway.

Dickman then explained the new plan to his brigade and regimental commanders and asked for their opinions.

Colonel Butts, having already declared it folly to place a strong force by the river, favored the plan. Colonel McAlexander was the only officer opposed to it. He went against the wisdom of elasticity and held out for a rigid defense of the river. Their opposing views opened a wound between the two Minnesota natives—even though a slightly different plan than that ordered by Degoutte was eventually agreed upon.

Butts thought that for him to hold almost three miles of the riverbank would be a "serious tactical error." Employing a rigid defense, he rationalized, "would fail to provide the necessary depth for security or for limiting the effect of surprise." He argued that a large force by the river could not be "effectively concealed, and during the attack their positions would be neutralized by enemy artillery and machine gun fire from the hills west and north across the Marne." The result, he pointed out, would be excessive losses in men. It would be impossible to reinforce the troops holding the riverbank. A total fiasco. "It was therefore conceded that the enemy would be able to cross the river when he should attack and that he could not be stopped by a strong force along or near the bank."

McAlexander felt his anger rising. "The plan finally adopted," he recalled, "was that the river should be held lightly and that the front line outpost detachments, if forced, would fall back on the main line and there make a firm stand while the artillery was to wreak havoc against the attackers. This plan aroused every ounce of hostility in me and I voiced my protest in most emphatic terms." As the old Indian fighter saw it, "We had in front of us an unfordable river which was the best possible obstacle; that the withdrawal of troops during an attack would be done in great disorder and that disorder would inevitably spread to troops in the rear; and that if we held hard to the river we had an easy job." Another issue he had with the elastic defense was that it required a "high state of efficiency and previous practical training to carry it out safely, besides being tactically rotten under the conditions as they existed on the Marne."

After the session had ended, McAlexander felt "disappointed and heartsick," realizing that soldiers could never be effectively commanded by committee—no matter how wise and experienced the committee's membership. In his mind's eye he saw a "scene where American troops would be giving way under an intense artillery and machine gun fire. What a magnificent target this mass of retreating men would make for the Germans. Utter confusion that must result from losses and abandonment of the fighting spirit."

If there was a single bright spot, however, it was the fact that his orders did not tell him how many men were to occupy the riverbank.

"The word 'elastic' all at once crystallized into 'rigid' for me. I would make a rigid defense. I had confidence in myself. I had confidence in the personnel of my regiment. I had Frank Adams, Guy Rowe, Maxon Lough and Harry Keeley as my field officers and a lot of splendid captains and lieutenants, and above all a certainty as to what my non-commissioned officers and privates would do under such a virile leadership."

He planned to fight the Germans at the Marne. Unlike the rest of the division, he'd have both feet in the water. He wrote to his wife, "We will be the only ones that can prevent the capture of Paris and we'll do it, be sure of that."

Then Dickman sent his artillery brigade commander down to see McAlexander. Inside the command post, Brigadier General William Cruikshank unrolled a marked-up battle map and McAlexander saw the letters "S.O.S." written over the area his regiment occupied.

"What does that mean?" he asked, with the sense of an alarm going off inside his head.

Cruikshank, who'd graduated from West Point in 1893, starred on its baseball team and been adjutant general of the First Division when it landed in France the year before, explained that the moment the 38th

Infantry was "driven out," as ordered by the elastic defense, his artillery would fire on that area.

"But we are not going to be driven out!" McAlexander protested. He and "Cruick" had served together in the First Division, and he hoped the newly promoted brigadier general, who'd only joined the Third Division a few weeks earlier, would let his men stay down by the river and, to avoid a deadly result, not fire on them. "I want that S.O.S. thing erased from your maps and kept out of your orders!"

Cruikshank replied that it was impossible, that the French had drawn up the plans and had designated his area as the "zone of fire."

"I don't want it and won't have it!" argued McAlexander.

Recalling that moment, he said that Cruikshank stood firm, insisting that the order could not be changed. "I then pointed out to him in an impassioned manner that it meant death to many of my men, that they were going to stay right where they were, and as sure as God was in heaven someone on either side of me would call for the S.O.S. barrage and I and my troops would get it in our backs."

His impassioned plea apparently convinced Cruikshank not to fire on his zone. "I was forced to accept his promise," McAlexander said, "knowing full well that [if he broke his promise] it meant death to many of us."

With that assurance, McAlexander went about setting up his defense at the river's edge.

CHAPTER 8

//

"THE 38TH WAS GIVEN THIS 'GATEWAY TO PARIS'"

After the Americans had gotten their own seven-mile strip of land to defend without all the shifting and the intermingling with Colonial troops and with the plan of elastic defense to follow, Dickman acted fast to put his troops into place. Although there'd be some more shifting within his sector before a final position could be determined, the general eventually divided his division into four regimental subsectors. He placed Brigadier General Fred Sladen's Fifth Brigade outside of Château-Thierry, with the 4th Infantry closest to the village, in the subsector named "Brasles," and the 7th Infantry alongside its eastern flank, in the subsector "Gland." The 7th's history went back to 1808 and the Battle of New Orleans in 1815, where it won its nickname, "The Cottonbalers." It was led by Colonel Thomas Anderson, described by historian John C. McManus as a "tough, blunt-speaking, hard-bitten Texan who had been commissioned out of the ranks twenty years earlier." General Sladen, West Pointer, Class of 1890, was the son of Civil War veteran Joseph Alton Sladen, who in 1872 was part of a detachment of cavalrymen that brought the Apache chief, Cochise, to the peace table. Backing up Sladen's two regiments was the Eighth Machine Battalion and the 76th Field Artillery. Next in line was Brigadier General Charles Crawford's Sixth Brigade, comprised of the 30th and 38th Infantries, the Ninth Machine Gun Battalion and the 10th Field Artillery. Crawford was grateful of the "fact that [his] Regimental Commanders were old Army officers." Butts's regiment took over the zone between the villages of Fossoy and Mézy, named "Mont-Saint-Pére." The responsibility of defending the division's easternmost flank, "Chartèves," went to McAlexander's regiment, from the railroad station at Mézy to near Varennes. It included straddling the Surmelin Valley where its river flowed into the Marne. The subsectors were named after the villages nearest their regiments, across the river in enemy-held territory.

Within the division's sector, between two hundred and eight hundred yards from the Marne, ran the Paris-Metz railroad over double tracks on a ten-foot-high embankment. From atop the embankment it was possible to look across the Marne into the German lines. On the south side of the railroad embankment an aqueduct paralleled the tracks, carrying water to the larger villages to the west. Also, paralleling the railroad tracks was the Paris-Metz National Highway, known locally as the Fossoy-Crézancy Road because it connected those two villages. More than one mile farther back from the railroad tracks was the Woods Line, as its named suggested a stretch of forested land. Along with the Outpost Line by the river, all offered three excellent defensive positions—along the riverbank the Outpost Line, then the Aqueduct Line and farther back the Woods Line.

Yet, from the start, Colonel Butts did not like his assigned piece of real estate. He sensed it was too immense. With meadows and ripening wheat fields and cherry orchards and patches of thick timberland, the lay of the land, he thought, was too unfavorable for a single regiment to hold. For one thing, where the 7th's subsector ended outside of Fossoy and his began, the Marne turned northward for almost two thousand yards and then made a right-angle turn to the east for fifteen hundred yards to where the 38th's subsector started. It was obvious to him that when the Germans attacked they'd hit him on his left flank as well as

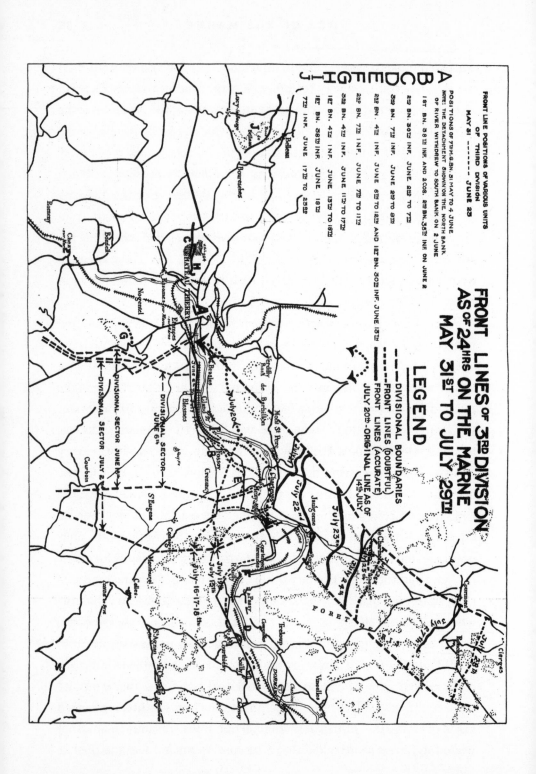

FRONT LINE POSITIONS OF VARIOUS UNITS
OF THIRD DIVISION
MAY 31 ------ JUNE 23

POSITIONS OF 7TH M.G.BN. 31 MAY TO 4 JUNE
NOTE: THE DETACHMENT SHOWN ON THE NORTH BANK
OF RIVER WITHDREW TO SOUTH BANK ON 2 JUNE

A   1ST BN. 38TH INF. AND 2 COS. 2ND BN.38TH INF. ON JUNE 2
B   2ND BN. 30TH INF. JUNE 2ND TO 7TH
C   3RD BN. 7TH INF. JUNE 2ND TO 7TH
D   2ND BN. 7TH INF. JUNE 2ND TO 9TH
E   2ND BN. 4TH INF. JUNE 6TH TO 12TH AND 1ST BN. 30TH INF. JUNE 13TH
F   2ND BN. 7TH INF. JUNE 7TH TO 11TH
G   3RD BN. 4TH INF. JUNE 11TH TO 17TH
H   1ST BN. 4TH INF. JUNE 13TH TO 18TH
I   1ST BN. 38TH INF. JUNE 18TH
J   7TH INF. JUNE 17TH TO 23RD

FRONT LINES OF 3RD DIVISION
AS OF 24 HRS ON THE MARNE
MAY 31ST TO JULY 29TH

LEGEND

— — — — DIVISIONAL BOUNDARIES
— — — — — FRONT LINES (DOUBTFUL)
————— FRONT LINES (ACCURATE)
JULY 20TH-ORIGINAL LINE AS OF
14TH JULY

head-on. He'd have to fight them off on two fronts. Back from the river the ground rose gradually to where he had made his command post. Butts believed that if the Germans were to advance south of the Marne they'd have to take the Bois d'Aigremont. He was sure that it was his subsector that would be their main target.

And Walker, after he'd been put in charge of the 30th's First Battalion and ordered to defend a three-mile front along the river, agreed with Butts. Having replaced Major Robert Livingston Denig, a Marine who'd fought at Belleau Wood, he, too, did not like the battalion's assigned position. "The enemy occupied the heights on the north side of the river and were able, because of the bend in the river, to concentrate their observation and fire upon our positions from three directions. On the other hand our men were forced to occupy the low, flat ground to the south of the river where every move in the daytime could be seen. This was the most difficult sector of the Division front to occupy by our troops and the most advantageous sector for the enemy to attack."

Walker's mission was simple, as it was for the front-line battalions of the other three regiments: to prevent the enemy from crossing the Marne, and "in case he should succeed in gaining a foothold south of the river, to drive him back. In any event the line of the Aqueduct was to be held. The mission was well understood by both officers and enlisted men."

Butts had set up his regiment according to the defense of elasticity. He assigned Walker's battalion to the north side of the Fossoy-Crézancy Road. Holding the river lightly was an outpost of two rifle companies. Supplementing the outpost companies, he added six machine guns and six light mortars with a short range of six hundred yards. The light mortars were to be used for harassing fire at night. He assigned Major Lindsey Silvester's Second Battalion and one machine-gun company from the Ninth Machine Gun Battalion to defend the northern and eastern edges of the Bois d'Aigremont. His Third Battalion was not available to him for his defense. It had been attached to the French corps near the village of Courboin. He located his command post near the northern edge of the Bois d'Aigremont, where he had good observation toward the Marne.

This defensive setup gave him four rifle companies of 250 men each, a single machine-gun company with twelve guns, and one trench mortar section of six light mortars. He also had a one-pound mortar, three .37 mm guns and one .75 mm gun.

Butts and Walker had positioned the two rifle companies down by the river, on the Outpost Line, so that Captain Kay McCallister's B Company was to the left of First Lieutenant Henry C. Switzer's C Company. In the Aqueduct Line, past the railroad tracks, Butts had placed three companies: A on the left flank, led by First Lieutenant Philip J. Sexton; in the middle, Captain John C. Adams's K Company that had been pulled in from the Third Battalion; and on the right D Company, commanded by one of the heroes of the raiding parties, Captain Jud Lasseigne. Beyond the Woods Line, Butts held in reserve the rest of the regiment, and that included two rifle companies pulled from the 38th Infantry.

The colonel reasoned that if he succeeded in holding the Bois d'Aigremont he'd ensure the success of the whole division. "Failure on my part to have possession of the Bois d'Aigremont at the end of the fight would mean failure of the division. It seemed to me that my regiment had been assigned the most important part of the division sector and there was no doubt that the Bois d'Aigremont must be held at all costs." He claimed that Dickman concurred. "[He] told me that he recognized that the sector assigned to the 30th Infantry was the most difficult to defend and therefore the one which the enemy would be most likely to cross in force."

In fact, it seemed that Dickman worried more about the Bois d'Aigremont than any of the other subsectors. To strengthen Butts's defenses, he had taken a battalion from the 4th Infantry, a company from the Sixth Engineers and, as mentioned, two companies from the 38th Infantry, and attached them all to the 30th. Crawford, the brigade commander who had issues with Butts, although he was pleased to have him as a seasoned veteran, carped that the colonel had "under his command one battalion more than his sector was allotted for its defense."

Dickman's decision to bolster Butts's regiment, had, in turn, weakened the 4th and 38th Infantries.

"An egregious blunder," growled McAlexander about losing two of his companies on the eve of battle. Even so, to the old Scot it didn't make any difference whether his regiment was down two companies or where it had been placed or what kind of terrain it had to fight on. He'd defend his subsector to the end because, as he constantly drummed into his troops, "they may kill us, but they cannot whip us."

What concerned him most was the French division assigned to protect his right flank up on Hill 231, the 125th, commanded by General Diebold, and its 131st Infantry Regiment, with L Company of the American 109th Infantry in reserve. The original line of defense gave the entire Hill 231 to the French to hold while McAlexander's 38th Infantry would defend the floor of the Surmelin Valley. Not trusting the French to stand their ground, McAlexander protested strenuously that he wanted his regiment to defend the entire hill. He had argued that if the French withdrew, then "it would be like shooting fish in a bathtub for the Germans to be high above us and on my right flank." He partly won his protest, gaining half the hill to defend.

General Diebold, it turned out, had a sense of doom when it came to the Allies' chances of victory. McAlexander sensed it. One of his captains had noticed how the French soldiers were "positively pitiful in their state of nervous tension. We were given orders to speak to French officers and men only in the most optimistic terms."

For his Outpost Line that ran between Mézy and over the banks of the Surmelin River and partway up Hill 231 to the village of Moulins, McAlexander brought up his Second Battalion. Not applying the strategy of elastic defense, of lightly holding the front line, he placed the battalion along the river and the railroad embankment—in full force. In support, in the Aqueduct Line, he positioned his First Battalion, now down to two companies, along the east bank of the Surmelin River. The Third Battalion he held in reserve in the trenches and dugouts back of the Woods Line.

Leading the Second Battalion was thirty-two-year-old Major Guy Ichabod Rowe, a granite-hard Vermonter and Norwich College graduate. He had served with McAlexander during the Philippine Insurrection, when they'd been with the 13th Infantry and both proven to be among the regiment's crack shots. The colonel trusted Rowe's instincts. He had him promoted to major on June 22, knowing that if any of his battalions could hold off the Germans it would be Rowe's.

A captain in Rowe's battalion said of him, "One of the most loveable characters I have ever known, vehement in his likes and dislikes, yet acting only on the soldier's principle of equity and fairness. Rowe at his best is in the midst of fierce, rotten battle conditions where his cool thinking, soundness of judgment and steadying hand, work wonders for those dependent upon him." After the battle, the captain added, "Rowe was one of the great constructive forces of the 38th Infantry."

Rowe's philosophy as a commanding officer was simple enough. He summed it up in a letter to McAlexander after the war: "I strove for mutual friendship, better understanding, more enthusiasm for the cause and harmony. This, boiled down, means morale."

The youngest of five siblings, Rowe had been raised in the small farm town of Peacham on the eastern side of the Green Mountains, by his aunt and uncle, after his mother had died in childbirth. He grew up thinking his sister and three brothers, who had stayed with their father, were his cousins. His uncle believed in *not* sparing the rod, and Rowe had been hauled behind the woodshed on many occasions. Because money was hard to come by, a college education was almost out of the question until a neighbor named Mary Gould loaned money to him and two other boys so they could attend Norwich, the first private college in the country to offer officers' training. He graduated in 1909 with a degree in engineering and a commission as a second lieutenant, and was the only boy to pay the loan back to Mary Gould. When he went overseas with the Third Division, he'd been married for nine years and he and his wife had two children.

Rowe had four "splendid" company captains, as McAlexander had characterized them, in his battalion to fend off the enemy at the Outpost Line by the river. At the time, however, it seemed there was some friction between the captains. Sensing this, Rowe demanded they iron out their difficulties, and quickly.

At first, Rowe placed E and H Companies on the front line, with G and F Companies in reserve. But McAlexander, after studying maps and walking his subsector, called Rowe into his headquarters. Showing his battalion commander a map, he said, "I want you to know the regimental disposition so you will know what to do when the time comes. Rowe, you hold the front line with two companies, don't you?"

Rowe said that he did, adding that he had two companies in immediate support.

"Well, there is just a little change in my present plan. Thicken up the front line by moving G Company in and start F Company at once digging these little echeloned trenches on the right flank as designated here." He tapped the section of the map that showed Hill 231 on the regiment's right flank, east of the Surmelin River.

Rowe then made the adjustments.

On the battalion's left flank, on the outskirts of Mézy, by the train depot and close to the railroad embankment, a front of six hundred yards, Rowe brought in G Company led by the Kentucky-born Captain Jesse W. Wooldridge, who a few weeks earlier had, on May 28, celebrated his thirty-third birthday.

As a youth, Wooldridge had gone to the Kemper Military Academy in Boonville, Missouri, and in 1905 he graduated from the University of Missouri as a civil engineer. He later moved to San Francisco and was in the banking business. Because he wore glasses, he looked more the banker than an infantry captain.

Wooldridge placed one platoon on the riverbank, one platoon just rear of the embankment and one platoon at the spur of the track south of the railroad station.

On the Surmelin River, where a railroad bridge crossed the small stream, and next to the 131st Infantry, a worn-out regiment of the suspect French 125th Division, with the 109th's L Company held in reserve, Rowe placed Captain Cornelius F. Dineen and his E Company. Dineen's company held a six-hundred-yard front with three platoons on the riverbank and one platoon garrisoned in the village of Moulins.

A twenty-five-year-old, six-foot, four-inch native of Brockton, Massachusetts, portrayed by one of his corporals as the hardest-boiled officer he'd ever met, Dineen had joined the army in 1916 during Pershing's Punitive Expedition into Mexico. Known to his family and close friends as Neil, but to his other friends as Con, Dineen was first stationed in Texas with the 19th Infantry Regiment. A promotion to corporal meant a transfer to the 57th Infantry Regiment at Fort Sam Houston. He was quickly made a sergeant, and two weeks later, on April 17, 1917, he vaulted into the officers' ranks when he earned a commission as a second lieutenant. Moving into officers' quarters, he found himself bunking with a young lieutenant named Dwight D. Eisenhower. During the time they roomed together, Eisenhower had been cramming to join the Masons, studying the society's secret rules, regulations, signs and the handshake. Although Dineen's religious faith opposed the Masons—he was a Roman Catholic—he readily helped the future hero of the Second World War and future U.S. president with his studies. Years later, when Eisenhower was being sworn in as president, one of the Bibles used had belonged to George Washington, from St. John's Masonic Lodge #1. In 1917, Dineen, an acting captain with the Third Division then in training at Camp Greene, had taken Christmas leave, gone up to his hometown and married eighteen-year-old Miriam Louise Maguire, who had recently graduated from Brockton High School and was a freshman at Bridgewater Teachers College.

In between Wooldridge and Dineen, Rowe moved in Captain Edward George Herlihy's H Company. The blue-eyed Herlihy, Eddy to his friends, liked to roll dice in a game of craps or play poker with other officers, especially with Captain Louis A. Merillat, Jr., a free-spirited graduate of West Point, where for two years, 1914 and 1915, he was a Walter Camp All-American end on the same football team with Dwight Eisenhower and Omar Bradley. Herlihy was a month shy of his twenty-fifth birthday, making him the youngest of the four captains. He came from Chillicothe, Ohio, and was an alumnus of Marietta College, Class of 1915, where he'd earned a degree in civil engineering. Like Merillat, he played college football and as a 175-pound lineman for four years had earned the nickname "Iron Jaw." At age sixteen he'd enlisted in the 4th Infantry of the Ohio National Guard, which was later federalized and became the 166th Infantry of the 42nd "Rainbow" Division. By the time he was nineteen he was a sergeant major. Before his twentieth birthday he'd been promoted to second lieutenant. He resigned from the Guard in 1916 and enlisted in the regular army as a private. After training at Fort Logan, Colorado, he earned his commission as a second lieutenant and, on the same day, June 24, 1917, got his silver bar as a first lieutenant. Two months later he was a captain. Perhaps that quick promotion came after he'd set what had been cited as a world record with a pistol. In rapid-fire competition he nailed ninety-nine out of a possible one hundred bull's-eyes.

On June 7, the day after the division took over its own slice of land on the Marne, the sharpshooter jotted in his diary, "Spent the day getting ready to go into the line. I hope the relief takes place very smoothly and quickly." The relief had gone smoothly, and much to his delight, he'd found that his command post, located in an old farmhouse abandoned by its owners, had been set up in a cellar stocked with wine. One scary morning the "Boche gave my P.C. hell. 41 shells. They have torn up everything but didn't hurt my cellar." Afterward, he brought a bottle to his battalion commander. In his diary he wrote, "Major Rowe doesn't like the drink I gave him."

To his disappointment, in the days to come, he'd have to move his command post closer to the river, closer to the Outpost Line and farther away from the wine. He also had to design and construct Rowe's new command post because of his engineering degree. When the job was done, he bragged to himself, "Am some architect."

Right behind G and E, in fact almost wedged between the two companies, came F Company, still in reserve, with Thomas C. Reid in charge. Born in Cherokee County, Kansas, in 1887, he'd married his high school sweetheart and gone on to become a doctor of osteopathic medicine in Demopolis, Alabama. He had a touch of sadness about him. His daughter had died the previous year, nine days before her second birthday. The officers of F Company, because of his initials, T.C., called him Tom Cat behind his back.

One of his lieutenants, Elmer J. Focke, saw that Reid's troops had been ready for some time. "Our boys are quite enthusiastic," the commander of the company's Fourth Platoon wrote to his father back in Dayton, Ohio, "and believe they will show the mettle they are made of when the time comes."

Behind the Aqueduct Line, Rowe had Companies B and D from the First Battalion. In the Woods Line, the rest of the regiment was lined up.

As his regiment was settling in, McAlexander had Rowe order their captains to have the men dig individual trenches, or foxholes, at right angles on the south side of the railroad embankment. The foxholes had to be two feet wide, five feet long and four feet deep. Since the angle of the slope was greater than the angle of falling artillery shells, it would offer "perfect physical security," according to the colonel. "A soldier could lie in one of them and be perfectly protected from the projectiles coming across the Marne. He could spread his poncho or shelter tent half over the top of his trench and keep out rain or sunlight."

Captain Eddy Herlihy called them cave shelters. On the 38th's left flank, Major Walker called similar foxholes that his battalion had been told to dig "graves."

A culvert ran beneath the railroad tracks, so that the soldiers between the river and the embankment could reach their foxholes without climbing up and over the embankment and exposing themselves to artillery and sniper fire. Inside each foxhole in Captain Wooldridge's section he had his men cut a niche in the wall where on the night preceding the attack he had extra ammunition stowed.

In the ground along the river, rifle pits were hollowed out at fifty-yard intervals. In front of the pits, the men strung trip wire low to the ground that would make it nearly impossible for the enemy to reach the rifle pits. At night each pit held four men, 1200 rounds of .30-caliber ammunition in addition to the 220 rounds each soldier carried. Also inside the pits were 50 hand grenades. During the day the pits were covered with brush, concealing them from aerial observation. Another line of rifle pits was constructed along the forward slope of the railroad embankment, on the opposite side of the foxholes.

After overseeing the construction of the foxholes and rifle pits, McAlexander and Dickman went up on Hill 231 to check trench fortifications between their men and the French. Both came to the conclusion that the French would flee once the battle commenced. McAlexander told Dickman they'd "skedaddle" the first chance they got. In fact, the 125th, a truly demoralized division, had already skedaddled in an earlier fight. When the Germans had attacked the valley of the Matz along the Oise River, a rupture occurred on the front held by the French. "The French 58th and 125th Divisions gave way under the shock," Marshal Ferdinand Foch recalled in his memoirs. And because the divisions had quit, the enemy, Foch went on to explain "was master of our second position on a front of seven and a half miles."

McAlexander had pored over the maps of his subsector and then walked the ground until he knew it by heart. With his Second Battalion down on the banks of the Marne, facing north where the Germans were sure to come, he felt he had to protect his right flank if the 125th withdrew. He ordered squad trenches dug—facing east—and for his men to be prepared to fight off the Germans, if they came from that direction, by themselves. Major General Charles H. Martin, a West Pointer who during the war commanded the 86th "Blackhawk" Division, described McAlexander as a "genius in defense" and claimed that his "uncanny visualization of the battle before it occurred caused McAlexander to dig trenches on his right flank between his regiment and the French division."

Dickman, who looked upon Foch as "a small dried up Frenchman," wasn't convinced the French would take off until he personally inspected their trenches. He'd been invited by General de Mondesir to see for himself how the French, after four years of facing fierce artillery bombardments, constructed their trenches.

At the 125th's headquarters, an officer proudly showed off a detailed map of their trench system, highlighted in "beautiful colors." Dickman realized that the map showed trenches that were only "contemplated." After the inspection, he shook his head because there had been very little work done on the trenches. To himself, he thought that the officer "did not know how sadly deficient those trenches were." He came to realize: "Why dig elaborate trenches if you don't intend to defend them?" He knew then, like McAlexander, that the 125th would indeed skedaddle.

Meanwhile, every night the Second Battalion had one rifle platoon from G Company and two rifle platoons each from H and E Companies moved up to the riverbank to prevent any crossing of the river. A rifle platoon was comprised of more than sixty men. It was organized with a headquarters, consisting of a lieutenant, a sergeant, an assistant platoon leader and four privates who served as runners, and four sections. Each section had its own role. The first, or hand bomb, section, was made up of two corporals and ten privates and privates first class divided into three bomber squads of four men each. The second section, rifle grenadiers, had two corporals, each armed with a rifle and a pistol, and seven privates and privates first class split up into three squads. The third section, all riflemen, had two squads under one sergeant, two corporals and twelve privates and privates first class. The fourth section, armed with rifles and pistols, carried one sergeant, two corporals, four privates first class with automatic rifles and eight privates. It was divided into four automatic rifle teams.

At daybreak, these platoons returned to their railroad positions at the embankment, leaving small detachments by the river to observe every ripple of water and, on the opposite bank, every bush, every tree, every blade of grass.

An order from Dickman, issued on July 5, stated that special precautions must be taken against possible attacks. "Patrolling of the banks of the Marne will be extremely active. All portions of the surface of the river will be kept under observation at all times, and no opportunity will be given for boats or single men to cross without being observed. Sentinels will not be posted singly, but by pairs or small groups."

As McAlexander bluntly put it, "These measures were taken to forestall any flighty French reports such as had driven me into a faint on the first night of our arrival in that sector."

During the first week of July, while McAlexander was still getting his regiment organized, Major Ziba L. Drollinger of the Ninth Machine Gun Battalion met with him at his command post to go over orders on where to deploy the machine guns.

About to turn thirty-three, Drollinger, who'd been a farm boy in Rolling Prairie, Indiana, was another West Point graduate, class of 1911. He'd served with Pershing during his Punitive Expedition into Mexico. When he first arrived in France, before his assignment to the Third Division, he'd been a student and then an instructor at the Army Machine Gun School at Langres. He had joined the division on June 30, and thus had been in its sector for only one week.

The major brought with him Dickman's "Plan of Employment of Machine Guns," the orders on how he wanted the machine guns placed. The key, obviously, was to afford excellent fields of fire. The order stated: "The Machine Gun defense of the sector will be such as will insure [sic] cross-fire on all critical points, flanking fire throughout the length of the river and along obstacles. A deep echelonment must be insisted upon, and the action of all guns in the Division Sector must be coordinated with one another and with the machine gun units on our flanks."

The guns were tripod-mounted French Hotchkiss gas-operated, air-cooled machine guns, fed with ammunition in metal strips and with an effective range of about two miles.

The decision on how those machine guns were to be placed was up to the commanders of the two machine-gun battalions after consulting with each regimental commander. But when he stopped by to confer with McAlexander, Drollinger, twenty years younger than the colonel, had already made up his own mind as to where to site his guns. By the time he reached the colonel's command post, his orders had been given and were about to be carried out. Earlier, he had scouted the 30th and 38th's subsectors. "The reconnaissance made at this time," he later explained, "was intended to acquaint [me] with the sector and to determine the state of machine gun defense existing in the area at the time." He discovered that there'd been very little work done toward the construction of permanent machine-gun emplacements, particularly for the regimental machine-gun companies, because of the shifting back and forth of the regiments throughout much of June and the fact the Sixth Engineers had been late in coming to the division. He noted that where the machine gunners had been placed at the edges of the woods, there was no protection from hostile fire.

"These positions," he reported, "had been hastily selected when the machine gun companies came into the sector. These positions were also faulty in that they did not always cover the most effective fields of fire. Nor were they in suitable locations to avoid gas attacks or hostile artillery concentrations that usually fell on wooded areas."

He saw the two main obstacles that faced the Germans were the Marne itself and, south of the river, the rising ground of the Woods Line that gave the Americans an open field of fire.

When Drollinger dropped into the command post on a dark night with the only light coming from candles flickering on a makeshift desk, the old colonel soon realized that the young major had, indeed, begun ordering machine guns into position. "He was imbued with the pernicious idea of 'elasticity' and was allowing a very few guns for the front line where they could fire on the river and beyond it, then a larger number of guns farther to the rear where they could not possibly have any field of fire until all troops had been withdrawn from the front."

Drollinger wanted most of his guns beyond the Woods Line, about two miles from the river. McAlexander wanted the guns closer to the river, where he believed they'd be more effective and not a danger to his own men if the bullets ever fell short of the river. Drollinger pressed the case, however, persisting in what McAlexander labeled the "elastic fallacy."

That had been enough! First Cruikshank! Now Drollinger!

"Major," the colonel said with a hint of sarcasm, "your attitude leaves me in great doubt as to who is in command of this sector. Is it you, or am I in command?"

Drollinger backed down. "Why, Colonel, of course you are in command."

"Fine, now that I know that I have the authority you will put your guns where I tell you! If we can't stop the Germans from crossing the Marne, we will never be able to stop them."

Later, Drollinger admitted that he and the other majors in the division's machine-gun battalions were merely acting as representatives of the regimental commanders "in effecting all technical details connected with the proper organization of the machine guns in their respective sectors."

Finally, he and McAlexander agreed on where to position the machine guns. The machine-gun defense for the 38th Infantry consisted of thirty-two guns dug in along the slopes on both sides of the Surmelin Valley, a few along the riverbank and two or three sections covering the roads to the south. The guns were sighted so that all ground between the Aqueduct Line and the river could be swept with fire by day or by night. The emplacements were coordinated in such a way that cross fire could be delivered against all important points. Machine-gun S.O.S. barrage lines were provided for along the banks of the river and a second line along the railroad embankment.

Placement then had to be coordinated with the artillery so that bullets and shells would simultaneously rake the enemy preparing to cross the Marne. Machine-gun emplacements were done under cover of darkness so the Germans could not locate them and knock them out with artillery fire or with bombs dropped by airplanes. The agreed upon positions were concealed from the enemy under apple and cherry trees and brush piles, behind stonewalls and "in the shadows of deep vegetation." Emplacements that had to be out in the open were hidden in dugouts covered with chicken wire and freshly cut clover "in such a way as to prevent detection even a few feet away." Certain vegetation could not be used, such as wheat, because when it dried out in the sun it quickly changed color and was easily detected by German aviators and then fired on by their artillery. Dirt dug up at night for machine-gun pits was dumped into sandbags and hauled over trails covered with gunnysacking into the woods, where it was then spread around.

Each machine-gun emplacement, which had a supply of spare parts and eight thousand rounds of ammunition in belts and boxes ready for use, had to be guarded by a sentry, day and night. Behind each regimental headquarters was a reserve ammunition dump stacked with 100,000 rounds of machine-gun ammunition.

"So effective were our secrecy measures," Drollinger reported, "that captured German intelligence maps, showing our dispositions about July 13th, contained information of approximately five or six gun emplacements in the entire brigade sector."

Now that the officers and men of the Sixth Brigade had settled into an uneasy position on the Marne, Wooldridge, after studying the terrain Rowe's Second Battalion had taken over, declared with some pride, "The 38th was given this 'Gateway to Paris,' the Surmelin Valley, to defend."

CHAPTER 9

///

"To Know That a Shot Is Aimed Carries a Dread"

As Drollinger's Ninth Machine Gun Battalion, in conjunction with the machine-gun companies of the 30th and 38th Infantries, was moving into position, constructing and camouflaging emplacements, and raids across the Marne to capture prisoners were a nightly event, and shells from both sides of the river shrieked through the black sky and exploded far back of the front-line troops, a lethal game of sniping between the opposing forces had begun.

First Lieutenant Lovejoy explained the constant dangers the men on his side of the Marne faced, so every officer and soldier knew the "feel" of darkness with the enemy watching, ready to shoot. Eyes and ears were sharpened as no other form of training could accomplish, he pointed out. "The soldier learned that he couldn't smoke during the night's vigil on the Marne. Less than fifty yards of a smooth swift river separated him from the Boche sniper. He must not patrol boldly along the bank in a bright moonlight, but, instead, crawl snakelike from bush to bush."

Snipers wounded two men in the 38th's B Company almost as soon as the regiment took up its position on the Marne. "This taught us to keep concealed even though we could see nothing to hide from," commented First Lieutenant Cleon L. Williams of the company's First Platoon. "It was far more impressive than all the theory that had been pounded into us on the use of cover."

C. William Ryan from Wathena, Kansas, knew what both Lovejoy and Williams had described was right—keep low and keep out of sight. A first lieutenant in the 30th's A Company, he'd taken his platoon on a night patrol down to the river where a dam crossed the Marne. Before they reached the dam, they heard shots being fired. When they reached the dam, they found two soldiers from another platoon killed by sniper fire.

Later that night Ryan made the near-fatal mistake of carrying a belt flashlight in the dark night. As an officer, he'd been putting his men in place, when he stumbled into a hole and fell. When he hit the ground, the impact accidentally turned on the flashlight.

"I had trouble to turn it off," he later wrote, "and covered it with my body while doing so." He didn't think the Germans saw it, but later, while he was walking parallel with the river, the "machine guns from across the Marne opened on me a time or two."

A German machine gunner, hidden in the woods opposite the 30th's First Battalion, made Major Walker's blood boil. Every night, when the food detail came up from Crézancy by wagon, a long haul that required a large detail of men, the machine gunner waited for it to cross over the railroad embankment. He would always greet the detail with a "burst and splatter" of machine-gun bullets. "The problem of getting over this ticklish spot and still remaining whole after reaching the other side was one of interest and excitement," Walker mused.

It was certainly too much excitement for two of the men on nightly ration duty, Sergeant John H. Goff and Private Newman Cook of H Company. It was the wagon they were driving, loaded with cooked food in marmite pots, cold food for two more meals, most likely stew or soup and hot coffee, that came under fire as it rattled up and over the railroad embankment. Both men were cited in division orders for bravery under fire.

Over in the 38th's subsector, in one instance, the men were not getting their hot meals regularly, and when that happened food details did not have to worry about snipers. McAlexander found out about the neglect during an inspection of one of his outposts. Chatting with a corporal from E Company and the men in his squad, he asked how they were getting along. The corporal said, "Oh, all right, sir." The colonel did not like the sound of "Oh."

"Are you getting your food regularly?" he asked.

The corporal hesitated before answering. "Yes, sir."

The answer bothered McAlexander. He wondered if the corporal was trying to protect someone. "When did you get your last hot meal?"

"Night before last, sir."

McAlexander discovered that on some nights the men of E Company were not getting their hot food. The captain was neglecting his duty. McAlexander thought, *Here are some of my splendid men being neglected, as food is the first essential in keeping up strength and courage. I cannot produce a high morale with such neglects existing.*

To the corporal he said, "You may say to the other men of this outpost that they will have hot food tonight and every night, even if the colonel has to carry one end of the marmite pole. But if the colonel carries one end, your captain will carry the other."

McAlexander saw a look of delight sweep over the corporal's face. It made him happy because the corporal knew his colonel was looking out for him.

When it came to sniping, McAlexander, on the other hand, was determined to exact an eye for an eye.

As a boy growing up in Minnesota, he'd been engrossed listening to his father and two uncles tell tales of the Civil War. He loved best the stories of the sharpshooters and the tricks they used to outwit their foe.

Sniping was a lost art, he thought. He'd change that under his command. At the Marne, he'd make the enemy front a danger zone to the depth of one mile. He'd "inflict loss on all moving things." As he rationalized, "the enemy is rendered exceedingly uncomfortable and soon loses in morale when he suffers losses without knowing the source of the fire. The fear of being hit by an aimed shot is disconcerting in the extreme, while a stray shot taking effect is negligible. To know that a shot is aimed carries a dread."

Almost from the moment his regiment took up its position along the Marne in early June, the colonel ordered his company captains to single out their best sharpshooters, only those who had the eyes of an eagle, had proven the best qualified on the rifle range and had hunted big game back in America and thus could pick off the enemy a mile away. They had to be "hardy, cool, calculating and sufficiently unemotional in their natures." He then issued each company four telescopic rifles. He told the snipers that they had to make direct hits, but if they missed then the "miss had to be so close as to give a 'popping' sound in the ears of the man aimed at and make him think of how close a call he has experienced." He learned the names of every one of the snipers, and at night when he inspected the front lines he talked to them, using their names.

At first the snipers had excellent places for concealment near the riverbank. They could fire into the enemy lines without worrying too much about retaliation. McAlexander had given orders that no one was to visit the snipers or even go near their posts. "I wanted perfect secrecy for the sniper."

One of his snipers, seeing a peasant woman on the north bank leading a cow down to the river for a drink, and remembering the colonel's order to kill everything that moved, shot her and the cow. Both the sniper and McAlexander believed that, in fact, she was a he and therefore a German spy reconnoitering a river crossing. McAlexander relayed the shooting to General Marchand.

In French, he blurted, "My God, have you killed a woman?"

It took a moment fumbling with his poor French for McAlexander to try to get Marchand to understand that the woman was a spy dressed in peasant clothes. Unconvinced, the general wanted to know how the sniper figured out that it was a man and not a woman.

McAlexander had had it with the French. He shot back, "Any damn fool sniper would know that in every French village there were always from one to four watering troughs for animals, and it would be no less than idiotic to try to water a cow in the Marne."

"Oh, yes," admitted Marchand, "now I understand."

When the regiment was shifted to the Surmelin Valley, places for concealment were hard to find because the ground there was more open. Some snipers became afraid to fire for fear they'd reveal their own positions and be themselves targets of German machine gunners.

In Wooldridge's company, McAlexander found out the snipers had not fired in several days. He decided to go down toward the river, inspect his troops and have more than a talk with his young captain. McAlexander's battalion commander, Major Guy Rowe, who'd served with him in the Philippines, asked to accompany him. He said no, that he did not want to put both of them in danger. In broad daylight, he strode down to where G Company had been digging in. Wooldridge was stunned to see the "Old Man" climbing the railroad embankment, showing himself to the enemy. A sentinel yelled for him to get down. "Sir, my orders are not to allow anyone to expose himself over this line. You'll draw fire there."

"Whose orders are you carrying out?" McAlexander asked the startled sentinel.

"The colonel's."

"Under the head of Military Necessity," McAlexander said, "I think we may change your orders so far as my observations are concerned."

When he and Wooldridge met, McAlexander told the captain that he'd heard no firing for several days. He asked where his snipers were, and Wooldridge had to admit that none had been posted. His excuse:

Every time they fired across the river, they'd receive return fire from enemy machine gunners. McAlexander then asked where Wooldridge had put the telescopic rifles. Wooldridge did not know, but he told a sergeant to fetch one.

"I gave that captain five of the unhappiest moments of his life while the sergeant was getting one of the four rifles," McAlexander recollected, believing then that the morale of his troops was "lowering."

When the sergeant returned, McAlexander grabbed the telescopic rifle and turned toward the shaken Wooldridge. "I want to bowl a couple of 'em over myself. Let's see how close we can get."

Wooldridge followed him as he crawled toward the riverbank until he found a clump of bushes and weeds that offered enough screening to keep them hidden from the Germans and still allow them to see across the river.

"Don't let anything show itself on the other side and live," he said in a scolding voice. Then he fired at every spot where he thought the enemy had a hidden machine gun. Wooldridge remembered that he fired two clips and the "results were disappointing."

Receiving no return fire, the colonel and his captain crawled back to the protection of the railroad embankment. The whole way, Wooldridge was jumpy because he knew "every square inch of our front was covered by German machine guns and one-pounders and every minute we stayed there our discovery was more imminent."

Once they had reached the safety of the railroad embankment, McAlexander informed his front-line officers huddled around him that at least there was one man in the regiment who could carry out an order. Having made his point, he climbed up the embankment to continue his inspection. He walked along the track toward his farthest outpost, daring a German sniper to take a shot. His men anxiously kept their eyes on him. One of them was Elmer Focke, the young lieutenant in Captain Tom Reid's F Company. Ten years earlier he and his family, who owned the Focke Packing Company in Dayton, "Home of German Made Wieners and Bologna," had traveled through France by train and had ridden over the same railroad tracks he now had been ordered to defend, and there was McAlexander as brazen as a streetwalker stepping along the tracks, his trench cane in hand. As McAlexander neared a stand of trees, Captain Reid, the practitioner of osteopathic medicine, shouted, "Colonel, don't go beyond the edge of the wood as the Boche always fire on that spot!"

Reid's warning angered McAlexander. *Too much timidity among his officers*, he thought. Yelling at Reid loud enough so that those within earshot could hear him, he ordered the Kansan to lie down in safety behind the embankment and not get up until he'd been given permission. He next directed every one to stay where they were. He continued down the track. Now that he was in front of his men, there was no way he'd back down and stop walking.

"I would have gone along that railroad then if it had been the last moment of my life," he said, justifying his actions to himself. *What*, he wondered, *was this damnable timidity that was sapping the courage of my men?*

The scraping of footsteps on the tracks behind him caused him to turn around. The sergeant major of the Second Battalion, William A. Walters, Jr., was trying to join him.

"Sergeant Major, what are you doing here?" a still angry McAlexander asked.

"I can't let my colonel go alone," Walters answered.

Moved by his actions, McAlexander let the sergeant major accompany him as he finished his inspection and returned to the officers, Wooldridge, Reid and the other captains, Eddy Herlihy and Con Dineen, huddled behind the railroad embankment. Then Wooldridge watched him as McAlexander turned and faced the Marne. "He squared his shoulders, swelled his chest, set his jaw and said, 'Let 'em come!'"

CHAPTER 10

//

THE
"FROSTY SONS OF THUNDER"

B ut when would the enemy come? And where?

Ferdinand Foch, the Allied supreme commander, like Dickman, Crawford, McAlexander, Butts and all the soldiers up and down the Western Front—French, British and Americans alike—was anxious to know when the attack would be launched and from where. He yearned to go on the counterattack the moment the Germans had been stopped. He understood that after the Germans attacked, the Allies would find the enemy's defenses less well organized to fend off a lightning-quick counterstrike. He wanted the strike primed and ready, a counterattack that he'd been planning since the fiasco at Chemin des Dames. But if the Germans succeeded in breaking through anywhere along the front that stretched for nearly one hundred miles, and that certainly included the sector held by the American Third Division on the banks of the Marne east of Château-Thierry, then a golden opportunity to switch to the offensive might be lost. He knew the Germans had the advantage in manpower. But he knew their armies were stretched too thin, that they were outrunning their supply lines. If he could preempt the Germans with a massive artillery barrage, count on the elastic defense to thwart any advance, and then beat them back, he felt it in his heart that he'd have them on the run. There'd be no more trench warfare; fighting would be on open ground. He had the Tenth Army of General Charles "The Butcher" Mangin poised on the Aisne River ten miles west of Soissons to spearhead the counterattack if and when the time was ripe and if the Allies held and then repulsed the Germans.

First blocking the enemy's advance and then attacking him, a one-two knockout punch, Foch called playing "this double game." But to play it "effectively" he had to use all available French forces between the Oise and the Argonne. But they first had to be rested and brought up to full strength. By adding American and British divisions, he'd then have an imposing mass of thirty-eight infantry divisions and six cavalry divisions. "This was enough to meet the requirements of our defensive front in Champagne and our offensive operations in the Soissons region," he believed.

But now, as the days ticked by in July, the enemy building its forces, bringing up what supplies and munitions were on hand, especially north of the Marne River, Foch found himself fretting through what he'd later call the "Period of Waiting." When would they attack? Where would they attack? Would it be against the British or against the French or both at the same time? Was Paris the main target? Or did the Germans plan to drive a wedge between the French and the British, split the Allies so they'd knock England out of the war?

"The Allies," he warned, had "to be ready to intervene anywhere on our front, from the North Sea to the Vosges."

Bolstering the French and British forces, Foch now had nine American divisions in the line. Each American division was twice the size of the other divisions on the Western Front—almost thirty thousand men per division. Four were regular army, the First, Second, Third and Fourth. Five were National Guard, the 26th from New England, the 27th from New York, the 28th from Pennsylvania, the 30th from North and South Carolina and Tennessee and the 42nd, whose twenty-six states and the District of Columbia covered America like a rainbow. One other American unit also in the line was a regiment of African-Americans from Harlem—the 369th, which had been ignored by Pershing and attached to the French Fourth Army, as if the black New Yorkers had never existed. As the 369th's commander grumbled, "Our great American general simply put the black orphan in a basket, set it on the doorstep of the French, pulled the bell, and went away."

Although it did not consider itself an orphan and had not been left on the doorstep of France like the 369th, the National Guard division from Pennsylvania, the 28th, had on the eve of the Second Battle of the Marne, been emasculated by the French. It had been dumped in the lap of the French 38th Army Corps, which was bad enough. When on July 8 the Pennsylvanians had moved up to the Marne, where they'd eventually fight side by side with troops from the Third Division, the French had quickly dismantled the 28th. Similar to what they'd done to the Third Division in early June, they broke up infantry regiments and assigned them to different sectors within the Marne region. Companies within regiments were yanked out and separated from one another and then sent off in different directions. The 28th was no longer a cohesive unit, at least not during the defense of the Marne.

For example, the 55th Brigade included the 109th and 110th Infantries and was attached to the French 113th and 131st Infantry Regiments of the French 125th Division, holding down the Third Division's right flank. The 56th Brigade, the 111th and 112th Infantries, joined forces with the French 39th Division on the Third's left flank—nearly a ten-mile separation between the two brigades. The rest of the 28th Division, scattered about, was held in reserve behind the Third. Then the French pulled out two companies from the 109th Infantry, L and M, and two companies from the 110th Infantry, B and C, forming the four companies from the two different regiments into a single battalion. On July 10, these four companies found themselves embedded with the French east of

McAlexander's regiment—B, C and M Companies with the French 113th Infantry and L Company with the 131st Infantry—and the old colonel, as earlier noted, held no trust in the staying power of the French. If they retreated when the Germans poured across the Marne, then the Pennsylvanians would have to fend for themselves.

A soldier in one of the companies sent to the 125th complained, "The American officers could never understand the character of this order, which divided our troops into such small elements. They realize at once the seriousness of the situation. Our methods of fighting differ from those of the French and the difficulties of language made intelligent liaison impossible."

In the days to come that difficulty of language and lack of direct communication between officers on both sides would prove disastrous.

Unlike federal units, National Guard units, for the most part, are homegrown. Soldiers come from the same place. They've grown up together, dated the same girls, graduated from the same schools and worked the same jobs. Within the ranks are fathers and sons, brothers, uncles and nephews, cousins and best friends and worst enemies. They are a reflection of their hometown's distinct character.

In the 110th Infantry Regiment, C Company, one of the four companies now with the French 125th's 113th Infantry, was such a unit.

It was made up mostly of soldiers from the closely knit county of Somerset, a sparsely populated region in the southwestern hills of Pennsylvania known as the Laurel Highlands, which border Maryland and West Virginia, a rich land of coal mines, farms and railroads, and the state's highest mountain. The coal mines were then owned by the robber barons—the Rockefellers, Mellons and Hillmans. Coal-mining strikes were common right up to America's entry into the war, and each time the 110th was called out to protect the mines and guard against violence—a difficult and conflicting duty for a number of the men in C Company who were themselves miners. The 110th had also been mobilized during the infamous Homestead Riots of 1892, one of the worst and most violent labor strikes in United States history.

Because Somerset County is situated within the highlands, the weather is usually colder and the winters longer than in other sections of Pennsylvania. Inhabitants of the county call it "Little Siberia." In the early days of the nineteenth century, General Alexander Ogle, who'd been a congressman and served in the state legislature for many years, while making an address at the state capital, proclaimed his constituents to be the "Frosty Sons of Thunder." The sobriquet stuck, and from then on the people of Somerset County proudly called themselves the "Frosty Sons of Thunder."

Like most of eastern America's National Guard outfits, Somerset's C Company had a heritage that went back to the Colonial days, when a number of the county's residents had been in the Continental Army during the Revolutionary War. The county had also mustered several militias that saw active service in the War of 1812. Four regiments had then been organized during the Civil War. In 1873, three years after Pennsylvania had established its state National Guard, the citizen soldiers of Somerset County became part of the 10th Pennsylvania Infantry Regiment. In the years leading up to the World War, the 10th Pennsylvania had put down riots, battled striking miners, fought in the Spanish American War, slogged through the jungles of the Philippines and Puerto Rico and, in 1916, patrolled the Texas border in support of John J. Pershing's Punitive Expedition into Mexico in search of the elusive bandit and revolutionary leader Pancho Villa. By then it had earned the nom de guerre "The Fighting Tenth."

In October 1917, after the United States had entered the war, the 10th was federalized, renumbered the 110th Infantry and assigned to the 56th Brigade of the 28th National Guard Division. Its men were drawn from the state's western counties, mostly from Beaver County northwest of Pittsburgh and Somerset. The other regiment in the 56th Brigade, the 109th Infantry, came from the opposite end of Pennsylvania, the eastern region around Scranton.

On July 15, 1917, a year to the day before it met disaster on the hills overlooking the Marne River, C Company, as part of the 10th, was formed and mustered into the regiment's First Battalion. One hundred fifty-eight "Frosty Sons of Thunder" made up the original roster, a motley group at first, some without equipment, others without uniforms, some with no military experience and others who had served on the Texas border and thus carried the swagger of a veteran. More than two thousand proud and patriotic county residents turned out to cheer them as they formed up for the first time on Somerset's North Street and then, accompanied by bands from nearby Meyersdale and Berlin, marched to their first encampment—the lawn of Somerset's County Courthouse a few blocks away.

The commander of C Company, thirty-five-year-old Captain W. Curtis Truxal, a 1904 graduate of Franklin and Marshall College, a prominent lawyer from Meyersdale and son of a minister, led the way. Among those marching with him were the superintendent of the Western Union telegraph lines, First Lieutenant Samuel S. Crouse, at fifty-four the oldest soldier in the company, and his eighteen-year-old son, Edgar, one of the youngest soldiers. The first to enlist once war had been declared was John Heitzman, nephew of the editor of the *Meyersdale Republican* newspaper. He was followed by brothers Corporal Samuel Boyd Salkeld and Private William Ralph Salkeld, grandsons of Civil War veterans, and Privates Charles and Frank Vannear. Eighteen-year-old Frank, nicknamed "Babe," had starred on Somerset High's first football team. Another recruit was Lawrence Hartle, just twenty years old, who had been working in the coal mines for three years.

Corporal Alvey Martz, a twenty-five-year-old from Glencoe who ran a remote mountain farm and was married with four children, trooped along, as did red-haired Herbert Foust, only five feet, six inches tall. A twenty-two-year-old laborer who had already served three years in C Company before being discharged in January 1916, Foust had eagerly reenlisted five months later to be part of Pershing's Mexican adventure. Alvey Martz's military lineage went back to the Revolutionary War. His grandfather, Herman Martz, had fought in the Civil War. At war's end, his family, having not heard from him for months, had no idea whether he was alive or dead. Then one day he came up the road to the family farm. Herman named his first son, Alvey's father, Abraham Lincoln Martz. Ironically, the Martz family was of the Dunkard faith, an old German sect that does not believe in military service.

Another farmer, Harry L. Stevanus, not yet twenty-three, was from Coal Run, a few miles outside of Meyersdale. He loved to hunt rabbits and squirrels in the woods and fields around the family farm. His girlfriend, Verna Imhoff, only sixteen, was among the crowd cheering the soldiers. They would tie the knot a week before Christmas. Although Stevanus proved to be a left-handed sharpshooter during rifle practice, he'd later be assigned as a cook, learning to bake biscuits, cakes and pies, but not bread.

Certainly, one of the spectators among the townspeople was sixty-five-year-old John Snyder, "Suse," as he was known around Somerset, a veteran of the Spanish American War. A year earlier, when C Company had marched off with the Pennsylvania National Guard to protect Texans against Villa, he begged Captain Truxal to let him go with the boys. After all, he'd been an original member of the company and was still on its rolls. Truxal told him he couldn't go.

"I would rather take you along for personal reasons than a half-dozen men," he said to Suse, according to a report in the Somerset *Herald*. "But you are past 64 years of age and a grandfather and my orders are to leave you at home."

"But Captain, I want to go. I was one of the original members of Company C and have always tried to do my duty and it isn't a fair deal to let me out now. I can keep up the march with any of them; won't you let me go along?"

"No, Suse," the captain said with finality.

The brokenhearted old veteran then burst into tears.

In the days and weeks to come, most of the company slept in tents erected on the courthouse lawn or in the basement of the courthouse, while others received permission to spend nights at home and even dine with their families. Those who did not go home messed in local restaurants. During the day, the citizen soldiers drilled in the streets of Somerset and in the fields outside of town.

On September 7, two months after being mustered in, C Company was shipped off to Camp Hancock in Georgia for intensive military training. To fill out the company with the required number of men, recruits were brought in from Texas and Oklahoma. But the company lost forty-two men from Somerset County who were dropped from the roles for health reasons or had been transferred to other companies. Of the 154 original members 116 remained.

Seven months later, as part of the 28th Division, the company left Hoboken, New Jersey, for the Western Front, landing in England in mid-May and then moving on to Calais, France.

During the 110th's short stay in Calais—getting their collective feet wet, hobnail boots and all—the regiment came under night attack, its first taste of war. One of its soldiers remembered the moment: "The hum of the German aeroplanes, the plying of search lights and the barking of the anti-aircraft guns, was the signal for the American boys to come out and observe what to them at that time was only a picturesque display. A little later, however, the men appreciated the great danger of the bombing planes, and took shelter along with their comrades among the Allies. From this time on until the close of the war the Regiment was never out of hearing of heavy artillery or out of danger from bombing or shell-fire."

On May 21, a few days after the night raid, the 110th Infantry pulled out of Calais, traveling in railroad boxcars to Lumbres and then on foot to Belquin, to a training center where the regiment was assigned to the 25th Northumberland Fusiliers for instruction. The Fusiliers had recently been hammered during the Battle of Lys as the Germans had tried to push the British back to the North Sea. As one Pennsylvania soldier noted about the Fusiliers, although they'd been badly cut up, they had "many high class officers and men left who were used as instructors" who "faithfully worked in assisting us in grasping the new methods of war."

In early June, following their training with the British, the Pennsylvanians were on the move, heading east toward the Marne to support the French. As they neared the front, the regiment traveled in trucks that belonged to the French and, to their surprise, the drivers turned out to be Chinese. Then they were on foot again.

"We sure did have to do some hiking before we reached our destination," Corporal William Leckemby reported to his mother. "And it was hot and dusty which made it much worse. We are stationed in an old-fashioned village among the peasants somewhere in France. I can't tell you the name of the place now."

Private First Class William O. Zimmerman, a thirty-eight-year-old bachelor from Somerset, dashed off a letter to his sister Rose, letting her know that there wasn't time enough for him to write letters. He added that writing paper was scarce. "Tell Carrie [his niece] I will write to her as soon as I can get paper for we only get paper once in a while and then it don't go around the company."

The countryside C Company passed through reminded the Pennsylvanians very much of the land around their hometowns.

"What I have seen of France is real nice," Corporal Alvey Martz, the farmer, penned in a letter to his "Dear Mother and All the Rest." "The land is rolling like the land back home. Most of it is farmed, and there is very little woodland. The season is late here. The apple trees are just blooming now. About all the crops I have seen are oats and rye. There are lots of horses here, all big horses, but not so many as through our country. Everything is behind the U.S.A."

Cook Harry Stevanus, a three-generation farmer, also took in the French countryside with a granger's sharp eye for the land. "The weather is fine here," he told his parents, who worked the family farm back in Coal Run. "The flowers are all in full bloom. The strawberries are ripe and some of the early cherries. The apple trees are full of apples and all other crops look fine to me."

The size of the eggs laid by French chickens astonished Captain Truxal. Although he was not a farmer, but a lawyer, Truxal had grown up in Somerset County's rich farmland. "Both France and England have us beaten on stock," he wrote home, pointing out that he had already seen a good bit of France. "Their poor stock is much better than our poor stock, and their good stock is far above our best. Even chicken eggs are bigger than ours."

Corporal John Heitzman wrote to his uncle, "This is a beautiful June Sunday. The weather is just perfect; everything around here is in cultivation and the flowers and blossoms are in full bloom. It reminds me very much of spending a Sunday in the country in Somerset county."

Private William Salkeld, in a letter to his "dear home folks," wrote that France was a pretty nice-looking country. "We are billeted in a small French village and have quite the time with the money. There must be quite a battle going on today. The heavy guns have been booming all morning. Let's hope they are shooting the dickens out of the Huns. I saw a couple of air raids already."

His older brother Samuel was keen on getting into tip-top shape. "The stronger we get the better we can fight," he wrote home. "My slogan is 'All muscle and no fat!'"

With all the marching and drilling and lugging one-hundred-pound backpacks and rifles, the C Company boys were getting stronger, their bodies hardening and their stamina increasing. Leckemby wrote to his family to tell everyone, "I'm as hale and hearty as ever."

Stevanus had been assigned to the officers' mess as a cook. His kitchen was in a farmhouse run by an old gentleman and lady. "They are very good," he informed his parents. "The old lady gives me a big dish of strawberries about every day and she had a small tree of cherries. My buddy and I picked them for her and then she gave us the half."

The closer to the front they got the louder the roar of the artillery became, and in the skies they witnessed dueling airplanes—French, German and American.

Captain Truxal told the folks back in Somerset, "We are quite accustomed to the rumble of the big guns and airplanes are as common as Fords."

Truxal spent a week in a farmhouse with Captains William Fish from New Brighton, commander of B Company, and Charles F. Linn of Monongahela, a surgeon in the 110th Infantry. Linn was a graduate of Washington and Jefferson College, where his father was an instructor, and the University of Pennsylvania. Their only diversion during this time, according to Linn, was watching aerial duels and German planes brought down by antiaircraft guns. In the evening they'd go out on the hills to listen to and watch the fireworks from the French artillery.

On July 3 word reached the division's commanding officers that the Germans planned a major drive on Paris the next day, America's Day of Independence. Under the dark cloak of night, the soldiers were rushed into the hills and valleys south of Condé-en-Brie, six miles from the Marne, and right behind the Third Division. They readied themselves for the attack in a long skirmish line. The attack never came. Another false alarm by the French. The alert was called off. But a week later, on the 10th, Companies L and M of the 109th Infantry and companies B and C of the 110th were taken away from the 28th Division and placed inside the lines of the French 125th Division.

And there they'd stay until after the battle, mixed in with the French and miles away from the rest of the boys in their division.

CHAPTER 11

//

"THE PERIOD OF WAITING"

Marshal Foch called it "the period of waiting."

The July days crept slowly by. The French were afraid that the monumental attack the Germans had been planning ever since Chemin des Dames would come at any time. To date, the Germans had been successful in keeping the moment of attack secret. And so every night, it seemed, from July 4 on, the French put troops guarding the front lines and those in reserve on high alert—meaning, so the troops thought, the enemy was going to begin their offensive that particular night. But every night nothing happened, except for the sporadic firing of the artillery from both sides and airplanes circling overhead like giant vultures.

"The French headquarters has been hollering 'Wolf' some more and all of our men were 'alert' again last night," Colonel Ulysses McAlexander, who had no faith in the French, wrote to his wife. "They sure do have the 'nerves' and a bad case of them." In another letter, he wrote, "I should have been glad if they had attacked for I am in a fine position to lick the tar out of those in front of me."

One of McAlexander's captains, Eddy Herlihy, jotted down in his

diary on July 12, "Very quiet, although we expected an attack at daylight. Another false alarm from the French!"

In the operations report of the 38th Infantry it was written, "The
troops were becoming more or less 'blaze' [sic] with regard to the alert
signals although they were thoroughly convinced that the attack would
soon be launched against them."

An antsy General de Mondesir of the 38th Army Corps was worried the Third Division had not done enough work in preparing
its "position of resistance." In a memorandum to General Joseph Dickman he warned, "While the enemy is preparing for an attack on a great
scale, in the course of which he will fire thousands of projectiles of all
kinds on your troops, not one man should be left without protection."
He ordered Dickman that his soldiers who were not manning combat
posts had better dig holes with earth parapets and those already occupying combat posts "should work unceasingly, under direction of their
officers, to obtain a continuous system of defenses."

As it turned out, the Third had been working on its defenses from
almost the time it had reached the Marne. The only problem had been
that de Mondesir kept shuffling the division around and it was impossible for an elaborate system to be constructed until a permanent position had been taken up.

After reading de Mondesir's memorandum, Dickman complied and
had his men redouble their efforts to dig in. Work details from the 30th
and 38th Infantries were sent out at night to help the men of the Sixth
Engineers construct trenches and erect barbed-wire entanglements.

"All night long and all today the woods have just been ringing with
the noise of picks and shovels," First Lieutenant Robinson Murray of
McAlexander's F Company, wrote on June 22 to Nurse Peggy Piersol in
Paris. "A squad of 8 men are digging me a little P. C. (post of command)
so I can duck into it if the shells begin to sing around here." He penned

his letter while sitting in a pup tent about one mile from the Marne, "not so far from you, either, so far as just distance is concerned."

Two hundred infantrymen from Walker's First Battalion were pulled from the line to work with the engineers. Infantrymen from other battalions were also ordered to dig trenches. Losing soldiers trained for combat to spend their time on work details did not sit well with Colonel Butts.

"This arrangement was unsatisfactory to me," he later complained, "for the reason that it reduced the effective strength during the night, the most likely hour for attack."

Not only did hundreds of combat soldiers work with the engineers, hundreds more had to carry food up from Crézancy to the men on the front lines. It angered Butts. He figured that both work details had stripped as many as 350 men from his three companies holding outpost positions on the Marne. His hands were tied.

"Orders from the Division Headquarters would not permit any delay of the engineer plan of field fortifications," he complained some more, "and it was impracticable to provide food carrying details for one battalion from another battalion."

Throughout the period of waiting and with orders to double up work on their defenses, tension ran high among the officers and men and, among some of them, doubts about their reliance on the French. Dickman and McAlexander had already seen the halfhearted trench system of the French division on their right flank, east of the Surmelin Valley. It bothered them deeply.

"We soon realized that the French divisions with which we were associated were not counted among the best, being depleted in strength and weak in morale," Dickman noted. "Their previous record, as told to us by French officers, was not such as to inspire confidence and set a good example to our men." He still held a grudge against the French for looting the backpacks of his men in the Seventh Machine Gun Battalion while they had been defending the bridges at Château-Thierry.

On July 10, McAlexander sent a letter of concern to his wife. "The attack is expected in two days; the French are on my right and I have been worried until I got enough of my own troops to guard me if they fall back, but now I am content; all I want is twenty-four hours more to complete my preparations, then Mr. Boche may come at me or us all he pleases."

Another officer disappointed in the French was Major Ziba Drollinger of the Ninth Machine Gun Battalion, which had relieved the Seventh Machine Gun Battalion at Château-Thierry. He had two great tasks to carry out, one involving the French—as he put it, "the construction of shelter and supplying machine gun emplacements with ammunition." He had the engineers cut deep, narrow trenches near each emplacement for the gun crews to take cover in during artillery attacks. The trenches were in the woods, hidden from aerial observation. He had one problem. "Very little had been done toward the construction of obstacles," he grumbled, "as the French had failed repeatedly to supply our division with the wire which they had promised us."

Along with the French, McAlexander had another problem to deal with. He found staff officers from division headquarters a bother because they were constantly nosing around his headquarters at Le Courtelin Farm, a mile or so south of Crézancy, as well as the command posts of his battalions and companies. It angered him that their commanders had given them permission "with no thought of the annoyance and inconvenience they would cause front line commanders." McAlexander looked upon them as "curiosity-indulging pests." He had a hunch that one reason they showed up was to spy on his regiment. "This sort of snooping made me furious."

It got so bad that he actually prayed a German sniper might kill one of them.

He had complained about it to his wife. "I don't mind the Boche. They don't worry me one hundredth part of what I am always getting from some fool staff officer away in the rear calling for eight state reports every day and special reports on every patrol, relief or what-not. It is aggravating the life out of me."

But when Dickman sent down his aide-de-camp, Captain Edward F. Smith, who had hinted to the major general that he wanted to be on the front line—commanding a rifle company—McAlexander had a change of heart. It so happened that he needed an officer to lead L Company, where there was a vacancy. The colonel assigned Smith to the company. A Vermonter from St. Albans, Smith had gone to the prestigious Hill School and graduated from Yale in 1915. He was the son, grandson and great-grandson of a dynasty of Green Mountain governors, senators and congressmen. At Yale he played football, ran track and as a classmate and competitor of the poet Archibald MacLeish won the prize for the best class poem. McAlexander recollected that Smith had protested because he'd never commanded a company before and had only been sent down as an observer. Dickman, however, recalled that Smith "made a direct request" for temporary assignment to the 38th Infantry, and it had been granted.

"Be it said to his everlasting credit," McAlexander later wrote about Captain Smith, "that he commanded that company during the subsequent battle with distinction, and afterwards spoke of the regiment as 'our regiment.'" In fact, Smith received the *Croix de Guerre* while serving under McAlexander.

McAlexander was in a foul mood during the whole first part of July, during the period of waiting. He moved his command post from the luxurious stone farmhouse to a deep dugout underground. He didn't shave for a number of days and "my beard shows white and the blinkety-blanked guns are shootin' worse and worse." His ears were sore from the constant racket of artillery shells, he was exhausted from sleepless nights, and then he tore a hole in the knee of his breeches. Putting on a new pair, he found they were too tight and didn't match his coat, and all his good shoes were worn out. "My boots won't last much longer," he told his wife, "and my temper is a bit frayed at the edges, and I don't give a damn."

Brigadier General Charles Crawford also felt the tension. He had gone to inspect the work of Colonel Butts's 30th Infantry. Not a fan of Butts or of Dickman's new chief of staff, Colonel Robert H. C. Kelton, he was disappointed that the regiment's trenches "had not been constructed to give much shelter as they should, not withstanding all the conferences and directions given." He ordered Butts and Major Walker to have their troops stop whatever else they were doing and devote themselves to their own trenches so that during the fight each man would have a trench for himself. The trenches he advocated were to be five feet deep, six feet long and two feet wide. When the German barrage came, they were to stay in the trenches until it passed and then mount to the surface of the ground and fight as individuals. To Walker he said that "company and platoon commanders would not be able to exercise any but slight leadership after their units were subjected to the enemy's preparation fire and barrage."

In recalling Crawford's inspection, Butts wrote that Crawford had approved his plan of defense. What worried Butts most was that the plans between his regiment and McAlexander's had not been coordinated. Butts, although not enamored with Crawford as a brigade commander, had still followed the called for defensive strategy of elasticity. McAlexander had not. The 30th held the riverbank lightly with a small outpost of riflemen. Its first main line of resistance was about a mile south of the river. The 38th held the riverbank in strength. It was McAlexander's intention to prevent a crossing at the Marne.

"This difference in plan between the two regiments of the same brigade," Butts later lamented, "was unfortunate." As he later complained, the difference "has been the cause of erroneous and conflicting impressions between the two regiments concerning the conduct of the defense."

While Crawford had been pushing Butts to strengthen his trenches, he'd also been arguing with the Sixth Engineers about the construction of his own command post. He didn't want an elaborate headquarters, just a simple structure squirreled away among

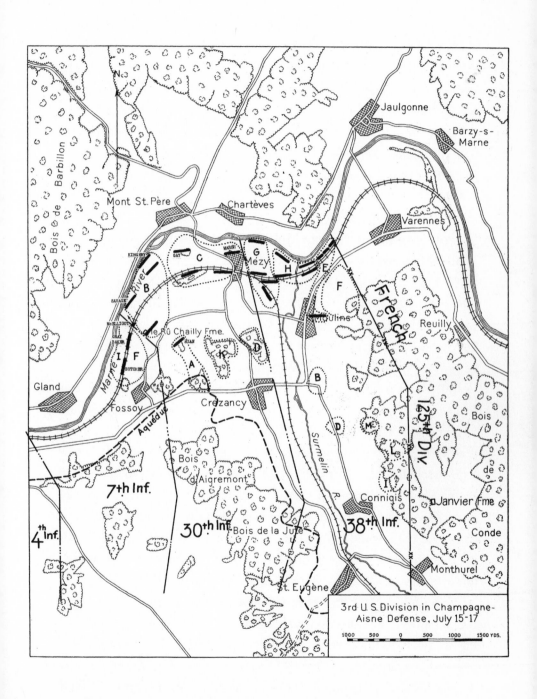

N

Bois de Barbillon

Mont St. Père

Chartèves

Jaulgonne

Barzy-s-Marne

Varennes

KING KY
GAY
C
MARIE
G
Mézy
H
E
F
B
SAVAGE
River
McELLIGOTT
GRAY
BAKER
RYAN
Le Rû Chailly Fme.
F
BUTCHER
I
P
A
D
Moulins
Reuilly

French

125th Div.

B

Gland

Marne

Fossoy

Aqueduc

Crezancy

D
M

Bois

de

Bois
d'Aigremont

Surmelin
R.

Conniqis

Janvier Fme.

Conde

7th Inf.

4th Inf.

30th Inf.

Bois de la Jute

38th Inf.

Monthurel

St. Eugène

3rd U.S. Division in Champagne-
Aisne Defense, July 15-17

1000   500   0   500   1000   1500 YDS.

the trees. The engineers went ahead anyway and built a "completely sheltered" command post, the roof made out of thick, metal arches called "elephant ears." When finished, it was as solid as a tomb. The division's Fifth Field Signal Battalion connected Crawford's command post to the command posts of Dickman, Butts and McAlexander and the forward units. The communications consisted of two independent field telephone lines, one buzzer telephone, one wireless system known as earth telegraphy, several runners and four pigeons.

I n the 30th Infantry's front, from east of the village of Fossoy, where the Marne angled northward to Mézy, to where the river then looped back to head once again in an east-west direction, Butts's First Battalion was ready. He believed that his position in the Bois d'Aigremont was crucial to the battle. General Dickman certainly thought so. "The heaviest [German] forces, very properly, were to be directed against the key of the position, the Bois d'Aigremont," Dickman wrote.

Butts and Walker had placed two companies, B and C, on the river and three companies, A, D and K, in the woods south of the Aqueduct Line and behind the Ru Chailly Farm, an outpost position about five hundred yards from the Marne. K Company had been borrowed from Major Paul Paschal's Third Battalion. It gave Colonel Butts five companies in Walker's battalion, one more than in a regular battalion. Butts also had in reserve two more companies taken from McAlexander's 38th Infantry. Crawford, the brigade commander, pointed out that Butts had a "battalion more than he needed to man his trenches." It was Butts's regiment, however, that, as Dickman stated, had to hold the Bois d'Aigremont.

Captain Kay McCallister from Saint Augustine, Florida, commanded B Company on the 30th's extreme left flank, protecting the east bank of the Marne. Here the river ran north to south. McCallister positioned two platoons on the riverbank, led by First Lieutenants Arthur Vandervoort Savage from Philadelphia's ritzy neighborhood of Chestnut Hill and James Rountree Kingery from the rural Georgia town of Summit.

Savage, called Art, had graduated the year before from Princeton, where he was considered the best oarsman in the university's history. His crew coach said of him, "I do not remember that we ever produced another oarsman quite like him for grit and fighting qualities." In a letter home, Savage wrote, "Fritz must be having fits, and then more fits when Penn's crew at last succeeds in beating him." Savage had four brothers, all Princeton graduates like their father before them and all in military service. Kingery, whose father, Johnson Beauregard Kingery, was named after the Confederate general Pierre Gustave Beauregard, had gone to the officers' training camp at Fort Oglethorpe, where he earned his commission. On the ship carrying the Third Division to France, the blond, blue-eyed Kingery, who could play the piano by ear, won $1,400 in a game of craps.

Behind Savage's and Kingery's companies Walker positioned A Company in the woods and fields around the Ru Chailly Farm. Where the Marne made a ninety-degree turn to the east at the German-held village of Mont-Saint-Pére on the river's north bank, Walker placed First Lieutenant Henry C. Switzer's C Company. He put two platoons on the riverbank, one of them a Stokes mortar platoon with five guns, commanded by First Lieutenant Frederick Winant, Jr. Like Lieutenant Savage, Winant, from a prominent New England family and a member of the illustrious New York Athletic Club, was a graduate of Princeton, where his three brothers had also gone. And like Savage's brothers, all of them were now in the service. A member of the university's crew team, Winant had already seen the war in Europe, soon after graduating in 1915, as a driver for the American Ambulance Field Service. When he came back, he then enlisted in the New York National Guard, serving with the elite Squadron A. The other platoon leader on the river was First Lieutenant Harry H. Marsh from Burnett's Creek, Indiana, a small town not too far from where the Battle of Tippecanoe had been fought. Thirty-four years old, Marsh, who was in the tobacco business, had married his hometown sweetheart, Miss Nellie Duffey, in 1906 and they had two children. He'd been commissioned a lieutenant after graduating from the second officers' training camp at Fort Sheridan, Illinois. His platoon was on the extreme right of the 30th's subsector in the village of Mézy and across the river from another enemy-held village, Chartèves, near the confluence of the Marne and Surmelin Rivers.

Next to Marsh's platoon on the right were companies of the 38th's Second Battalion. Commanded by the Vermonter Major Guy Rowe, the battalion's formation had not changed at all since it first took over McAlexander's front-line defense. The company on Marsh's right, on the outskirts of Mézy, G Company, belonged to Captain Jesse Wooldridge. The bespectacled banker from San Francisco had kept his First Platoon, commanded by First Lieutenant David C. Calkins from Jacksonville, Florida, on the riverbank. Three other platoons were then echeloned back of Calkins's platoon to the railroad track—one in front of the embankment and two behind it. The platoon in front was the Second Platoon of First Lieutenant Mercer M. Phillips from Georgia's Chattanooga Valley.

Captain Herlihy's H Company had been set next to G Company. The Ohioan had two platoons hidden in the willows on the riverbank, one on the west bank of the Surmelin and the other on the east bank where the river flowed into the Marne. In direct support of these platoons he placed his other two, each close behind the troops on the riverbank. Captain Con Dineen's E Company came next. The Brockton, Massachusetts, native put three platoons on the east bank of the Surmelin and a fourth platoon in reserve in the hillside village of Moulins. In support of the riverbank companies, Major Rowe kept Captain Tom Reid's F Company close behind the others—ready to counterattack when the time was right.

Defense of the Aqueduct Line was given to the First Battalion, although it was down by two rifle companies. Its mission was to counterattack if the Germans crossed through the Second Battalion. The Third Battalion, minus K Company, had been assigned the Woods Line and had taken up a position east of the Surmelin River, with L and M Companies placed well up the slopes of the Moulins Ridge and a bit south of the village of Launay. Two companies of the Sixth Engineers, B and C, had been attached to McAlexander's regiment and were in reserve in the Aqueduct Line and on the hill west of the village of Courtelin.

The 38th also had thirty-two machine guns on the slopes on both sides of the Surmelin River, several on the riverbank and three more covering the roads leading to the south. The emplacement of the machine guns, which included A Company of the Ninth Machine Gun Battalion, commanded by Captain Stuart R. Carswell, and its own machine-gun company, led by Captain Sidney Young, a West Pointer from Utah and grandson of Brigham Young, had been coordinated so that a deadly crossfire could be delivered against key points between the Aqueduct Line and the Marne.

Even though Rowe had stayed with his original line of defense, the protection of his right flank was worrisome, not only to him, but also to his commanding officer, McAlexander. From the start he and the colonel felt certain that the moment the battle started the French soldiers up on Moulins Ridge, designated Hill 231 on military maps, were sure to bolt. Rowe was grateful there were freshly dug trenches up in the woods at the brow of the hill facing east. Maybe it was time to move Reid's company into the trenches to strengthen his right flank—just in case.

Meanwhile, Crawford, after meeting with Butts, checked McAlexander's defenses. Crawford liked the colonel, who had graduated two years ahead of him at West Point. He found his defenses to be "progressing satisfactorily." He had no suggestions for improvement. Instead the two West Pointers talked about the "almost complete absence of activities on the part of the enemy which presaged a formal attack."

The one activity that troubled them and everyone in the division was German aviators and their endless control of the skies over the Third's sector of the Marne. Watching them throughout June and into July, Crawford described them as daring. The planes flew in low, skimming the tops of the trees, the machine guns sweeping the open fields. The French antiaircraft guns fired at them, but never brought down a plane. "It seems as if I saw a million shots fired at these hostile planes without results. The parts of bursted projectiles were always falling about, and it seemed strange that there were not casualties from this source."

Captain Donovan Swanton, a West Pointer who commanded the machine-gun company in Butts's regiment, commented, "The illusion of a smiling, peaceful countryside was disturbed only by the enemy planes which flew across daily, usually followed by shelling for ten or fifteen minutes, particularly over the village of Crézancy."

Southeast of the Third, the companies from the American 28th Division, as they began to move up to the front line, also had endured German planes. Corporal Alvey Martz from C Company, described by a Somerset County newspaper as a peace-loving soldier, wanted to hide anywhere from "old Fritz so he can't see us from his flying machine and drop a bomb on us. We see him quite often as he passes over us nearly every night."

The harassing planes, Dickman sensed, "had a worse morale effect than anything else." He reported that his men felt they were not being looked after. "They were willing to go without food, if necessary, but when they were hovering over us our aeroplanes had gone home, then the Boche came over us with machine guns." He reported how they "flew over our lines only high enough to avoid hitting trees; they would look through the trees and fire on our troops."

Observed an American engineer, "Enemy planes had almost undisputed possession of the air. . . . Allied planes were seen only occasionally."

Colonel Butts remarked that the "German airplanes practically flew at will, and were able to spot our various lines and headquarters of both Infantry and Artillery units and to take photographs of the same."

Kelton, Dickman's chief of staff, compared the German air service to the French, with a jab at the French for not challenging the German superiority over the harassed American lines. "The German flies when he's told," he remarked during a conference at division headquarters, "and the French flies when he thinks he ought to."

Another mark against the French.

The Germans also sent up manned observation balloons, hovering above the river, but not close enough to the American side. On a windy July 7, a French soldier shot one of the balloons. It erupted into flames. The observer parachuted out. The wind blew him over the Third Division lines. He was captured and gave up some good information. McAlexander wrote home, "The captured German says that the valley where I am is to be filled with gas when the attack begins; there is this about that, if the gas comes you may be sure Fritz won't, for he can't stand gas as well as we can."

Most of the men slept during the day in their shallow dugouts. At night, they climbed out of their foxholes, stretched, walked around for some exercise. Many of them sat in open fields and, as Walker observed, listened "to the singing of the artillery projectiles as they shrieked across the sky above them, in both directions seeking out some suspected location. . . . Much time was devoted to the description of the sounds of the guns, their probable location and flashes, their caliber and the intention of their crews."

In the 38th's subsector, Captain Dineen, in a letter to his father, described that not only were he and his men well fed and he'd put on weight, but "I shave in my dugout every day, and now and then take a sponge bath, which is the most refreshing thing over here."

Lieutenant Murray thought of Peggy Piersol back in Paris. "Know what I'd like to do tonight?" he wrote to her. "To put on summer clothes and run off with you somewhere for a little dance, where we could dance when we pleased and go outside and rest when we wanted and drink punch or lemonade, with a salad, maybe, and get back at any old time at all."

Corporal Bill Fitzgerald, in Butts's regiment, felt safe in his foxhole. He wrote in his diary, "I am living in the woods south of Crézancy in a little dugout three by ten where I have plenty of cigarettes, plenty of magazines and papers and plenty of time to read so why should I care if Germany wants peace? Many aeroplanes overhead. Bang! That's the little seventy-fives just to send Fritz a few messages. If he don't send gas but tries to come across the Marne in front of us, I can say what my Lieut. Col. said: 'The Marne will be so full of dead Boche that you can walk across on them.'"

One of Walker's platoon officers down by the river had been keeping an eye on the small German-held village of Mont-Saint-Pére on the north bank. A long stone wall ran in front of the village. Each night when Walker went to visit the platoon, the officer asked him to have the artillery blow down the stone wall—sure there was something hidden on the other side. During the day, the officer watched the village and the stone wall very closely. He told Walker that he believed that behind it were munitions and that every night from behind the stone wall several machine guns and *minenwerfers*, the German equivalent of trench mortars, fired on his position. After repeatedly asking for an artillery strike, he finally got his wish. The Americans shelled the stone wall and the ground behind it. There were no munitions. Instead, hidden from view were bridging and pontoon material ready to be thrown across the Marne the night of the big attack.

"A lucky move on our part," sighed a relieved Walker.

CHAPTER 12

"AT LAST WE WERE READY"

D ay after day the period of waiting dragged on. Artillery shells whistled back and forth like a vicious rally at a high-stakes tennis
match. The Americans and the French also fired gas shells, including for
the first time mustard gas. General Dickman reported that on two suc-
cessive nights his own artillery had fired nine thousand gas shells into
the forest above the Jaulgonne Bend. A German grenadier described how
the forest was soaked in "thick clouds of gas." On several occasions the
wind shifted and vapors from the gas drifted back across the Marne and
the men in the 7th and 38th Infantries had to don their respirators.

In the meantime, as part of the 38th Army Corps, reinforcements were
brought up in support of the Third—the French 73rd Division, which had
been designated the counterattack division, and half the forces of the
National Guardsmen of the 28th Division. The other half of the 28th was
placed in the French 3rd Army Corps. The Pennsylvanians to fight in the
38th Army Corps were still split three ways—one section sent to the Third's
left flank, one section directly behind the Third and one section of four
companies from the 109th and 110th Infantry Regiments to the right flank.

On July 10, the men of C Company from Somerset County and the men of B Company from Beaver County received their orders to be part of the French 113th Infantry Regiment of the 125th Division near the village of Courthiézy. Courthiézy was about five miles east of the Surmelin Valley and the start of the Third Division's sector. A day later, under the dark of night, Somerset Captain W. Curtis Truxal and Captain William Fish from New Brighton moved their men into their assigned outpost positions on the Marne. They found themselves bunched between platoons of French soldiers. The American officers now reported to the battalion commanders of the 113th. Truxal's subsector, near the village of Courthiézy, was halfway between Dormans to the east and Crézancy to the west. The same railroad track that ran through the Third Division's sector, the Paris–Metz line, also ran through C Company's subsector, offering a natural defense fifty to one hundred yards from the Marne. Truxal placed his Third Platoon, commanded by First Lieutenant Robert J. Bonner from Philadelphia, one of the few officers not from Somerset County, on the river with five automatic rifle squads, covering five hundred yards. Along the railroad track, behind Bonner and his men, Truxal lined up his First and Second Platoons under the commands of First Lieutenants Samuel E. Crouse and Wilber E. Schell, as well as his automatic rifle squads. In support, two hundred yards back of the railroad track, he put his Fourth Platoon. Leading the Fourth was twenty-seven-year-old noncommissioned officer Sergeant Robert A. Floto, a cigar manufacturer back in Somerset County and a former cavalryman before reenlisting in C Company in 1916.

Captain Charles F. Linn, the surgeon from Monongahela, and several men from the medical detachment, came up to the front line for a few days where the French were encamped to get a sense of the place and the facilities. Linn slept in a deep underground shelter with a French surgeon. His bed was a stretcher. It was "most uncomfortable," he recalled. Later, he moved into a freshly dug shelter with a tent over it, sharing it with his men. He slept on the ground "most comfortably with 75s and all the larger guns booming over our heads." In a letter to his relatives, he wrote, "I'm afraid that when I get home I will not be able to sleep anywhere as comfortably as on the floor unless it may be on the cellar floor with a lot of giant firecrackers going off over my head every few seconds."

If the Germans were on the verge of another major offensive, then those Pennsylvanians had very little time to prepare their fortifications. Overnight, they needed to carve out at least twenty rifle pits along the riverbank. As a historian of the 28th Division described their arrival to the front, "There was no sleep that night, even had the excited fancies of the men permitted. Up and down, up and down, went the sturdy young arms, and the dirt flew under the attack of entrenching picks and shovels."

By morning the pits were miraculously dug and manned. For C Company and the three other companies from the 28th Division now part of the French 125th, the period of waiting had begun. It was July 11.

Back at the Third Division's sector, several inventive officers in Walker's battalion figured out a way to lob hand grenades clear across the Marne and far enough into the woods and villages to disrupt the Germans and maybe put an end to their bothersome nightly machine-gun fire that disrupted their place by the river. The 30th Infantry's machine guns could not reply in kind. They'd been placed in such a way that they could not fire back into the enemy's defenses. Instead, Walker's machine guns had been set up to stop the Germans from gaining a permanent foothold on the south bank. But there had to be a way to make the Germans pay for their constant harassment.

The officers' idea for payback went back to the Middle Ages. They'd construct a catapult.

"The catapult [*sic*] was the very instrument for the purpose we wished to use it," Walker explained. "The idea was to set the throwing arm, pull the pin from the grenades, place it in the pocket of the arm and pull the trigger. The grenade would pass through the air and reach the ground on the enemy side of the river in just about the time required for the bomb to explode after the pin was pulled and the lever released."

In the village of Crézancy, protected and hidden from the Germans, the officers went about designing and building their catapult. They decided to test it out on the night of July 14, Bastille Day.

O n the 13th, the day before the unveiling of the catapult, the French reported they had detected significant movement of the enemy on the north bank of the Marne. Observers were hearing distinct "unloading noises." They surmised that the Germans were bringing up ammunition depots. They also spotted a line of floating mines near the bank between the villages of Gland and Brasles. The mines were believed to be meant to deter raiding parties from crossing the river and capturing prisoners. An order went down to General Dickman to have his artillery on July 14 destroy the depots and floating mines.

Dickman ordered his artillery to hurl high-explosive shells for three hours into the woods south of Brasles and Mont-Saint-Pére commencing at 5 a.m. on the 14th. The division's infantry outposts opposite the two villages were to be withdrawn by 4 a.m. to the safety of the railroad embankment. Machine guns and automatic rifles were to be trained on the north bank and "fire upon any bodies of the enemy which may be driven out of the cover by artillery action."

The division commander then ordered sufficient ammunition dumps moved nearer to his combat positions. The amount of ammunition: two hundred rounds for each rifle, one thousand rounds for each automatic rifle and fifteen thousand rounds for each machine-gun section. Walker counted 420 rounds per rifle for his battalion and a "good supply" of hand grenades and rockets delivered to each platoon on the night of the 13th.

Along with the ammunition came word there would be "no retreat when the attack should come."

Dickman warned that the enemy would most likely cross the river with an attack of fog or smoke to conceal their movements. He warned of "chaos" and that officers had to use rockets to show the artillery the location of the enemy. In daylight they were to use the Very pistol. At night they were to send up a high rocket with a large white star.

With all this action on both sides of the river, was Foch's "period of waiting" about over?

M ajor Rowe, who believed in harmony between his men, saw a problem between two of his captains. Wooldridge of G Company and Herlihy of H Company had a falling out. In a message to Wooldridge the major wrote, "Better go over and make peace with Herlihy. We must have harmony and cooperation."

In his diary, Eddy Herlihy was blunt about how he felt about his fellow officers. A captain in one of the battalion's companies he wrote was "full of prunes" and "makes me tired." Another captain he labeled a "big boob."

Rowe also decided that another raid across the river on the night of the 14th might result in collecting good intelligence. If he got permission from McAlexander, he'd send a patrol from Herlihy's company to do the job.

At 8 p.m. in his war diary for the 14th, Rowe reported he had 30 officers and 859 men available for duty. He had well over one million rounds of ammunition for his riflemen. He noted that his battalion was still working on the construction of trenches and the work had been going on for a number of days. The weather was good and on the front line it was "very quiet."

Herlihy, whose company was in the center between the companies of Captains Wooldridge and Dineen, pointed out that every one of his rifle pits had 1,200 rounds of .30-caliber ammunition in addition to 220 rounds carried by the men. Each trench on the river had been supplied with 50 hand grenades.

Lieutenant Focke, in Captain Reid's company, which was still in support of the other three companies, remembered that each soldier was given three bandoliers of ammunition that were thrown over his shoulder. "One thing I remember was that this made me so hot that I threw away my trench coat."

Dickman had sensed from the beginning that, as far back as their training days at Camp Greene in North Carolina, when the soldiers were on the firing range, "they had confidence in their skill with rifle and machine gun and in their own mental and physical qualities." With enough ammunition now being brought to the front, that confidence had to be growing.

First Lieutenant C. William Ryan, in charge of A Company's Fourth Platoon, was positioned a few hundred yards south of the Ru Chailly Farm, in a little stand of woods on a hill with a broad view of the Marne Valley. A lawyer from Kansas, Ryan was impressed with the crew of a one-pound gun in the center of his position, manned by a sergeant and seven men. "There was a large dugout a few yards back of their gun," he remembered, "abundantly, almost luxuriously, it seemed to me supplied with cooking utensils and an oversupply of army rations, with canned heat to use for cooking." Talking to the sergeant, he found him quite capable, but on the night of the 14th, the sergeant and his crew were relieved.

In his dugout in the 30th Infantry's subsector, Corporal Fitzgerald saw that his rifle and pistol had gotten rusty, so he gave them a thorough cleaning, read an old copy of the *London Daily Mail* and then fell asleep.

First Lieutenant Johns Hopkins of K Company, a University of Pennsylvania graduate, Class of 1915, another commissioned officer from the Fort Oglethorpe training camp, who'd been transferred from the 30th's Third Battalion to Walker's First, climbed into his foxhole dug underneath a rock and like Fitzgerald went calmly to sleep.

Alex J. Artman of the 38th's B Company, told his sister back in Sheboygan, Wisconsin, "Well, sister, you need not worry about me—no German is ever going to get me, at least not if I see him first. I have been sleeping with one eye open for the last two months."

A day earlier, on July 13, Dickman thought it fit for him and his headquarters staff to honor the commander of the 38th Army Corps and his staff with a dinner the following day to celebrate the anniversary of *La Fêe Nationale*, the storming of the Bastille and the start of the French Revolution on July 14, 1789. He sent out invitations and received acceptances from de Mondesir and his general staff.

But there was now a feeling among the Allies that the Germans were ready to strike. The French generals politely withdrew their acceptances. Dickman had to know something was up, and he almost canceled the dinner. "We refused to be stampeded and finished our dinner as per menu and schedule." He then wondered what the French thought of the American attitude under such circumstances. "Did they admire our confidence or did they pity our ignorance?"

If indeed an attack was imminent, as Dickman now sensed, then he and his staff needed to pack up the division headquarters' papers, personal effects and office equipment and load them on trucks "ready for a swift move to south or west." But Dickman's staff had failed to load any trucks, and the general wondered if the French officers saw this failure as more evidence of the Americans' lack of experience. But Dickman would be damned. "What would our watchful commander-in-chief have done to a subordinate giving such exhibitions of weakness and lack of confidence on the eve of battle?"

Around the time the officers were dining, in the skies north of Château-Thierry, Quentin Roosevelt, the youngest son of President Roosevelt, was shot in the head during a dogfight. His plane crashed. He had died instantly.

July 14, another night. Before checking on the raiding party he'd approved in Herlihy's company and then heading out to inspect Major Rowe's Second Battalion, McAlexander penned a letter to his wife telling her of the day's goings-on. "This is France's 4th of July and it made a holiday for us, but we work just the same as every day, Sundays included."

Herlihy had been getting his men ready for the raid across the river for two days, making sure the boats were in good shape and, if they needed it, repaired. He didn't want anybody drowning on his watch.

He'd picked two second lieutenants from New York City to lead the patrol, Jefferson Healy and Paul Plough. Healy, Brooklyn-born, had been a star at Boys High School and then the captain of the undefeated 1916 Columbia University football team, where he'd earned the nickname "Big Jeff." Plough, born in the Bronx, was a 1917 graduate of Amherst College. Both young men had earned their commissions at the Plattsburg Officers' Training Camp.

"We had got the boats ready," Plough wrote to his brother Harold, "and the lightness of the night caused us to put it off till the next night. Major Rowe sent us back to a little town in the rear of the line to sleep and rest up."

The little town was Crézancy, and here the inventive officers of Walker's battalion finally rolled out their catapult, ready to test it down by the river. As we'll soon see, they never got a chance to use the catapult to lob a live grenade across the Marne.

E ast of the Third Division, in the Champagne region, the French Fourth Army, under General Gouraud, captured twenty German prisoners after a savage knife-and-bayonet fight. They were then interrogated at once. One of the Germans, an officer, had tucked inside his tunic battle plans that included the exact time when Ludendorff's Peace Assault would start. Just hours away. Ten minutes after midnight on July 15.

That evening at 11:45 Dickman received an urgent communiqué from corps headquarters, telling him of Gouraud's raid and the capture of the prisoners.

"Twenty prisoners have just been taken this evening by the Fourth French Army, they say that the launching of the attack of their army will take place tonight towards 1:00 o'clock (German time). As a consequence the army now decides to immediately launch the C.P.O." (C.P.O. stood for the French to preempt the German bombardment with their own.)

"This remarkable piece of good fortune came to us in the nick of time," Dickman recalled.

All units in the division were put on "Alert A." They were warned that the German attack would be preceded by a "violent and short preparation . . . with heavy well organized use of gas shells." As Colonel Kelton phrased it "to discomfort our troops" during the German attempt to cross the river. When the gas barrage hit, the front-line troops were to withdraw to the railroad embankment and "hold out to the last." But strangely only the artillery had been told the exact time of the attack. As a result, according to an after-action report of the battle, "All the working parties were caught under the bombardment some distance from their battle positions."

In the meantime, rolling kitchens brought food to the men, their only hot meal of the day. The YMCA sent chocolate and cigarettes to the front lines. The medical aid stations prepared for the coming battle. The 30th's aid stations were in the Bois d'Aigremont south of the village of Crézancy. The 38th's aid stations were in the village of Connigis, about one thousand yards southeast of Crézancy, as well as in Moulins and Paroy, both villages on the slopes of Hill 231. The facilities at Connigis and Paroy were set up in wine cellars, offering good space for the surgeons and better protection than the other aid stations.

As the midnight hour approached, Captain Wooldridge, huddled next to Kenneth P. Murray from Mount Vernon, New York, a young first lieutenant who'd just turned twenty-one. Wooldridge "felt there was a general awakening in the consciousness of the men that brought on a stiffening in the back of our necks." He noticed restlessness in "K. P." Murray, a West Pointer, Class of 1918, former academy hockey star and famous around the campus for sleeping.

"What is it?" Wooldridge whispered to him as they looked across a ripe, shoulder-high wheat field marked with red poppies toward the river.

"Seems mighty quiet on the other side, sir."

No signal rockets or Very lights—just quiet, Wooldridge thought. *Ominous, foreboding quiet!*

To K Company's Second Lieutenant John Henry Hilldring, a former student at the University of Connecticut, Class of 1918, and a resident of Westport, a "death-like stillness" pervaded the Surmelin Valley.

McAlexander, meanwhile, had gone to Rowe's command post hours before Dickman had received his communiqué, to inform him that he and his men were not going to be relieved as promised. Both front-line battalions of the Sixth Brigade, Walker's First and Rowe's Second, had been scheduled to be relieved in mid-July. Butts, even though he had been warned on the 13th by Chief of Staff Kelton "to keep my command constantly on the alert for an impending battle," went ahead with the relief, bringing up Major Lindsey Silvester's Second Battalion to take over for Walker's First. The battalion was on its way.

McAlexander, on the other hand, told Rowe to expect the Germans to try and cross the river at any time. He thought it better for Rowe to continue to hold the front line because his battalion knew the ground better than the other battalions in the regiment. Rowe's men had to stay. Rowe said there was no other place he wanted to be until after the attack than defending the front line. Earlier he had written to his sister in Peacham, Vermont, telling her that he hadn't had a bath in weeks and had his clothes off only twice since moving into the front line, adding, "In spite of home sickness, lovesickness and good food sickness, I would not be elsewhere in the world."

McAlexander looked at the Vermonter, a man he'd served with in the Philippines, and thought a less courageous man would have begged to be taken out after ten days of untiring vigilance. He was glad to have Rowe as a battalion commander.

As he always did at least once every day so that "officers and men know the 'Old Man' is around," the colonel moved on to inspect his troops to make sure they were ready and to buck them up. He believed that "to be a colonel in wartime is the nicest command there is on earth. All I want is a good, clean regiment that will stand any test." It was the one question buzzing through his mind: *Will my men stick to their job?*

He talked with privates and noncommissioned officers, anxiously searching for "that something in their voices and attitudes for which I had striven from the first moment I joined the regiment." When he reached the extreme right flank of his subsector, across the Surmelin Valley, where farther to the east the French and the four companies of the 28th Division were entrenched, he stopped to talk to a sergeant, to feel him out.

"How are the men getting along?" he asked.

"Fine, sir, but we are awfully tired of waiting for the Boche to come over," the sergeant answered.

"What will you and your men do if the Germans come over?"

"Oh, if the colonel will only give us the chance we'll show you what we'll do to them."

McAlexander believed the sergeant and felt a glow fill his insides when "I realized that at last we were ready."

CHAPTER 13

//

"WITH GOD,
FOR KAISER AND THE NATION"

O n the rainy, foggy night of July 14, three miles back from the
north slope of the Marne, the German Seventh Army's 23rd
Corps, Corps Kathen, led by guides who had scouted their route during
the daytime, moved up to the river. The corps, ready for the big attack
code-named *Strassenbeau* ("Road Construction"), consisted of the 10th
and 36th Infantry Divisions, including the 47th, 128th, 175th and 398th
Infantry Regiments and the Fifth and Sixth Grenadier Regiments.
Held in reserve was the 10th Landwehr Division. Its job was to mop up
after the other divisions overran the enemy's front.

The success of the attack hinged on two things. The first was absolute
surprise. The second thing the Germans counted on was their engineers.
They had amassed everything they believed was needed to make a successful crossing of the Marne. There were two corps bridge trains, eight division bridge trains and twenty pioneer companies primed to construct the
river crossings. In the corps bridge trains the engineers had to push forward a combined total of twenty-six complete pontoons and twelve half
pontoons to ferry the infantry across the river and carry material for a light

bridge two hundred yards long. To bring the bridge and the pontoons up to the Marne in the corps bridge trains alone required 275 engineers, 60 wagons and 340 horses. Landing sites on the south side of the river had already been located, selected by generals and other high-ranking officers who had slipped down to the river's edge dressed as privates and carrying rifles or spades. The ideal landing site was where the Paris–Metz railroad line was farthest from the Marne, so the infantry battalions would have the most room to deploy behind the embankment before reaching the enemy's first line of resistance. Along with bridging material, boats and rafts, the engineers had three ferries to carry the troops to the south bank. For a number of weeks, the corps had been practicing river crossings near Fismes on the Ourcq River, having to march twelve miles each way from its encampment to the river in blazing sun and swirling clouds of dust. The corps was now ready to make its move.

The timetable for the battle had been calculated to the minute. At 12:10 in the morning the artillery would open up. At 1:55 the pontoon bridges and footbridges, pontoon boats and ferries would be thrown into and across the Marne. At 2:10 the first infantry units would cross the river. At 2:30 the infantry would reach the railroad embankment. At 3:50 a.m. the rolling barrage would begin and, as at Chemin des Dames, the rout would be on.

The operation's orders had been issued to the troops quite late, most likely to keep the attack secret. Lieutenant Kurt Hesse of the Fifth Grenadiers was going over the orders, figuring what the men under his command were to do. On the eve of the battle "a perfectly strange grenadier reported to me," Hesse recalled. "Very much excited, but modestly, he asked if it was true that there were Americans opposite us, and that the attack had been betrayed." Hesse reassured him and then asked about what the men were thinking. "I found there was complete confidence in the leadership, but here and there was an uncertain feeling as if the affair would not succeed. 'The infantry has an instinct,' as old soldiers used to say."

Hesse had his own doubts, too, about whether the enemy knew about the attack's time and place. He knew German prisoners had been taken. He'd heard that one of them was a photographic officer who had been carrying important maps in violation of orders. And there'd been desertions.

General Max von Boehn of the Seventh Army and General Hugo von Kathen, the corps commander, had calculated their troops could cover the two-mile march to the river in two hours. Although the rain had cleared out, they hadn't counted on a night as black as any the soldiers had ever seen. According to Lieutenant Hesse, "In the woods we could not see our hands before our eyes." Making it worse, there had been insufficient reconnaissance of the routes to the river, and units became lost.

In the near-blinding dark, the army marched toward the river, toward the jump-off points that had been earlier scouted.

Each soldier carried rations for three days, mostly bread and canned goulash. With gas masks on, lugging boats mounted with machine guns, burdened with their rifles, automatic rifles, machine guns, bandoleers of ammunition, pistols and bayonets, along with life-saving belts and ropes, plugs for stopping up any holes in the pontoons, extra oars and foot bridge equipment, thousands of soldiers groped their way forward. Horses pulled artillery, pontoons and supply wagons with hooves and wheels wrapped in burlap and rags to muffle the sound, while dogs struggled with the smaller supply wagons. The soldiers banged into trees, suffered scratches from branches and slipped on ground slick from the earlier rain, while now and then they heard the whine passing overhead of a heavy artillery shell fired by the enemy. The brush was so dense, Hesse wrote, and impossible to get through and there was "scarcely a tree thick enough to afford protection against a rifle bullet." Several times the guides got lost. One absurd reason: the engineers, after all their planning and scouting and picking out the exact landing sites, had failed to mark paths through the woods or erect road signs to point the way. The march took four hours, not two. When they reached their assigned destination in the woods close to the river, Hesse remarked, the trip had been unusually hard on the men. "There had been casualties during the advance, great exhaustion of the troops, some sick and missing. But they were in their places as ordered." Yet after their ordeal in the woods, especially for Hesse's Fifth Grenadiers, who had been shelled and had men killed, they were tired and nervous. The Sixth Grenadiers, on the Fifth's right, and the 398th Regiment had made it to their assigned destinations close to the river unscathed because they had started out in daylight and therefore weren't harassed by artillery fire.

About eight hundred yards from the river, in the middle of deep woods, there'd been a few shelter holes dug for the soldiers to climb into while awaiting zero hour. They'd be hunkered down during the course of their own bombardment and then at 3:50 a.m. a rolling barrage would commence and they'd fire up smoke bombs to hide their movements and follow the barrage across the river, staying a few hundred yards behind the crashing artillery and gas shells. And again, as at Chemin des Dames, with surprise on their side, they expected little opposition. The enemy would be pulverized, gassed and ready to flee—if they hadn't already fled in terror. The Surmelin Valley would be theirs. And then it was on to Epernay to meet up with the Crown Prince's First and Third Armies after they had taken the Rheims salient. At Epernay, the Seventh would peel off toward Paris while the other two armies would continue toward Châlons-sur-Marne and from there march down the west bank of the Aisne River to St. Mihiel. About two weeks later to the west the Army Group Crown Prince of Bavaria would strike the British in Flanders.

Meanwhile, General von Kathen's immediate goal had been for his corps to reach the Marne in two hours, cross it in one hour and take the railroad embankment from the Americans and capture the heights of the Surmelin Valley. He and von Boehn still believed that "our offensive intentions have been kept secret. We expect to take the enemy by surprise."

The mission for the Americans and the French, who had a surprise of their own—they now knew when and where the attack would take place—was to stop them. Fall back, and then counterattack. The defense of elasticity. If it worked, Foch planned to mount his offensive right away, as the enemy, in disarray, withdrew back across the Marne.

Before the German drive had been launched along the more than sixty-five-mile front from Château-Thierry to east of Rheims, the crown prince, as he'd done many other times when his army group went on the offensive, addressed his troops. "Comrades," his standard rallying speech went, "things are going hard with us. They are bitterly difficult. It is a case of life and death for you and for all that we Germans have. Whether we shall pull through I do not know. But I have every faith in you that none will desert the other or the cause. There is no other way out of it; and so, forward, for God and with God, for the Kaiser and the realm! For all that you love and refuse to see crushed."

This time, when the crown prince looked upon his troops on the eve of battle, he felt anxiousness in his heart. Earlier in the war, he had awakened every morning with pleasure. Now his mornings were bitter. "The troops," he remembered, "though still almost everywhere perfect in discipline and demeanor—willing, friendly and cheerful in their salutes—were worn to death. My heart turned within me when I beheld their hollow cheeks, their lean and weary figures, their tattered and dirty uniforms." The German army also suffered from the Spanish influenza epidemic that raged through its ranks.

In fact, a July 14 British communiqué painted a grim picture of the German soldiers. "Out of a batch of 800 German prisoners captured on July 4, 30 men reported sick with influenza within 24 hours. The medical officer who examined them states that their influenza is of a much severer type than ours, their temperatures were higher as compared with those of our men suffering from the same complaint, and there was a good deal more prostration, possibly due to malnutrition, as a number of men complained of short rations."

In hindsight, instead of attacking, the crown prince thought that it would have been smarter to have "moved far enough from the enemy to give our severely fatigued and morally depressed troops time to rest and recuperate."

The crown prince most likely thought that *Friedensturm*, the "Peace Assault," was Germany's last chance to end the war on its own terms.

In contrast, his father, Kaiser Wilhelm II, was so optimistic of success that he bragged, "I will be in Paris by midnight of July 17, 1918." In fact, his staff had already so counted the Americans beaten and the French in full retreat that they even prepared place cards for a celebration dinner at Paris's posh Hôtel Majestic, where the kaiser would raise a toast to his troops marching down the Champs-Elysées as his grandfather's troops had done in the Franco-Prussian War.

Between Château-Thierry and the Argonne Forest, Germany had 3 armies, 47 divisions and 650,000 men. Opposing the Germans were one million equally battle-weary French and untested American soldiers. On the eve of the battle, the kaiser arrived on the battlefield, urging his troops on, according to the War Diary of the 10th Division: "With God, for Kaiser and the nation!"

CHAPTER 14

"ALL THE DEMONS OF HELL"

The Second Battle of the Marne opened at precisely twelve midnight on July 14–15, on a night "with a darkness," the soldiers remembered, "you could feel." Ten minutes before the Germans planned to fire on the Allies along a more than sixty-five-mile front, the French and American artillery struck first. In the sector held by the French 38th Army Corps, their shells rained down on the hills and villages north of the Marne, catching out in the open the German 10th and 36th Divisions, including the 128th, 175th and 398 Infantry Regiments and storm troopers from the Fifth and Sixth Grenadiers as they moved up to the river.

Fifth Grenadier Lieutenant Kurt Hesse had been dozing in a dugout waiting for the German bombardment to go off. The roar of artillery and exploding shells snapped him awake.

"At last!" he thought, the attack was under way.

He checked his watch. It was midnight. Why had the attack started at 12:00 and not 12:10, as planned? Had a mistake been made? The moment he jumped out of his hole, Hesse realized that shells were falling on Corps Kathen's position, not on the enemy's. The French and

Americans had preempted the German bombardment of high-explosive shells and mustard gas. He jumped back into his hole.

Ten minutes later, as scheduled, the German artillery, eighty-four batteries targeting the Bois d'Aigremont and the Surmelin Valley and able to reach all the way to Montmiral, roared to life. The line of batteries spewed high explosives throughout the Third Division sector plus more than one thousand gas shells per square kilometer that fell in the meadows, wheat fields, woods and on the trenches and dugouts of the Americans.

Recalled Crown Prince Wilhelm, "And then there was a tremendous roar, as if the end of the world had come."

The night exploded into flashes of orange and red and blinding white light and noise so terrible eardrums were punctured and the ground shook and split open. On the American side, trees were uprooted, their limbs torn off and splintered, flying through the woods like giant spears. Fierce fires swept through Crézancy. Its smoldering buildings tumbled into heaps of bricks and stones. Soldiers in Major Lindsey Silvester's Second Battalion of the 30th Infantry, marching in to relieve Major Fred Walker's First Battalion, as well as two battalions of the 7th Infantry on Silvester's left and soldiers still on work details digging trenches or bringing up food, were all caught with no place to hide. Men shook uncontrollably while others were blown into nothingness, no traces of their bodies ever found. In horror, Silvester's medical officer, Captain William E. Boyce, working without a gas mask because it was a hindrance, saw that "dead animals lay everywhere in the tangled, broken woods . . . and everywhere were torn human bodies." He tended the severely wounded, more than 250 men, many of them "raving maniacs. . . . Some of them cursed and raved and had to be tied to their litters; some shook violently . . . some trembled and slunk away in apparent abject fear of every incoming shell, while others simply stood speechless, oblivious to all surroundings." There were so many wounded it was impossible to carry them back to the dressing stations. Major Paul C. Paschal's command post was close by, and he gave up his dugout so it could be used by the injured, exposing him to shellfire.

A first lieutenant serving under Captain Boyce, Thomas R. Royster of Virgilina, Virginia, did not have enough room at his dressing station to handle all the wounded being brought in. Many of them had to be cared for out in the open. According to a regimental report, "Forgetting all dangers to himself and in spite of the dense gas he went fearlessly among the injured, dressing them and continued at this work during the whole bombardment which lasted ten hours."

Over in the Fifth Brigade's sector, with gas permeating one of the dressing stations of the 76th Field Artillery, the doctors and medics there, working frantically on the wounded, gave up using their gas masks unless the concentration was so strong they had to slip them back on for a moment or two. Captain Percy G. Black saw a sergeant just as his head had been blown off. A soldier staggered in, his arm in shreds. "The road to Battalion Headquarters was a veritable deathtrap, and it was impossible to evacuate the wounded."

When the bombardment had subsided, Chaplain George Ridout of the YMCA tended to a soldier probably shocked to the point of no return. The soldier said to him, "Chaplain, I am not crazy, I am all right." But a shell had struck so close to him that it ripped the head off one of his friends. "I went over where he lay," the grief-stricken soldier went on, "and picked up his head and put it on again and said, 'Buddy, come along now with me,' and I tell you, Sir, he wouldn't come along."

Wrote Captain Jesse Wooldridge, down by the river with his men of G Company, "All the demons of hell and its ally, Germany, were unleashed in a fierce uproar that transcended all bombardments of the past. It thundered and rained shells, high explosives, shrapnel and gas. They swept our sector as with a giant scythe, and as far back as their guns would reach." But inside the foxholes dug in the railroad embankment, Wooldridge and his men "leaned our heads in genuine affection against the dirt side of our little slit trench and began to marvel at its motherly shelter. How they could churn up the whole world and never drop one in!"

French veterans swore the bombardment was worse than anything they'd seen at Verdun in 1916.

The shells were landing everywhere. In the 38th's A Company, First Lieutenant Robert Crandall, who'd successfully led a patrol across the river a month earlier, directed his men to shelter holes dug in the woods and cared for the wounded. A piece from a high-explosive shell pierced Crandall's helmet, knocking him out and seriously injuring him. His sergeant, William C. Hardie from Jersey City, sensing Crandall had been hurt, searched for him in the bitter dark, ignoring the shells landing all around him. When he found Crandall, he administered first aid and, without any assistance, dragged the lieutenant from Stamford, Connecticut, to a slit trench. When it was light enough, First Lieutenant John B. White and Sergeant George Gerard, both later killed, carried him to the dressing station in Crézancy. There at the dressing station Crandall, married with two children, died.

First Lieutenant Clarence E. Allen of the 30th Infantry's E Company, encouraging the men of his platoon amid the shells and gas, directed them to their dugouts in the woods near Crézancy. He helped care for the wounded until a shell took his life.

So intense was the bombardment according to First Lieutenant Frederick Winant, Jr., commanding a Stokes mortar platoon, it was nearly impossible to determine how the troops in his company were making out. "The best a man could do," he remarked, "was to hug his cover."

The sudden roar of the bombardment and the shaking of the ground jolted Johns Hopkins from his sleep. The K Company lieutenant poked his head out from under the rock to see what was happening and was "confronted with a sight I cannot ever forget. Trees were falling all around, some of them completely uprooted."

From where he was he could see Major Lindsey Silvester's Second Battalion taking cover among the trees. The German artillery had its sights on the woods, shells landing like hail from hell. First Lieutenant Clarence E. Allen, in command of the Second Battalion's E Company and one of its most popular officers, screamed at his men, "Keep out of the woods! Get off the road into the field and lie down!" Twenty-five-year-old Hopkins, who'd grown up in a wealthy neighborhood of Philadelphia and was the 1915 class poet at the University of Pennsylvania, watched in horror as a shell fragment tore into Allen's chest, ripped clear through his body and exited out his back. "Although he lived all night," Hopkins recalled, "suffering intense agony, he died about daybreak cursing the Germans with his last breath."

Soon after the bombardment had started, Hopkins smelled gas as it spread across the ground. With his heart pounding, he slipped on his gas mask, wiggled back into his hole and "tried to settle myself as comfortably as possible." But he had hardly gotten settled when a soldier landed on top of him, making his heart pound faster. At first he thought the soldier was a messenger sent by the captain of K Company, John C. Adams, ordering him to be ready to form his platoon. "A feat I knew to be impossible midst the wild din, and in that inky inferno streaked with bursting shells."

Finally the soldier made himself known. He was the company clerk, a corporal named Lavine. He had put off digging his own foxhole. His only protection was a blanket that he had wrapped around himself. Running about like a rooster with its head cut off and without donning his gas mask, looking for any shelter, he'd found Hopkins's dugout. Throughout the night they shared the tight quarters beneath the rock. Because he had inhaled plenty of gas to make him "ghastly sick," Lavine vomited into his gas mask. With gas everywhere, the poor company clerk had to keep his mask on. "Although I was far from comfortable," Hopkins wrote, "his plight was many times worse than mine."

An artillery officer, with the flashes of the guns piercing the darkness, "all at once heard a curious sound quite distinct from the commotion raised by our guns. It was a steady whir overhead, like a high wind whistling through the trees, yet there was no wind." As he later learned, "it was the noise of Boche shells passing over us in a continuous stream."

One of McAlexander's sergeants major, Walter Peterman from Indiana, Pennsylvania, elaborated in a letter home, "If you can imagine what it would sound like to have hundreds of shells exploding within 50 or 100 feet of you, throwing dirt and debris all over you, combined with the terrible noise of our guns in the rear sending thousands of shells over to deal death and destruction to the Germans you will have an idea of what the night of July 14 was like. In addition to the noise there were terrible fumes from the gas shells to contend with."

In his small dugout, as the shells fell and the horrible explosions grew closer, Chaplain Ridout prayed fervently. He recited an old hymn by Charles Wesley, "Jesus, Lover of My Soul," slightly changing the lyrics to deal with the "hail of iron" outside his dugout:

Hide me O my savior, hide
Till the storm (of shell) is past;
Safe into the (morning) guide,
O (protect) my soul at last.

As the explosions pounded so close to his dugout, he prayed, "Cover my defenseless head with the shadow of thy wing."

Then shrapnel struck the roof covering Ridout. Dirt showered down on him. He clambered out of his dugout and ran for the captain's, deeper and more fortified. Climbing into the captain's dugout, Ridout was surprised to see it was crowded with soldiers, several of them wounded. He sat down to wait out the bombardment and thought of the words from the Bible, Jeremiah 49:8, "Dwell Deep." "It is a good thing on the danger line to dwell deep. Spiritually it is likewise so. The soul that dwells deep in God may have a thousand enemies pursue it, but it is safe from the enemy."

Corporal Fletcher Benson from Wooldridge's G Company, who had dropped out of divinity school to enlist, a stalwart soldier who did not smoke, chew tobacco, drink or swear, was fearless in the midst of the barrage because of his faith in God. His only protection was the walls of a hastily dug trench. While all around men were being killed or frightfully maimed, he felt secure. As with Ridout, a hymn kept singing through his mind.

I shall not fear the battle
If thou art by my side.

To Ridout, he later confessed, "I felt in a strange, peculiar way that there was One standing at my side and when the shells were bursting all about me I felt that He was shielding me from the shrapnel and comforting me so that all terror left me and I was not afraid."

Nine men in the ten-man kitchen force of the Sixth Engineers' C Company, attached to the 38th's Third Battalion and stationed along the Aqueduct Line between the village of Le Chanet and Courtelin, were killed. In the corral, thirty-six of the kitchen force's thirty-seven horses were destroyed. Forty percent of C Company were casualties.

A shell landed in the midst of A Company of the 30th Infantry and killed two men. One of them was Pierson McGee. A saddened Lieutenant C. William Ryan mourned him. "Pierson McGee, as fearless and faithful a man as I found in the war, my orderly and most dependable runner." When Ryan later came across McGee's grave and that of another soldier in a covered-over trench, he looked down at their dog tags and helmets that had been placed atop the grave. "In the very center and exactly the same place in each helmet was a bullet hole, which evidently penetrated the center of the forehead."

Earl E. Opel, a corporal in E Company of the Sixth Engineers who coincidentally came from Summit Mills in Pennsylvania's Somerset County, described the artillery attack to his mother and sister. "'Demon Bill' [Kaiser Wilhelm II] sent over some material. Several foundries, a railroad track and a battleship came over by aerial line. And after he done his 'woistest' he found he had a lot of tough-skinned Yanks left whom he could not lick." Opel told them he was feeling fine and "never received a scratch."

The roaring German artillery fire awakened another engineer, Sergeant Philip Frank Lund, a carpenter and native of Deep River, Connecticut. In his diary, he confided, "Decide to stay in dugout rather than get in safety trenches. . . . Lts. Anderson, Ralph, Bromwick and Crane are hurt. Monteith, Hard, Glendenning, Cooper, Barry, Brown and Olsen are killed, and all horses but two."

A shell blew up over the head of Private William Byrnes from Syracuse, knocking out the 30th Infantry private for more than two hours. When he awoke, he discovered that his coat had been shredded and ripped from his shoulders. Hot shrapnel had singed his back. To his family he wrote that "you cannot imagine how close to death I have been." He admitted, "My nerves are all gone." But he then assured them that what had saved him was the "good Lord and your prayers."

O n the German side of the Marne, the Seventh Army had its infantry in place for the attack across the river. An hour later, the 398th Infantry Regiment had reached the river. Once they were there, however, it was clear that the French and American artillery had been causing as much harm to the Germans as the German artillery had been doing up and down the Marne Valley. There was not a spot spared, Hesse pointed out. All communications had been destroyed. One battalion of the 47th Infantry, still at division headquarters, had been routed, with many killed and wounded. By two o'clock the artillery fire from the Allies had slackened. The valley was blanketed in fog, smoke and green and yellow gas.

The Sixth Grenadiers had made it to the river opposite the American Sixth Brigade without suffering any losses and without "being harassed seriously by the enemy," according to the regiment's tactical report written after the battle. "Machine-gun fire was heard only now and then in the valley of the Marne."

The Fifth Grenadiers were having a harder go of it. The Allied shelling was taking its toll. Lieutenant Hesse described how the regiment's First Battalion had been "caught by a fearful artillery fire in the narrow lane leading down to the river." When officers from the Sixth Grenadier's regimental staff headed for the river, they ran into elements of the battered First Battalion, which had come to a standstill. They ordered the commander of the battalion to move his surviving troops forward. He refused, replying that several direct hits had already struck one of his companies and that "it was impossible to cross the river."

The roar of the bombardment bellowing from batteries on both sides of the river carried all the way to Paris. At first there were three tremendous explosions followed by a constant roll of guns. The first thought was another air raid had started. But when no air-raid sirens heralded another enemy bombardment of the city, citizens there realized the great battle had finally begun. Thousands of them raced to the top of Montmartre to crowd around the base of the Church of Sacré Coeur to witness the eastern skies on fire. Others rushed to the rooftops of the tallest buildings in Paris to see in horror a horizon aflame in red and orange.

Colonel Billy Mitchell, commander of the American First Air Brigade, eating a midnight meal in Paris before heading back to his headquarters near Château-Thierry, had just been joined by Donald Brown of the American Red Cross, when "we heard the reverberation of guns to the north, [and] looking in that direction, could see tremendous flashes in the sky." Certain the main German offensive had just been launched, an excited Mitchell turned to Brown and said, "If you want to see the greatest battle in history come with me!"

They jumped up from their meal, dashed for Mitchell's automobile and then raced for his headquarters almost three hours away to grab an airplane and fly over the battlefield. Mitchell had flown reconnaissance over enemy lines numerous times without any escort because he had not wanted to be slowed down. Now he wanted to see the battle for himself.

Hell broke loose," recalled Pittsburgh native and veteran of the Spanish American War Captain Robert Woodside, whose M Company of the 38th Infantry, acting in a "sort of free lance support," was back in reserve on the western slope of Hill 231 digging trenches when the bombardment started. Since his company was surrounded by American artillery emplacements from the 10th Field Artillery, he'd taken the precaution of preparing squad dugouts for his men because he knew German artillery would zero in on the division's big guns and the shelling would be severe. He was right. "We thought Satan and all his imps were busy overtime that night."

The moment the shells began to whistle down from the black sky, Woodside made certain his men were safe in their freshly dug trenches. Behind the trenches was a small brick hunting lodge used by the French as a canteen. They had it stocked with wine in celebration of Bastille Day. With gas bombs spreading their vicious vapor through the woods and meadows and along the Marne and Surmelin Valleys, the French inside the hunting lodge started a fire to burn off the gas fumes and then proceeded to drink all the wine, as Woodside quipped, "to keep the Boche from getting any. After they had completed this task they crowded into our dugouts until the barrage had passed over and then we saw them no more."

Unfortunately, when one of Woodside's working parties returned to the trenches, there was no room for the men because of the French soldiers who had packed themselves into their trenches. The Americans, with their gas masks on, had to seek shelter elsewhere.

In the 30th's C Company, First Lieutenant James Gay, Jr., from Philadelphia and a University of Pennsylvania man, was leading a patrol along the river. "Suddenly the entire skyline north of the Marne lit up with a flash."

Lieutenant Ike Lovejoy, atop a hill above the Marne, found that the men in the rifle platoons could hear nothing "save the continuous whine of the whistling shells as they passed high overhead." He added, "There was no break, no pause, no stop. Men in the companies along the hills which flanked the valley looked down toward the flat expanses of cultivated land near the Surmelin and saw that the flame-bursts and flashes seemed to fade into one great screen of fire." He described how huge tree trunks "snapped completely in twain; a roof here or a stone wall there came tumbling down; a cloud of smoke and flying pieces of dirt would drift away and leave behind it a gaping hole the width of a road."

————

The platoons on the river scrambled for their foxholes, which had been dug into the railroad embankment, and burrowed in like rabbits in a warren. Luckily for them the German shells whistled past, exploding farther back in the open fields and patches of woods and small villages along the Surmelin, seeking out enemy artillery emplacements. There was nothing for the soldiers in Major Rowe's Second Battalion to do but to wait out the bombardment and then rush back to their outpost positions. A soldier over in the 30th Infantry, it was told, once inside his foxhole fell asleep and slept through the entire bombardment. When he awoke, he was covered with dirt and the dead were all around him.

One of the dead was Sergeant Edward T. Marum of A Company. From New York City, Marum had been scheduled to leave the regiment in the morning to return to the United States as an instructor. His commander called him "as fine a soldier as we sent to war and a favorite with officers and men. He died miserably." A trench mortar platoon in the 30th's First Battalion had no place to hide from the bursting shells. Commanded by Second Lieutenant Harrison E. Barringer, an attorney from Jacksonville, Florida, the platoon had to give up ground west of the Ru Chailly Farm—ground it had been working for weeks to fortify— and move to the other side of the farm. Barringer's men were digging new holes in a narrow strip of woods when the bombardment hit them hard. One of his corporals and the corporal's squad were struck and never seen again. First Lieutenant Dennis C. Turner of B Company, whose platoon was in the rear of First Lieutenant James R. Kingery's platoon, yelled at Barringer to get into his dugout in the railroad embankment. Before he had a chance to huddle, someone yelled that two men had been killed and they were trench mortar men. Barringer asked Turner if he had a first-aid man. Turner said he didn't have one, but Kingery had one down by the river. Turner ordered Barringer to go to Kingery, get the first-aid man and find out what was going on.

Barringer crawled out of the dugout. A shell went off close to him and he thought he was dead. He sprinted across an open field to Kingery's platoon and in twenty minutes located the first-aid man and brought him back. He let Turner know that Kingery and his men were safe by the river at the moment because no shells were landing where they were.

German tracer rounds, red in the dark sky, flew over the heads of Barringer and Turner, fading into the woods while the first-aid man went to work on the wounded.

B ehind the men in the foxholes, machine gunners, concealed in the woods and villages, fired over their heads and into the hills north of the Marne. From the village of Moulins, Captain Sidney H. Young of McAlexander's machine-gun company, kept his guns pouring lead into enemy territory. One of his lieutenants commanding a machine-gun squad went crazy from shell shock and had to be taken back to the dressing station at Crézancy.

Another gunner, First Lieutenant Chester Boothe Blakeman from the Ninth Machine Gun Battalion's A Company, with gas filling the woods, stayed at his position even though the only part of his gas mask he had left was the mouthpiece. From a well-known Mount Vernon, New York, family, with three brothers in the service, he and one other soldier kept firing across the river. Blakeman operated his gun for more than two hours. He was then evacuated to a hospital, suffering from gas wounds.

A ll telephone and wire communications had been destroyed in the barrage. Commanders were cut off from their front-line troops and had no idea what was going on down by the river. Thirty minutes before the start of the bombardment, Sixth Brigade commander Brigadier General Charles Crawford had tested the communications between his command post and the command post of Colonel Billy Butts. It had worked.

In a field message sent to division headquarters at 4:50 a.m., Crawford stated that there were no reports of the enemy's infantry attacking. "There are shrapnel falling on Courboin and roads leading out from there. Mounted men from Syracuse [code name for the 30th Infantry] left there at 12:30, arrived at 4:10, reports woods shelled. Few men at Bochage not wearing gas masks. French artillery near us, all communications out."

Twenty-five minutes later, he sent another message, stating that the French 125th Division reported violent bombardment at Jaulgonne Bend and poison gas in the Surmelin Valley.

Inside his command post in the Bois d'Aigremont, Butts wasn't sure if the bombardment was the prelude to the German attack. His French liaison officer, Lieutenant Leon Marchand, who'd been at Verdun, showed signs of uneasiness. He told Butts the shelling at Verdun had never been this terrible. He asked him if he thought that this bombardment meant an attack.

"Surely it is the beginning of the attack," Butts answered, "for they are using some very large caliber shells."

Butts reasoned that the "large caliber shells would not be used unless destruction was sought and that destruction of field works and command posts was always attempted just prior to the attack."

Assembled inside his command post along with Marchand was Butts's second in command, Lieutenant Colonel Cromwell Stacy, a former assistant inspector general of the United States Army; his Headquarters Company commander, Captain Turner Chambliss, a 1914 graduate of the Virginia Military Institute; his adjutant, Captain Sterling Maxwell; his intelligence officer, Second Lieutenant Lewis C. Beebe, a University of Oregon graduate and formerly with the Oregon National Guard; runner Edward Bzoch, a thirty-year-old private from Chicago, where he owned a well-known real-estate company; and Butts's artillery liaison, First Lieutenant George P. Hays, from the division's 10th Field Artillery's Second Battalion. The 10th's Second Battalion headquarters and its line of batteries that included twelve American 75-caliber guns lined up next to twenty-six French batteries, eighteen

77s and eight 55s, was set about one thousand yards south of Butts's command post, on a hill at Grèves Farm with a clear view of the Marne. Grèves Farm was described as more of a medieval manor than a farm.

Hays was short, five feet, eight inches tall, and slightly built, but a man who gave off an aura of quiet confidence. He'd been born in China, where his parents were Presbyterian missionaries. He grew up on a farm in Oklahoma and learned to ride a horse as well as any cowboy, a gift that would soon save his life. At the start of the war he dropped out of Oklahoma A&M College (now Oklahoma State University) in his junior year to enlist. He earned his commission at the officers' training camp at Fort Root, Arkansas. In World War Two he'd be the founding general of the famous 10th Mountain Division. Perhaps of all the soldiers under his command, even if he was a liaison officer from another unit, Butts trusted Hays the most.

At the moment Butts and his staff were totally isolated from brigade and division headquarters and from their own battalions and front-line companies. The enemy artillery had severed two field telephone lines, a buzzer telephone and a telegraph that had kept all commanders in constant contact with one another. Even the four pigeons, trained to deliver messages under frightful conditions, were disoriented and thus useless.

"All means of signal communication with the regiment had ceased to function when the bombardment began," Butts recounted. "It was of no value during the battle. This was unexpected."

Repair parties were unable to fix the equipment. Even Colonel Stacy, who spent much of his time trying to figure a way to fix the problem, found it impossible.

The only way to find out what was going on and to give or receive orders was by using runners, many riding for their lives on horseback. Private Bzoch, the Chicagoan, then got his first assignment—take an order to a wireless station, give it to the officer in charge and see what was left of the station, if anything. Maybe the wireless could be repaired. When Bzoch got there, he saw that a shell had flattened the station and all the men inside had been killed. Not knowing what to do, he left the written order on the body of the station commander and headed back to the headquarters command post in the Bois d'Aigremont. On his return, he was twice wounded and was evacuated to a dressing station and then on to a hospital.

Finally, a runner came in with the news the Germans were assembling three pontoon bridges and ferrying soldiers across the river.

Butts wanted the river shelled, the bridges and boats destroyed.

Hays tried to get on the box telephone to reach his artillery battalion commander, Major George W. Easterday, to give him Butts's order to shell the river. But an enemy shell had struck the 10th Field Artillery's dugout in which the telephone switchboard and its operators were huddled. The switchboard had been gutted and the operators killed. Hays quickly sent two messengers to link up communication between his battalion and the 30th's post command and make sure Butts's order was carried out. The runners took off, but never returned. And with Bzoch wounded and out of action, it was now up to Hays to be his own runner and carry orders from Butts to his artillery batteries.

Hays dashed out of the command post and ran toward a horse corral, shells lighting up the sky and shaking the very ground he was running on. Reaching the corral, he saw to his despair that the animals had all been killed. He now knew he had to reach battalion headquarters on foot. Galloping toward him was a private on a big horse. He drew up next to Hays and said he had a message for the colonel and needed to know the location of regimental headquarters. Hays pointed out where it was just as a shell hit nearby with a huge explosion. The private jumped from the horse, yelling, and sprinted in the direction of the dugout. Hays grabbed the terrified horse by the neck and leaped onto its back. He rode off to battalion headquarters, through the woods where trees were being uprooted by the enemy's artillery, falling across his path, their sharp branches whipping at his face. As rider and horse closed in on Grèves Farm, another shell crashed close enough to wound the horse. It reeled forward to the stone wall that encircled the manor house and then collapsed. After vaulting the stone wall, Hays raced the rest of the way to the battalion command post that had been mostly destroyed by German

Men of A Company, Seventh Machine Gun Battalion, hold off the Germans from crossing the Marne River at Château-Thierry. *Signal Corps*

One of two bridges the French blew up to keep the Germans from capturing Château-Thierry. *Signal Corps*

Major General Joseph T. Dickman had been a cavalry officer before leading the Third Division. He was one of the oldest front-line generals in the AEF.
U.S. Army Photograph, Fort Stewart Museum

"They may kill us, but they cannot whip us" was the fighting principle of the commander of the 38th Infantry, Colonel Ulysses Grant McAlexander.
Signal Corps

Commander of the 30th Infantry, Colonel Edmund L. Butts believed his regiment's defense of its subsector was the deciding factor in turning back the Germans. *Signal Corps*

On the road outside Montmiral, on June 1, men of the 38th Infantry's Second Battalion meet French refugees fleeing the German army. *Signal Corps*

Part of the Third Division convoy on its way to the front, June 2. *Signal Corps*

On June 2, troops of the 30th Infantry march through the village of Viels-Maisons on their way to the Marne River. *Signal Corps*

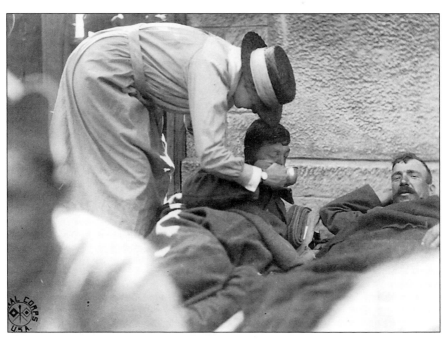

Red Cross nurse Mary Withers tending to wounded British soldiers at Montmiral. *Signal Corps*

Above: Leading the 38th Infantry's Second Battalion, Major Guy I. Rowe battled superior enemy forces attacking his men from three different directions.
Robert B. Ferguson

Right: Major Fred L. Walker, commander of the 30th Infantry's First Battalion, received the Distinguished Service Cross for his actions during the battle.
Signal Corps

Colonel Robert H. C. Kelton, Third Division's chief of staff, is credited with calling Colonel McAlexander the "Rock of the Marne." *Signal Corps*

A captain in McAlexander's regiment, Jesse W. Wooldridge proudly proclaimed, "The 38th was given the 'Gateway to Paris,' the Surmelin Valley to defend."
U.S. Army Photograph, Fort Stewart Museum

Left: Captain Edward Herlihy of H Company, 38th Infantry, earned the nickname "Iron Jaw" as a star on the 1911–1914 Marietta (Ohio) College football teams. *Daniel E. Herlihy*

Right: Captain Cornelius Dineen, commander of the 38th Infantry's E Company, had bunked with young Dwight Eisenhower during General John J. Pershing's 1916 Punitive Expedition into Mexico. *Dineen-Klingenberg Family*

Left: Captain Thomas C. Reid and his men in the 38th Infantry's F Company saved the Third Division's right flank after it had been left unprotected by retreating French troops. *Signal Corps*

Right: A lieutenant in Reid's company, Elmer Focke hailed from Dayton, Ohio. *Dayton Metro Library*

Left: Winning more than one thousand dollars in a craps game on the way to the Western Front, the 30th Infantry's Lieutenant James Rountree Kingery's luck ran out on the banks of the Marne. *Roger Snyder*

Right: Coming under his first artillery bombardment on June 4, 1918, Corporal William Fitzgerald of the 30th Infantry (on the right of fellow soldier Harry Lewis) wrote, "Shells whizzing overhead—getting near the firing line. Oh boy!" *Rick C. Fitzgerald*

Lieutenant Robinson Murray of the 38th's F Company carried on a courtship with Peggy Piersol, a nurse in Paris. After the war, while still in France, they were married. *Anne Murray Morgan Papers, Radcliffe College Archives, Schlesinger Library, Harvard University, Cambridge, Massachusetts*

In position along the railroad tracks near Mézy, a soldier from the 9th Machine Gun Battalion keeps watch across the Marne. *Signal Corps*

Soldiers from the 30th and 38th infantries, gassed on July 15, leaving a first-aid station for the hospital at Courboin. *Signal Corps*

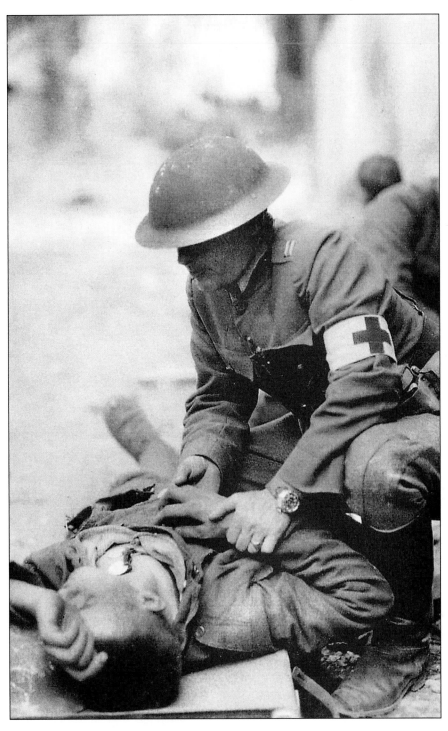

A Third Division surgeon examines one of the casualties during the Aisne, Marne operation, July 22, 1918. *The National Archives, Modern Military Records Branch*

Soldiers burying horses killed during the opening bombardment on July 15.   *Signal Corps*

German prisoners of war waiting for mess after their capture at Gland on July 25.
Signal Corps

Dead German soldiers fill a trench on the outskirts of Mézy. *Signal Corps*

A captured German piano taken by American soldiers in the village of Gland. *Signal Corps*

A camouflaged pontoon bridge thrown across the Marne River by H Company of the Sixth Engineers. *Signal Corps*

AEF Commander, General John J. Pershing, and his staff meet with Major General Joseph Dickman after the Second Battle of the Marne. *Signal Corps*

Corporal Alvey Martz of C Company, 110th Infantry, surrounded by Germans, led his men to safety, killing eighteen of the enemy along the way.
Historical & Genealogical Society of Somerset County

Captain W. Curtis Truxal, commander of C Company, 110th Infantry, revisits the fateful battleground after spending most of the war in a German prison camp. *Historical & Genealogical Society of Somerset County*

Left: Private William O. Zimmerman from Somerset was celebrating his thirty-eighth birthday when he and Lieutenant Samuel Crouse were ambushed by a German patrol and killed. *The Family of William O. Zimmerman*

Right: Cook Harry Stevanus of Coal Run, Pennsylvania, killed six Germans before taking a bullet below the left knee that cost him his leg. *Larry C. Bodes*

artillery. Dead American artillerymen were strewn everywhere; the wounded were being carried to a nearby first-aid station. The batteries were firing their 77-millimeter shells across the Marne into the woods beyond the north bank. Close by, batteries of the French artillery were thundering away, sending their 155-millemeter shells hurtling toward the far side of the Marne. Amid the chaos, Hays found Major Easterday. He told the major to fire on the river and take out the enemy's bridges and boats. He next went to each of Easterday's batteries and explained what needed to be done. The officers then trained their field pieces on their new targets. Hays raced over to the French batteries and had them redirect their fire. Back at Grèves Farm, he was informed that one of the pontoon bridges had been hit.

Satisfied, he borrowed a horse and headed back to the 30th's command post at a gallop. Into the woods he rode, the German shells banging all around him, trees cracking, breaking and crashing to the earth. The stench of gas was heavy and the smoke bombs filled the land like a fog. Halfway to Butts's headquarters, a shell fragment hit his horse. The animal stumbled sideways and rolled to the ground, dead. Again on foot, Hays completed his return trip. He then got the news that the Germans had crossed the river and were fighting their way south toward the Bois d'Aigremont.

Hays soon found out his day was far from done.

Like Hays's Second Battalion, the 10th Field Artillery's First Battalion, nicknamed "Ragamuffin," was also cut off from any communication. Attached to the 38th Infantry, it was commanded by Captain Jonathan Waverly Anderson from Chattanooga, Tennessee. A 1911 graduate of the Naval Academy, Anderson had transferred into the army a few years before America entered the war. McAlexander found him a fine officer and liked the fact that he could keep an eye on Anderson and his batteries to ensure they did not fire on his own men as he was sure was going to happen from the artillery batteries to his left, those assigned to the 30th Infantry.

Anderson's command post was set up in a farmhouse near the village of Saint-Eugène, on the northeastern edge of the Bois d'Aigremont and close to McAlexander's command post, which on the 14th the colonel had moved from Connigis to Saint-Eugène.

Its Battery A was close to McAlexander, only five hundred yards away, at Janvier Farm. Nicknamed "Arthur" because its commanding officer was Captain Arthur Brigham, Jr., its four gun emplacements, or gun pits, each about two feet deep and separated by ten yards, were in the sector held by the French 125th Division's 126th Infantry Regiment across the Surmelin River, on the eastern slope of Moulins Ridge. Although the battery was close to McAlexander, it was out of the Third Division's sector and, in effect, detached from the rest of Anderson's battalion. Also, the battery was out in the open. Its gun pits were partially screened from the enemy by a line of trees and covered with a lengthy camouflage netting that stretched across all four emplacements, and a trench ran behind the pits, offering protection for the soldiers, three to a gun, when enemy bombardment got too hot.

Both Anderson and Brigham, who'd been commissioned from the ranks, and Brigham's executive officer, First Lieutenant Joseph W. Loef, knew Battery A was in a dangerous position.

"The enemy air service was very active," Lieutenant Loef stated, "making frequent reconnaissances, apparently unopposed by allied planes; in fact I do not recall seeing any allied planes at all during the two days preceding the attack."

Prior to the German bombardment, Brigham and Loef had two wire lines running over separate routes connecting them to battalion headquarters. Shelter pits for the men and for ammunition had been dug. An observation post had been placed well in front of the battery, on the top of Hill 231, east of Moulins. When the French forces withdrew during the early morning of the 15th, the observation post was overrun and the men lost. The wire communications were severed. The only communication was by mounted messengers, and that meant, with artillery shells exploding nonstop and gas sweeping over the valley, riding down the steep slopes of Hill 231, splashing across the Surmelin River and up the other ridge to either Anderson's battalion command post or to McAlexander's regimental command post, a harrowing three-mile dash, and then back over the river and up the hill.

Battery A's orders were to fire five rounds per minute for five minutes and then three rounds per minute for ten minutes on the edge of the woods immediately across the Marne, at its confluence with the Surmelin. Other targets were north and northwest of Mont-Saint-Pére, concentrating on a deep wooded ridge called the Bois de Barbillon. But with the observation post gone, the gunners were not sure if their shells were landing on enemy lines or on the backs of McAlexander's men. Riders had been sent to locate the observation post, only to find it was gone, the men captured.

There was more bad news. Ammunition was running low. At 2 a.m. an orderly who had ridden up from battalion headquarters, with the message from Anderson to "continue firing at your own discretion," was sent right back, carrying a verbal message from Brigham: "Need more ammunition badly. Send some as soon as you can."

But it was impossible to resupply Battery A because the heavy bombardment made it too risky to move artillery shells across the Surmelin Valley. Brigade ammunition trains could not make the long climb up Hill 231 under the endless artillery fire. And the French infantry that covered Battery A's front began its withdrawal. A French officer tried to get Brigham to reposition his guns in front of his infantrymen who were then getting reorganized a distance behind Brigham's batteries. "The Boche are advancing on this hill from three sides," the officer informed the American. "I have received information that they are attacking Conde to cut off our rear."

There wasn't much Brigham could do with his batteries almost out of ammunition.

The good news, if there was any, was the French artillery, which had also pulled back, had an ammunition dump cached near Janvier Farm, not too far from the battery. Volunteers raided the dump and lugged back 250 rounds, but suffered a number of casualties. The additional rounds taken from the French ammunition dump didn't last long, and the battery was soon put out of action.

Resupplying Battery B, commanded by West Pointer Captain Alfred K. King, was another nightmare. Ammunition dumps of any size were being blown up and wagons lugging ammo up to the battery were being destroyed, their men and horses killed or wounded. "Scattered ammunition, particularly from French positions, was about all that we could count on," noted Anderson, "and the search for, and location of, such ammunition was carried on with enthusiasm akin to that found in an Easter egg hunt."

While this was happening, French soldiers began to filter through Battery A's position. "At first it was thought that these were slightly wounded going to the dressing stations," Loef recalled. "But later, as their numbers increased rapidly, investigation showed that the first line was falling back." French officers informed Loef that their entire line had been broken and they were forced to withdraw. The lieutenant then reported to Brigham, telling him about the retreating French. If the Germans had crossed the river, then Brigham ordered him to fire south of the Marne.

Like Batteries A and B, Battery C was also having a difficult time keeping its guns resupplied with ammunition. The only ammo brought to it had to be carried by hand through thick woods where wagons could not penetrate. Led by Captain Homer Cook, the battery suffered the most of any during the bombardment. Anderson believed the reason was that Cook's guns were located near the "storm centre" of the German artillery preparation. Two of the guns were hit, with one officer and six men killed and forty wounded.

Captain Anderson was worried because he kept getting conflicting reports about what was happening. With one battery out of action, and soldiers pulling back on his front and on his left, it looked to him that there was an "excellent chance of being completely surrounded." He considered for a moment pulling back his guns, in case he was overrun.

He hurried to McAlexander's command post at Saint-Eugène to consult with the colonel, knowing that if the regiment should withdraw to the rear "we would be in a rather serious position."

McAlexander looked at the captain and stated in "no uncertain terms that he was going to stay where he was, so we patterned our plans accordingly—dug in a little better, and left the horses with the echelon."

The 30th Infantry's First Battalion commander, Major Walker, like everyone else, was also without any means of communication except by runner. A number of his men were out trying to fix the wires leading into his command post. The shelling wounded several of them. They were carried into the shelter fourteen feet beneath the ground, where their wounds were dressed by candlelight. Even though they were deep underground, the concussion of the exploding shells kept snuffing out the candles.

Twenty minutes after the start of the German barrage, at 12:30 a.m., Lieutenants Raymond B. Jauss, who in June had led one of the first raiding parties across the Marne, and George B. Henderson, the scout officer of Silvester's Second Battalion then on its way to replace Walker's battalion, slipped into the dugout wearing gas masks. They informed the major and his staff that the division's entire sector was under horrific fire and that their subsector had been swept with mustard gas. They had run into a detail of engineers caught in the open. Most of the men had survived, they said, but that many were lost, wandering around the woods as stragglers.

Earlier, Jauss and Henderson, along with two sergeants, had been on a scouting mission close to the river, giving Henderson a chance to know where to position the men of his battalion marching in to make their relief. At midnight, the French and American artillery attack hit the north side of the Marne, many of the shells striking directly opposite the scouting party. One shell hit an ammunition dump and it burst into a huge ball of flames. When the Germans answered, Jauss and Henderson and their sergeants darted for the safety of Walker's dugout, slapping on their gas masks as they ran. When they reached the edge of the woods, where Walker and his staff were holed up, the enemy's exploding shells formed a box around the dugout. The four men were not able to enter through the front door of the dugout and had to skirt around to the back door to get in and descend the stairs to the bottom of the bunker.

Down inside the command post, they found Walker and his adjutant, First Lieutenant Harold L. Reese, anxious to know what was happening to their battalion. Walker had sent out runners to his company commanders and not one had yet returned. They were either killed or lost in the utter darkness or unable to get through amid the rain of shells and obstacles on the roads and paths. Runners from the companies on the front line were also not getting through to Waker's headquarters. Finally, a runner from D Company made it, Private Garland Green. From Baker's Creek, North Carolina, he'd been wounded in the arm and had bound up the wound himself. He refused medical attention, received a message from Walker to carry back to his commander, Captain Francis "Jud" Lasseigne, who had led the first successful raid into enemy territory a month earlier. Private Green bolted from the command post into the evil night. He had to work his way back to Lasseigne, who was sharing his dugout with First Lieutenant Iverson Lawton south of Crézancy in a place ominously called Cemetery Woods, so named because there was a village cemetery encircled by a stone fence there in the woods. Private Green was one of the few runners from D Company who had dared to venture out. The others trying to reach Walker's headquarters could not find their way. Several of them were killed. Lawton, from Greenville, South Carolina, remembered that some of the runners had gotten lost "in the utter darkness and terrified to an awful extent by the terrific shell fire which hailed down hard and fast on our position."

Then a runner from C Company reached Walker, all out of breath and very agitated. Walker had him sit down and rest for a bit before the runner made his report. When he was ready, he said the Germans had crossed the river, entered Mézy, greatly outnumbered the men in his own company, and those men were "being wiped out!" He said there was gas everywhere and he had to slip by many Germans who were between Mézy and battalion headquarters. Getting to Walker's command post, he added, was like running through hell.

A third runner, this one from A Company, made it through. All officers in his company had been killed, he claimed, and he'd seen his company commander, First Lieutenant Philip Sexton, "lying before his post of command with both feet shot off."

An officer from A Company staggered in, confirming the runner's report. The Germans had broken through on his company's right flank. He then collapsed, saying he'd been gassed. He was placed on one of the bunks and administered to.

Another runner, wounded in the hand, arrived from the Ru Chailly Farm. From B Company, he, too, had terrible news. The Germans had crossed the river and destroyed two platoons. His company commander, Captain Kay McCallister, was now begging for reinforcements.

Walker realized the "difficulty of attempting to move any troops during this terrific bombardment and darkness." He decided no troops would be brought up as reinforcements. He was sure they'd be annihilated. "The original plan of each isolated unit fighting on its own ground and following the judgment of its natural leader was not to be tampered with."

There could be no reinforcements at this time, not until after the bombardment had ended.

Walker then sent a field message to Butts. It was 2:15 a.m. and Butts did not get it until 5 a.m. "We have had some gas. All groups of woods south of Railroad on line with P.C. are being heavily shelled. Heavy machine gun fire in vicinity of Mont St. Pere since 2 a.m. Have received no news from front line companies. I believe all lines are out.

"Capt. McCallister reports that he needs re-enforcements and that his two front platoons have been driven back. Cannot depend on any method of liaison. Better base your actions on what you observe from your P.C."

When all the runners had left to return to their companies, leaving Walker without any enlisted men to carry messages, he turned to Jauss and Henderson and another officer, a heavyset captain.

"Now that my runners are all gone," he said, afraid his battalion was being overrun, "will you men try and make the journey to get information back to me about what's going on." He had to find out if, in fact, the enemy had crossed the Marne and were now destroying his platoons on the river or were the reports exaggerated or even false. The three officers agreed. Jauss was to go out to "ascertain the whereabouts of the enemy's line." The heavyset captain was to try to make regimental headquarters. Henderson was to locate K Company and put them into the line. Walker, in his telling of the moment, had sent Henderson out "to observe the enemy's activities." Henderson was gone for a short time and returned, reporting that "the Germans were only fifty yards in front of our station," Walker recounted. "[Henderson] also reported that an enemy machine gun crew was posted on the Fossoy-Crézancy Road near Company A's position and that it could fire on any troops that might cross it."

Henderson wrote, "Jauss and I left the dugout at the same time as we intended to go out of the woods through the same path."

They split up. Henderson reached K Company, his letter stated, and gave the commander there Walker's orders. He then headed back to the First Battalion headquarters. Jauss, meanwhile, hadn't gone far when a fragment from a high-explosive shell ripped into him, mortally wounding the recently married first lieutenant from New York City's Gramercy Park.

After Lieutenant Henderson's harrowing return trip through the rain of shells, he made a safe arrival at battalion headquarters. When he climbed down into Walker's strongly fortified earthen command post to give his report, he found it eerily deserted. Walker and his staff had vanished.

In the 38th's subsector, Colonel Ulysses McAlexander, just back from checking on his troops down by the Marne, was sitting with his staff in his command post in a dugout near the small village of Connigis on the Surmelin River, when his adjutant brought him a letter from home. Before he had a chance to read it, the German barrage kicked off. One of the first shells to hit burst ten feet from the château. It blew out windows, destroyed two bicycles and damaged two others. No one was wounded. "Did you ever turn a stone over in the fields and see the bugs scatter from under it?" he wrote to his wife in the midst of the bombardment. "Well, the rest of my bunch started to move out of the building while the 'Old Man' still stays in his room and will continue to stay as long as there are four walls and a whole ceiling."

Earlier he had written home stating, "I was never born to be ended by a shell."

In Moulins, the village on the hill east of the Surmelin River, Captains Tom Reid of F Company and Con Dineen of E Company, along with First Lieutenant Ralph Eberlin and two platoons from Reid's company, were eating their supper when the bombardment lit up the valley. Reid immediately ordered Eberlin to reach the First and Second Platoons, commanded by First Lieutenant Carl C. Cramer and a Sergeant Campbell and get them under cover.

"What are my orders?" Eberlin asked.

"Move to the trenches in case the French fall back on our right."

Near H Company's command post under the railroad bridge close to the river, Captain Eddy Herlihy was making the rounds with the commander of the Second Battalion, Major Guy Rowe, his adjutant and his sergeant major when, as Rowe put it, "the ball opened." They saw the sky erupt into a sheet of flame. Rowe later told McAlexander, "That was my one big moment of fright."

"Shells were bursting everywhere south of the river," Herlihy wrote. "For a few minutes the railroad, every woods and every village in the Surmelin Valley was ablaze with exploding shells." For almost two hours the bombardment passed over the heads of Rowe's battalion on the river, hitting areas farther south. "The Germans did not waste ammunition on a mere 'outpost position.' Their fire was directed on the wooded slopes of the Surmelin and on the villages and roads in the rear areas," Herlihy added.

Herlihy revealed that the merciless bombardment had permanently affected the nerves of everyone. "For days we jumped every time a shell burst near us—sometimes we would flinch at the crack of our own cannons. I thank the good Lord that I am here, not a shapeless mass of flesh, and I will never forget His mercy. The only thing that saved me was the fact that I wasn't ready for death. I shall be ready in the future."

Corporal William Fitzgerald of the 30th Infantry became a nervous wreck, writing in his diary on the 17th, "Every auto truck startles."

Throughout the bombardment, Captain Herlihy kept visiting the outposts of his company, calming his platoon officers and squad leaders. A captain in another company noted that with disregard to his own life, Herlihy "went out and helped carry in the body of Private Leon P. Goff, a runner who was severely wounded." Goff, while slung over Herlihy's back, crapped on the captain's trench coat, and the excrement mixed with blood made Herlihy smell "like a latrine." "Good grief," he later worried, "my boys will think I did a job in my breeches."

Prior to the French and American artillery send-off and before making the rounds with Rowe, Herlihy had been away from his command post, checking his troops. He had crossed the railroad bridge when a "flare lit me up like a Christmas Tree," the 1915 Marietta College graduate put in his diary. "Had vision of Heinie making me look like Swiss cheese with M.G.'s. Nothing happened. They can't hurt me—it isn't scheduled for me—I'm too young to die."

After Rowe, his adjutant and his sergeant major had hurried back to their command post, the major sent a field message off to his "CO," McAlexander.

> *I was at the river bank when she started. Have been back about ½ hour. Much gas, some chlorine and a bit of tear gas. They are not shelling the river bank yet.*
>
> *I believe every one is standing it well. We will hold them.*
>
> *Rowe*

Rowe then ordered F Company's Captain Reid to get three of his platoons up on the Moulins Ridge east of the Surmelin River and occupy McAlexander's fire trenches. His right flank had to be protected. Rowe kept Reid's Fourth Platoon under his direct command.

P aul Plough and Jefferson Healy, the second lieutenants in Herlihy's company, both of whom had been ordered by Rowe back to a village to rest up, hadn't yet gone to sleep when a shell hit the house they were in. They ran down into the wine cellar. Healy said he'd try to get back to the company. Plough opted to stay in the wine cellar until the barrage lifted, knowing the Germans wouldn't attack across the river until after the artillery attack. There was nothing either could do while shells dropped down on them.

But the six-one, 188-pound former captain of the Columbia football team, a Latin scholar with a reputation as an orator, was determined to rejoin his company. With gas mask on, Healy started running as if he were back on the gridiron, dodging shells and machine-gun bullets ripping up the ground around him.

"Healy tried to get through," Plough recalled, "but was killed."

He was struck by a bullet and mortally wounded. He lingered until August 11. When a Delta Gamma fraternity brother heard that Healy had died, he wrote about how "Big Jeff" had a spectacular way of catching passes. "I can see him now tearing up and down the football field at Columbia, using every inch of his six feet and every ounce of his weight in perfect abandon to bring victory to Columbia."

Captain Harold W. James from Wilkes Barre, Pennsylvania, and a West Point classmate of Dwight Eisenhower, reported that "many acts of heroism and bravery were performed by these messengers who went from one post command to another through the hail of shell and shrapnel when it was so dark that one could not see his hand before his face."

He pointed out the night was so dark in the woods where most of the 38th's troops were hidden and wearing their gas masks, it was "almost impossible to move anywhere. There was nothing for the infantry to do but wait for daylight to come."

Thus the long night wore on," Rowe later wrote, "with no news from the front. No news is supposed to be good news, but at such a time one wonders if he hasn't forgotten some vital provision, and thoroly [*sic*] longs for just a message that all is well."

"For hours that seemed weeks," Captain Wooldridge wrote, "we huddled in our tiny splinter proofs [a shelter against shell fragments] or open slit trenches in the horrible confusion of it all, but we lovingly patted, as yet, cold steel and awaited the second shock we knew would come—the shock of bodies, material bodies that we could see, feel and fight—something tangible so that we could release our mad lust to kill this great snake that was slowly coiling around us, this furious beast that was volcanically tearing at our vitals."

CHAPTER 15

//

"IT WAS SOMETHING AWFUL"

Before the bombardment, Colonel McAlexander had a gut feeling that the French 125th Division, then holding Hill 231 on his right with elements of the American 28th Division, would withdraw once the fighting got too hot. He had sent his F Company, commanded by Captain Tom Reid, up the hill to shovel out another system of trenches. The trenches were sited so they could cover the right flank of the Second Battalion in case the Germans gained a footing to the east. It proved a smart move. During the bombardment, the French, in fact, retreated without telling anyone, leaving McAlexander's right flank exposed. The Pennsylvanians in the four companies of the 28th attached to the French were now without their main support, and once the Germans crossed the Marne, they'd be surrounded and in dire trouble.

Shells struck C Company of the 110th Infantry, the men from Somerset County, in as deadly a way as it hit the men from the Third Division. The historian of the 28th Division noted, "During the entire night that followed Bastille Day the cross fire of the two famous artillery preparations whistled over the Marne and thundered and crashed into every yard of ground for miles on both sides of the river."

Another historian, H. G. Proctor, wrote, "Crashing, ear-splitting explosions came so fast that they were blended into one vast dissonance that set the nerves to jangling and in more than one instance upset completely the mental poise of our soldiers, so that they had to be restrained forcibly by their comrades from rushing out into the open in their temporary madness."

Captain W. Curtis Truxal; twenty-eight-year-old First Sergeant Martin L. Markel, a miner from Somerset; and the French interpreter Renato Geruto were on the river inspecting the outpost of First Lieutenant Robert Bonner's Third Platoon, located near the headquarters of a French company, when the bombardment began. It was mealtime and for all the troops in the company who hadn't had a chance to eat it would be a long, hungry night. One of the kitchen details, bringing up food for the front-line platoons, dodged incoming shells and scrunched up behind a road bank for protection.

Corporal Alvey Martz had charge of a work detail stringing barbed wire when the shells started landing all around them. He nonchalantly said to the men in his party, "It looks like a big attack. I guess we will have to take cover." Carrying their shovels, they crawled over the railroad embankment to one of the hastily dug trenches to wait out the shelling. Discarding their shovels, they grabbed their rifles.

William Martray, a private first class in the medical detachment, wrote to a friend, "We certainly did get hell while it lasted for we had just arrived the night before and we hadn't any time to dig ourselves in. We sheltered ourselves along the road and some times in shell holes and in the open. You may think the Fourth of July is noisy, but when high explosives and shrapnel start to burst over your head then it's time to think of home."

Reuben Rakestraw, a forty-one-year-old hotel manager and bartender from Humbert, described to his mother how high-explosive shells and shrapnel kept coming, exploding around them every second. "It was something awful, and your prayers pulled me through. They shelled us all night Sunday night and came over early Monday morning. Shells were dropping every second all around us. Some were killed and many were wounded by the shrapnel during the night." In another letter, he wrote, "We had to lie there with gas masks on all night; the fellow lying next to me was wounded in the leg, several were dead and many were wounded. . . . It was awful and makes me tremble to think of it."

Another Somerset County soldier, Samuel Landis of Rockwood, a corporal in the Second Platoon's automatic rifle squad, watched in dread from the railroad track as "Privates Paul Bills, Charles Olson, Nathan Arndt, Charles Kelley and Luther Streng were killed by the barrage of artillery fire. Of course there were lots more wounded among them myself hit in the back."

The moment First Lieutenant Wilbur Schell saw Landis's wound, he ordered him back to the dressing station. Landis refused to go. As he saw it, "I couldn't leave the boys."

The French soldiers didn't have the grit Landis showed. As soon as the German shells crashed into the 125th Division, they pulled back, exposing both flanks of the two companies of the 110th Infantry, one from Beaver County and the other from Somerset. One American soldier, staying in his freshly dug trench and ready to stand his ground, observed that "a constant stream of panic-stricken French were rushing to the rear and for a time it looked as if the whole line would give way." A lieutenant from the 109th Infantry, the brigade's liaison officer assigned to the 125th's divisional headquarters, knew something was up the moment the bombardment broke over their heads. The French officers, he reported, had packed their personal effects, burned maps and records and then slept on straw strewn on the floor of their command post. It was "plainly evident" to the American that a "withdrawal was contemplated."

When daylight finally came and the Pennsylvanians had endured a night so terrible, powerless to do anything for themselves, they poked their heads out of their trenches and foxholes prepared to stop the enemy on the banks of the Marne. They would soon be startled to see that with most of the French gone, they were hopelessly surrounded!

It would now take more than grit to fight their way out. It would take luck and many acts of extraordinary heroism.

CHAPTER 16

//

"OUT OF A NIGHT AS BLACK AS THE MOUTH OF HELL THEY CAME!"

Brigadier General Charles Crawford declared that for the Third Division the Second Battle of the Marne was "exclusively a Sixth Brigade fight." Major General Joseph Dickman noted that the enemy did not attempt a crossing in front of the Fifth Brigade, although Brigadier General Fred Sladen's men suffered heavily during the ghastly bombardment, and one battalion of the Seventh Infantry took terrible losses during a counterattack that shook the confidence of Colonel Billy Butts, whose 30th Infantry was on the Seventh's right flank fighting for its life. Not only was it a Sixth Brigade fight, it was a company and platoon commanders' fight where generals had little chance to influence the course of events. It was a running gun battle, a clash of close-range-rifle and automatic-rifle fire—the rattle of machine guns, the pop of pistols, the bang of hand grenades, exploding artillery shells, the sharp ring of steel on steel, and the agonizing screams of men in a death struggle.

"Bayonets, butts, fists and teeth!" was how Captain Wooldridge vividly remembered the battle. "Did you ever turn yourself loose in a mad passion that knew no limit? Were you ever blinded by blood and lust to kill and let yourself go in a crowd where you could feel their bodies crumble and sink to the depths below you, then brace yourself on them and destroy, destroy, destroy?"

It was a fight where communications had broken down and where confusion and rumor and false information swept over the battlefield as thickly as the clouds of smoke and gas that now covered the Marne Valley from Château-Thierry to Varennes. The eyewitness reports that Major Fred Walker had received during the early stages of the bombardment in which frightened runners and some lieutenants, including First Lieutenant George Henderson, said they had seen the enemy crossing the river and wiping out platoons were at the time mostly false or exaggerations. The lesson Walker learned: "Verbal messages are unreliable and information transmitted verbally will be greatly exaggerated. The officer in command must not consider the unfavorable reports from his subordinates as correct."

It was these exaggerated reports that forced Walker to abandon his command post for fear it was about to be surrounded and overrun, and forced him to seek a new, more secure position—five hundred yards farther back from the front line to a ravine south of the Fossoy-Crézancy Road.

Walker's adjutant, First Lieutenant Harold L. Reese from Mahoney City, Pennsylvania, later blamed Lieutenant Henderson for the sudden change of command posts. Walker had ordered him to reconnoiter the battalion's front to discover the exact location of the enemy—had they crossed the river and cleaned out his companies? According to Reese, Henderson was gone only a short time. He reported that German machine gunners were covering the battalion's left rear at the edge of a hill covered with woods that was occupied by K Company. Because Walker had not been able to communicate with K Company, he assumed it had been driven back. Walker then gave orders for his headquarters to fall back.

"Of course," wrote Reese, "later developments showed that the information given by Lt. Henderson was incorrect and personally I doubt this officer ever left the west opening of the dugout."

In fact, K Company had not been driven back. It was still holed up on the hill in the woods. Its commander, Captain John C. Adams, with all communication broken down except for runners, sent one of his men to Walker's command post. The soldier returned and said there was no one there. Adams thought he was lying, afraid to venture far from his own dugout, that he had "shown a yellow streak." Adams looked at First Lieutenant Johns Hopkins and ordered him to get to Walker's command post. Hopkins discovered it empty and returned and said to Adams, "When I got there I found it as the man said, no one was there." For some unknown reason, he said to Adams, "Major Walker and his staff had vacated their headquarters without notifying us."

Adams turned to Hopkins and, taking a deep breath, said, "Hoppy, I don't believe a man in this Company will come off this hill alive. Our orders are to stay here until further orders, and here we stay, unless we can get word from regimental headquarters."

Walker believed his new location would give him more control of the battle, that he'd have a better line on the action and be more accessible to runners. Soon after Walker had left his original command post, a shell struck its roof, caving it in; the move had saved him and his staff from being entombed. Adding to the confusion, many of the officers in his battalion, as well as Butts and Crawford, were still not sure where he'd gone until he was able to get runners out to them. He immediately sent messages to A, K and D Companies between the Ru Chailly Farm and the village of Crézancy, finally telling their commanders of his move.

He also ordered First Lieutenant Donald N. Swain to carry a grim message directly to Butts: that many in his headquarters had been killed or wounded; the woods north of the Fossoy-Crézancy Road had been torn to pieces by shellfire; he still had no communications from his front-line commanders; and from stragglers drifting back from the river the news was that the Germans had crossed near Mézy and Ru Chailly and were closing in on the railroad embankment and moving southward.

Because it had gone back by more than a quarter mile, Walker's move was misinterpreted by Captain Jud Lasseigne, whose D Company had been posted on the northern outskirts of Crézancy. Reading Walker's message, he thought the battalion was withdrawing, perhaps believing this was part of the defense of elasticity. He then moved his own troops back, taking up a new position on the south side of Crézancy.

At that moment, a few hours into the battle, according to a study published twenty-one years later in the *Infantry Journal*, Walker "knew neither the location of his own front line nor that of the enemy. In fact, he did not know if his two forward companies were still in existence. He was unaware of the situation of the units on his flanks—if they were holding or if they had been withdrawn. He had to judge by surmise, and part of that surmise was incorrect."

Most of the runners were not getting through. Walker had sent five messages back to regimental headquarters and none of them apparently got there. Butts refused to be stampeded by alarming reports, Dickman noticed. In fact, the colonel sent a field message to Crawford stating he was "sticking and would stick."

At the first crack of daylight, an anxious Butts still had no news from Walker. Over the near deafening noise of the bombardment, he occasionally heard machine-gun and rifle fire.

"I had great confidence in Major Walker," he later wrote, "and I knew that he and his company officers had a high sense of duty. I felt that the 1st Battalion was doing an excellent piece of work. Otherwise I felt the Germans would have broken through and would have appeared before the Bois d'Aigremont by this time."

Still, he needed to know firsthand what was happening at the river's edge. He ordered Lieutenant Beebe to immediately send out three patrols. Captain Turner Chambliss personally went down toward the river to check on the men in the trenches and shelter holes. Then Butts sent a message to General Crawford just to let him know that "I still was present for duty."

Beebe returned to the dugout with the grim news that Major Lindsey

Silvester's Second Battalion, moving up to relieve Walker's battalion, had been hit in the open with hardly any place to take cover. He said that many had been killed and wounded and the rest of the battalion was finding makeshift shelters to wait out the bombardment. Then Chambliss reported in. He did not like what he had seen. It looked as if his Headquarters Company was 50 percent wiped out. All the horses and mules were dead or screaming in agony from their wounds. The rolling kitchens and water carts had been destroyed and were useless. He feared there'd be no food or water for some time. When he reported all this to Butts, the colonel, upset about the casualties, seemed not too concerned about the loss of food because all his men carried two days of emergency rations. But the lack of water—that was a problem: "I could imagine my men fighting in their trenches until exhausted by hunger and thirst." How was he going to bring water to his troops without animals and carts? While he worried about it, a message arrived at last from Major Walker. It had been sent at 2:15 and it was now three hours later—the first news from the front since the shelling had started.

> *We have had some gas. All groups of woods south of railroad line with P.C. are being heavily shelled. Heavy machine gun fire in vicinity of Mont St. Pere since 2 A.M. Have received no news from the front line companies. I believe all lines are out. Bombardment began at 12:00.*
>
> *P.S. Capt. McAllister reports he needs reinforcements and that his two front platoons have been driven back. Cannot depend on any method of liaison. Better base your actions from your P.C.*
>
> *Walker*

Rereading the message, Butts realized that the only thing he could base his actions on was what he could observe from his command post. All communications had been obliterated and most runners were not getting through. Walker was not going to be able to gather vital information and send it on to him. "I had learned nothing in five hours except by sur-mise," Butts admitted, "and surely his [Walker's] headquarters personnel was operating under conditions at least as difficult as my own."

Amid all the confusion and rumors and falling shells and gas bombs, the first reported Germans to reach the south bank of the Marne on the early morning of the 15th were members of a reconnais-sance patrol of a half-dozen men that came over in the midst of the bombardment. A little after two the patrol penetrated the American line between the platoons of Harry Marsh of the 30th Infantry and David Calkins of the 38th. The Germans slipped into the outskirts of Mézy looking to take prisoners. At the time Calkins was out inspecting his rifle pits on the riverbank, making sure his men were alert and primed to fight once the bombardment slackened or ceased altogether. In fact, all the platoon leaders made frequent rounds of inspections during the first two hours of the bombardment because the enemy shells landed far back of them. On one of his rounds, Calkins spotted the Germans and mistakenly thought they were Americans. He walked toward them through a wheat field, the ripened grain over three feet high. As he approached, one of the Germans swung his rifle up, aimed at Calkins and fired. The bullet smashed into the lieutenant's right hand. He fell back into the high wheat, blood pouring from the wound. Pulling his pistol from its holster with his left hand, he crawled through the wheat to the river's edge. He got himself into the midst of the patrol. Jumping up, he fired at the Germans, hitting two of them. Before he got off another shot, a rifle butt crashed into his head. Calkins pitched to the ground, senseless.

Sergeant Peter G. Martinsen from Brooklyn heard the shots and, wondering if Germans had landed, went to find his lieutenant, with pistol in hand. When he approached the place where Calkins had been captured a German loomed up out of the wheat, pointing his rifle at Martinsen. "Giff me your rifle, you are a prisoner!"

Without a moment's thought, Martinsen shot him dead. Then he yelled to his own men, "Yes, they are Germans! Give 'em hell!"

The surviving members of the German patrol, carrying Calkins and its own dead and wounded, quickly retreated across the Marne. When Calkins came to in enemy territory, he found himself a prisoner of war. He was taken to the regimental commander and interrogated. The young American told the commander that opposite him in the Surmelin Valley were nine divisions from the United States with eight French divisions in reserve. The Germans knew he was exaggerating. They laughed at him and kicked him, yelled that he should have gone back to America and played baseball, and hauled him off to a hospital in Trélon in the northeast of France, close to the Belgium border. The hospital was a converted woolen mill. "Food was scarce and very poor as evidenced by many deaths from starvation," Calkins later reported. "Anywhere from four to seven were buried every day!" From Trélon, he was taken to a prison camp in Poland, and later to another camp, in Rastatt, Germany, and then to Villingen, Baden, a camp for only American officers. While he was being moved about, Calkins was listed as killed in action. After the war, to the surprise of his own fellow officers, he rejoined the 38th Regiment in occupied Germany.

Shortly after the capture of Calkins, German engineers from the 20th Pioneers, leading the main force of Corps Kathen, reached the river at Chartèves, opposite Mézy. It was 2:30 a.m. They threw their bridging material for six pontoons over the river and pushed boats and ferries into the churning water. At the same time, snipers from the 17th Machine Gun Battalion, set up in the woods, fired at the Americans. "So beautiful was the arching canopy of tracer bullets over the Marne at this time," thought Captain Herlihy, "that it was almost impossible to realize that these damn slugs were lethal."

At about three o'clock the German artillery concentrated on the Aqueduct Line, pounding the south bank and hitting the Fifth and

Sixth Brigades. Thirty to fifty minutes later, the rolling barrage started. It landed on the front-line platoons for three minutes and then jumped one hundred yards to the south, to the Aqueduct Line. Then three minutes later it jumped another one hundred yards, reaching the Woods Line. But the German 398th Infantry Regiment, the 17th Machine Gun Battalion—eighty-five handpicked men known for their sharpshooting skills—and the kaiser's famed storm troopers from the Fifth and Sixth Grenadiers, supported by the 47th and 175th Regiments, were all late crossing the river and lost most of the covering protection of the rolling barrage. Still, under cover of smoke and tear and sneezing gas, they rushed out of the woods to the water's edge, jumped into their machine gun–armed flat-bottomed pontoon boats and ferries that were pulled back and forth by ropes stretching across the river, or stepped onto the hastily erected floating pontoon bridges, and headed for the south bank of the Marne River, through the thick smoke and fog and deadly gas rising off the river like a scene out of a horror story.

The sight of them thrilled the Americans. Captain Wooldridge declared, "Out of a night as black as the mouth of Hell they came!"

The enemy boats, Lieutenant Lovejoy recalled, were "loaded to the gunwales."

The platoons of the 30th and 38th Infantries, holding the riverbank, rose up to meet the enemy head-on as they crossed the river. Their Springfield rifles cracked to life. Machine gunners from the Ninth Machine Gun Battalion and the machine-gun companies from the two regiments fired their Hotchkiss guns until the barrels glowed red.

Major Ziba Drollinger, commander of the Ninth Machine Gun Battalion in support of the Sixth Brigade, also remarked how his Hotchkiss gunners had to cease firing frequently "to let the red hot gun barrels cool."

Lieutenant James Rountree Kingery of the 30th's B Company, commanding one of the platoons closest to the river's edge, stood on the bank and heaved hand grenades at the approaching enemy boats. His bravery and perhaps foolhardiness "surprised and bewildered" the Germans, according to a Third Division historian. Lucky enough to win over a thousand dollars in a craps game, would Kingery's luck hold on the banks of the Marne while he kept lobbing grenades at the enemy's boats or would it run out?

It was in front of Kingery's company, led by Captain Kay McCallister, First Lieutenant Henry Switzer's C Company, and the 38th's G, H and E Companies, under control of Captains Wooldridge, Herlihy and Dineen, where the German forces were the heaviest. The enemy also struck across the eastern slope of Moulins Ridge, Hill 231, where the French 125th Division had quietly withdrawn during the bombardment, without telling a soul. It left McAlexander's right flank exposed.

C olonel Butts—huddled in his command post in the Bois d'Aigremont with his staff, Lieutenant Colonel Cromwell Stacy, Captain Sterling Maxwell, French Lieutenant Marchand and First Lieutenant George Hays, who kept galloping back and forth between the 30th's command post and his artillery batteries to give orders and to see how they were doing—had no idea what was going on down by the river. At the command post, Hays kept pressing Butts for targets, but the colonel could not designate a single one. All he could do was to send out more runners to locate Walker, but they never returned. Was it possible the runners were being wounded or killed en route? Butts wondered. What was the situation on his right with McAlexander's regiment? What was happening on his left, with the 7th Regiment? "Did Brigade or Division Headquarters have any information I should have? We could only guess the answer. The battle had been going on for three hours and I knew practically nothing of the situation."

At this time of the year, dawn came early on the Marne. As the morning light spread over the battlefield, Butts decided to make a personal reconnaissance to see if he could find answers to any of the questions that had been pestering him and his staff since the opening of the bombardment. He left his command post, hidden away in the woods. Maybe out in the open he could spot something that would give him a clearer picture of the battle. He walked along the northern edge of the Bois d'Aigremont, past Major Paschal's Third Battalion hunkered down in the trenches. "They were huddled in the corners of their shelters," he later wrote, "most of them apparently unconcerned although they were being shelled unmercifully."

Smoke and gas obscured the Marne Valley. Looking north toward the Fossoy-Crézancy Road, all he saw were shells falling and erupting into bright flames between the woods and the road. He could see nothing that would shed light on what was going on. He returned to his command post.

Inside he found Captain Curley P. Duson of the Ninth Machine Gun Battalion's B Company. Duson reported to him that he'd brought his company up to the Bois d'Aigremont to relieve the Ninth's D Company. He told Butts that almost all of his horses were dead or wounded, that his men had to pull the machine-gun carts up by hand. Butts directed him not to relieve D Company, but to keep it where it was, and to place his guns along a firing line of his, Duson's, own choosing, call for 100,000 rounds of ammunition to be put in reserve and then be prepared to "repel the attack."

Then Butts got in touch with First Lieutenant Francis Winslow of A Company, Sixth Engineers, attached to the 30th Infantry. During the lead-up to the bombardment, Winslow's men had been digging trench fortifications for the regiment. Butts had Winslow's men take up a reserve position in the trenches at La Chanet Farm. This position commanded the Fossoy-Crézancy Road. When Butts ordered up A Company, it had been searching through its shelled encampment for fellow engineers wounded during the artillery attack. After the wounded had been tended to, Winslow turned to the maimed horses. He placed gas masks over the heads of the horses to save their lives.

Butts now had bolstering his regiment two machine-gun companies instead of one and a company of armed engineers. To Captain Duson of the Ninth Machine Gun Battalion, he said, "We are going to fight it out at all costs on the edge of the Bois d'Aigremont."

Colonel McAlexander, meanwhile, was having his own problems amid the confusion. He'd already made up his mind to stand and fight on the riverbank, and not pull back as part of the defense of elasticity. He'd fight not with one foot in the water, as General Degoutte had pictured it, but with both feet in the water. It was simpler for him to know what was going on. His men were fighting where they stood. He just didn't know how they were faring. His main problem came from brigade and division headquarters.

Earlier, leading up to the battle, he'd found "such confusion of thought at Higher Headquarters that I did not dare let my officers know of the conflicting currents with which I had to fight, so I kept all information from them, except what was necessary for them to know." Now, to his utter dismay, the division seemed to be restricting his options on the battlefield rather than offering any kind of assistance. As he later put it, "Before and during the battle I had had so many demands from Division headquarters transmitted partly through the brigade, but mostly direct to me that I wholly disregarded the least important of them so that I could give attention to my troops, then engaged in a life and death struggle on my front and both flanks." His anger growing, McAlexander also wrote, "I took the course of attending to the enemy first, letting the higher headquarters sizzle in their own juice until I could attend to such trifles."

While the officers in Dickman's headquarters were "sizzling in their own juice" over what the commander of the 38th might be doing, or not doing, McAlexander, like Butts, decided to make a personal reconnaissance of the front. Only he planned to go down to the river.

CHAPTER 17

///

"THE RIVERBANK IS CARPETED WITH GERMAN DEAD"

The two battalion commanders defending the front lines were both trying to get a fix on what was happening to their men. Major Walker of the 30th's First Battalion had moved his command post back to a ravine. Major Rowe of the 38th's Second Battalion felt he, too, had to relocate his command post. He was getting no useful information where he was. But no news is good news, he thought, and he wondered if he hadn't forgotten some vital provision. He longed for a message that all was well. He could only hear the horrible clash of fighting down by the river. He could see nothing of it because of all the smoke, gas and fog. As soon as it was light enough, he and Sergeant Major William Walters, Jr., and others in his staff moved up the hill in a heavy mist on the east bank of the Surmelin River, to near the village of Moulins.

"I had no intimation of what was going on," he wrote. But on the way up the hill he finally received his "first real report and," as he later explained bitterly to McAlexander, "that was a damned lie." He was now to experience the same thing Walker was experiencing over in the

30th's subsector—falsehoods and exaggerations by frightened men in combat for the first time.

Here came a company commander up from the river "wild-eyed and followed by a few wild followers." To Rowe he said, breathlessly, "You will have to get out of here right away! The Germans are across and everything is lost!"

Looking at the officer and the men with him, Rowe anxiously asked, "Is this all there is left of your company?" The officer said it was; and that was the damned lie, although Rowe didn't know it at the time. The company was pretty much intact, repelling the enemy from getting a foothold on the south bank of the Marne. Rowe wouldn't find out the truth until much later. If he had known the truth at that moment, he confided to McAlexander, he would have shot the captain on the spot. He quickly ordered the captain and "his gang" into a nearby trench, forming a thin line of resistance that covered the road where it made a turn just north of Moulins. If the officer's story was true, as Rowe believed, and the Germans had indeed crossed the river, wiped out his company and were fighting their way south, the line would have to hold. It would serve as a rear guard for the other companies on the river—if they were also driven back.

Then the mist cleared and the fog by the river lifted. Rowe could see the Marne and the village of Mézy and the railroad embankment covered with soldiers, bayonets flashing in the early morning sunlight. He and Sergeant Major Walters were unable to tell if the soldiers were Americans or Germans. In front of the embankment Rowe saw the wheat field that marked the subsector of Captain Wooldridge's G Company. The wheat field had been trampled down, flattened as if a tornado had ripped through it. Filling the wheat field were scores of Germans, and as Rowe watched, they kept coming from the river, trying to reach the railroad embankment.

Hearing the "racket" coming from the river, Second Lieutenant Harry J. Bush from Lackawanna, Pennsylvania, a platoon leader in Captain Reid's company, came down to where Rowe had set his rear guard and said to him that if there was a fight he wanted to get into it. Rowe decided to send Bush and his platoon to the embankment, between Wooldridge's and Herlihy's companies and have him report to Herlihy. Removing Bush's platoon from Hill 231 weakened Reid's company, and Rowe later regretted his decision.

After watching the fight below, believing that one company had been destroyed and sensing trouble on the other side of Hill 231, Rowe sent a field message at 4:50 a.m. by pigeon to McAlexander.

"The Boche have penetrated Mézy and the French are falling back on my right. Will you guard my flanks? Rowe."

What had actually happened down by the river when the Germans first attempted to cross the Marne in front of both regiments? What had happened before Rowe and Walker moved their command posts and before the fog had lifted? And what was happening now?

Following the rolling barrage at three-thirty, the Germans of the 10th Division, led by two battalions of the 398th Infantry and a battalion from the Sixth Grenadiers, had first poured across the Marne on their pontoon bridges or armed pontoon boats. With shells falling on the American companies holding the riverbank and enemy machine-gun bullets zipping over the water and into the American defenses, it would seem all was lost. In fact, even before the Germans had gained a foothold on the south bank they were already annihilating Wooldridge's First Platoon. It was here that machine-gun fire was the most intense. When the enemy landed on the south bank, every man in the platoon was either "killed or put out of action." Wrote Lieutenant Ike Lovejoy, "The river platoon, whose leader had been Calkins, was almost completely wiped out of existence. One or two men were later accounted as wounded, but other heroes fought those hordes of onrushing Germans to a finish—their own finish."

Among the dead was the sergeant from Brooklyn, Peter Martinsen. When his body was later found, there were twelve dead Germans in a heap in front of him. Under Martinsen's body were his pistol and rifle, both empty of bullets. He was twenty-four years old. Lovejoy saw another of Calkins's soldiers, a private, "surrounded by five of the enemy, all killed by bayonet, but his own rifle clutched in his hands ready for more when the bullet from a machine gun stopped his work."

One of the few survivors was a Sergeant Celero. Slightly wounded, he'd been working his way back to report to Wooldridge about what had just happened to his First Platoon.

In another platoon on the riverbank, Sergeant James E. McFadden's squad was almost completely surrounded as it tried to hold its position. Everyone in the squad was either killed or wounded. McFadden, himself wounded, reported to his platoon commander and, refusing to go to the rear to have his wound dressed, served as a liaison between his platoon and Wooldridge's company headquarters.

The German 10th Division's war diary reported that by 3:50 a.m. the two battalions of the 398th, backed up by the 47th Infantry, had landed between Fossoy and Mézy, opposite the Ru Chailly Farm, where Butts, applying the elastic defense, had not placed his front-line battalion on the river in full force. It left McAlexander's left flank open—which Butts later refuted. The plan for the 398th called for its troops to wheel to the right, capture Fossoy and the high ground around La Rocq Farm, where it would establish a defensive position between Butts's regiment in the Bois d'Aigremont and Colonel Tom Anderson's 7th Infantry south of Fossoy. The 47th Infantry followed at daybreak only to be heavily shelled by artillery and blistering rifle and automatic rifle fire. Yet three companies from the regiment made it across the river.

Meanwhile, the Sixth Grenadiers sent a message to headquarters that its First Battalion had gotten across in front of Wooldridge's company and had reached the railroad embankment east of Mézy with slight losses. Its mission was to take Crézancy and then push southward along the ridge leading to the Bois d'Aigremont. Once there, it was to establish a defensive position, linking up with the 398th so that the two regiments formed a continuous line.

At the moment the Grenadiers in front of the 38th Infantry were in the wheat field, which went from the Marne up to the embankment. It was here that Calkins's platoon was being overwhelmed. With Calkins already captured from the earlier raid and with his platoon shredded almost to a man, the enemy was about to capture Mézy. After battling through Calkins's platoon, the Grenadiers took aim at the embankment, firing their rifles and hurling stick grenades. They rapidly set up their machine guns in great number.

"They drenched my main line (every fifth bullet being a tracer of burning gas)," Wooldridge later wrote to McAlexander, "until it was light enough for their infantry, the 6th Grenadier Guards composed of men all over six feet and the flower of the Kaiser's soldiers, to charge my line."

A German major, the Iron Cross pinned proudly to his breast pocket, had led his men up to the railroad embankment and was setting up his machine-gun squad on the embankment when Wooldridge saw him amid the confusion and roar of battle. He realized that the machine gunners had to be taken out or the damage they could do to his company in a short period of time would be terrible. Corporal Barney F. Salner heard Wooldridge yelling, trying to direct his men toward the machine-gun squad. "But the firing was so intense," Salner recalled, "that he was not sure that he was heard." Wooldridge had to act fast. With some of his enlisted men, and hollering at them to take out the Germans, he ran at the machine gun, firing his pistol at the major. Singling out the American, the German major returned fire with his own pistol. Both Wooldridge and the major advanced, their pistols hot in their hands. One of Wooldridge's shots hit the major's gun arm. He switched the pistol to his other hand, but it was too late for him. "They were within one yard of each other," Salner recalled, "when Captain Wooldridge killed the German officer."

The rest of the machine-gun squad surrendered. With bullets whizzing over the ground, Wooldridge and his prisoners were forced to crawl back to the railroad embankment. As he ducked down next to the dead major, Wooldridge yanked off the Iron Cross to keep as a souvenir.

"It is beautiful," he wrote to a friend, "laid in heavy silver."

In front of Herlihy and Dineen's companies, the Fifth Grenadiers and the 175th Infantry of the German 36th Division were unable to land. Automatic rifle fire and hand grenades from the Americans sank twenty boats. Wire entanglements strung underwater and not seen by the Germans had ensnared many of the boats, keeping them from landing.

Corporal John Connors from Pawtucket, Rhode Island, when his squad from Dineen's E Company had been put out of action by machine-gun fire, manned two automatic rifles by himself. He kept them leveled at the approaching boats, and when he ran out of ammunition, he unpinned a hand grenade and was ready to toss it when it blew up in his hand, killing him.

Corporal Billy Abrum, another of Dineen's men, like Connors, stood on the riverbank hurling grenades at the incoming boats, until he, too, was wounded, but not mortally. No boat landed near him. Another of Dineen's corporals down by the river, Abe Short from Aurora, Arkansas, who'd receive two Distinguished Service Crosses before being killed in the Meuse-Argonne, although wounded in the arm, kept his squad firing their automatic rifles at the boats. His squad sank three boats.

When the attack first started, Wooldridge was surprised that the enemy had crossed in force in front of his company. Although his First Platoon had been destroyed, he had three more platoons in position to fire on the Grenadiers now caught in the open. The Germans dropped to the ground and "wriggled themselves, in combat groups, all over our front, many to the very foot of the railroad bank. Every remaining clump of tall wheat and shell holes became a living thing. They rested, then charged the bank, were hurled back, rested, threw stick grenades, charged again and again."

His Second Platoon, commanded by First Lieutenant Mercer Phillips, with bayonets fixed, charged off the embankment with a roar into the midst of the Germans, bayonets against bayonets. Mercer took a mild wound to the head. While he was having it hurriedly dressed, a German officer attacked him with a pistol. Grabbing a rifle from the soldier who was binding up his wound, Mercer stuck the officer five times with a bayonet. The officer fell and, as he was dying, pressed his elbow to the ground to steady his arm and then shot the lieutenant from Georgia through the brain.

Wooldridge himself was nearly shot by a Grenadier officer. The officer leveled his pistol at the captain, but before he had a chance to pull the trigger he was bayoneted by one of the captain's men. Wooldridge was startled to see the soldier who'd just saved his life. "My water cart driver," he recalled, "the littlest fellow in our outfit, skidded and dodged his way for two miles to join us on the front line."

"What are you doing here?" Wooldridge blurted.

"I thought my place was with my comrades when the fighting started," he answered.

In fact, cooks and other kitchen personnel had all joined the fight. First Lieutenant Thomas Bresnahan, a Fitchburg, Massachusetts, resident and graduate of Vermont's Middlebury College, organized a small detachment of orderlies, runners and casuals from McAlexander's Headquarters Company. He led them in an attack against a German patrol, completely wiping it out.

G Company's acting corporal Alexander Newell of Chicago, his own squad decimated, picked out two surviving men from another squad and led them on their hands and knees into the wheat field, toward enemy machine guns. Amid the confusion of hand-to-hand combat, the roar of rifle fire and exploding grenades and the desperate shouts of soldiers on both sides, the three Americans were able to outflank five enemy machine gunners and put them out of action. They then continued on to the river and carried back two wounded men and, in the process, captured thirty-three prisoners. Newell wasn't done yet. Alone, he crawled back to the five machine guns that he'd put out of action and destroyed them all so they couldn't be used again.

Corporal Lewis Nunley from Hulette, Kentucky, duplicated Newell's feat. Alone he advanced toward a machine gun squad, attacked the enemy and killed the entire crew. He carried the gun back to his own lines. He next picked out nine men and they flanked the enemy, killing a number of them and capturing twenty-five.

Wooldridge told the story of a Private Dickman, "a Jewish lad from the sweatshop district of New York" who spoke very little English. Dickman was the "most uncoordinated man living. He ruined every formation he was ever in. He was a perpetual accident on the way to happen." Wooldridge was behind him during the early stages of the fight. He watched as Dickman patted the back of an "excited comrade."

"Don be afrait, vatch, vatch, you see dat one? Now vatch me (bing) you see dat? Go aheat and shoot 'em, they can't hurt, go aheat and shoot 'em. Vatch I get annoder."

Wrote Wooldridge, "Thus he proved himself a leader of men."

As hard as it fought, the Second Platoon, like the First, was slowly and bloodily being "eliminated." Wooldridge had two platoons left.

To Wooldridge's right, Captain Herlihy, having thwarted the Fifth Grenadiers from crossing the river, had to face a large force of troops from the Sixth Grenadiers, more than three hundred of them that were filtering over from in front of G Company. Standing on top of the railroad embankment, he saw them coming up from the Marne through the mist and first thought them to be from one of Wooldridge's battered platoons withdrawing from the riverbank. He sent a small party down to meet them. The Germans opened fire. For the next two hours, the men in H Company battled the enemy in a firefight at close quarters. Herlihy was astonished to see that the "cooling jackets on the Chauchats melted and hand guards on the Springfields caught fire, but the shooting was dead accurate." A number of the riflemen had to spit on their rifles' bolts to try to cool their guns down.

With the Americans firing so rapidly, the Germans began to take cover in the wheat.

Leading Herlihy's left support platoon, First Lieutenant Frank L. Young from Chicago, had his men fire into the wheat field, but at a slower rate, cooling down their automatic rifles. It also gave them time to better aim at the Germans hiding in the wheat. With deadly accuracy, each time a Grenadier tried to wiggle forward, an American picked him off. While directing the firing, Lieutenant Young left himself exposed. A shell, shot from the woods north of the river, hit him. He died instantly.

First Lieutenant Stanley F. Griswold suffered a life-threatening wound that pitched him into the wheat field. Private Tigner, with the great first name of Major, scrambled out of his rifle pit and, exposing himself as Lieutenant Young had done, with machine-gun bullets flying every which way, reached Griswold and brought him back to safety, and in doing so saved his life. Acting alone, Sergeant Alfred G. Bailey from Eli, Oklahoma, personally knocked two enemy machine guns out of action and then captured a German and his machine gun.

In Herlihy's left front-line platoon on the riverbank, led by Sergeant William Unkauf from Syracuse because Second Lieutenant Paul Plough had yet to return from Crézancy, he found that the enemy had gotten behind him. It made it impossible for his platoon to fire into the Grenadiers without hitting their own men from the support platoons holding the railroad embankment. Instead, he had his men fix their bayonets and, tossing grenades, led a charge. It killed a number of Germans and resulted in the capture of sixty prisoners.

When Unkauf and his platoon, with their prisoners in tow, reached the embankment, Lieutenant Plough showed up at last, having worked his way back from Crézancy. Plough had no idea what was happening. He thought Unkauf had ordered his platoon to retreat. Angry with Sergeant Unkauf, he took control of his men and in a counterattack led them back across the wheat field to their trenches on the riverbank. When the platoon got there, Unkauf was missing. He'd been wounded and was somewhere in the wheat field. Mess Sergeant Otto Wolz from Rahway, New Jersey, volunteered to rescue Unkauf. To Herlihy, he said, "I probably won't make it in the face of that shelling, but I will try it for my pal." He didn't make it. He was hit with shrapnel in the head, chest and arms, but survived. Then Private First Class Steve J. Harelis from Boston, dodging fire from both Germans as well as Americans shooting from the railroad embankment, made three daring attempts to bring in Unkauf. He succeeded on his third try. Plough's counterattack resulted in the capture of twenty-two more prisoners. According to Herlihy, this action threw the Grenadiers into confusion.

On Herlihy's right, Captain Dineen was struck by gas. He had fought for about four hours, but found his gas mask too much of a hindrance and kept taking it off. According to Herlihy, "He left the field in an ambulance." Dineen's senior lieutenant, Howard Foster Ross, a four-sport athlete at Miami University and former teacher, coach and athletic director at the high school in Troy, Ohio, took over command of E Company from Dineen. He immediately ordered his men to counterattack. They drove the Germans back, again causing confusion in the ranks.

At about 5 a.m., the Germans who had crossed in front of Wooldridge's company and then swung over to attack H and E Companies dropped back toward the river. Herlihy took this time to try to make contact with Captain Wooldridge, whose company was getting the worst of the fight. He couldn't find Wooldridge, but found instead the remnants of a leaderless platoon—no officers or noncommissioned officers, only fifteen men. He raced back to his command post to get Captain John A. Minnis from Montgomery, Alabama, a Marine Corps officer attached to his company as an observer, to take charge of the platoon. Minnis, his skin almost as dark as the Senegalese soldiers who had been part of the division when it first reached the Marne, had been a bayonet instructor before his assignment as an observer. The Marine reorganized the men, had them fire directly into the advancing Germans and then counterattack with their bayonets. He faced a German in a bayonet duel witnessed by Herlihy. The German, who had almost reached the railroad embankment, made a "rushing long thrust at Minnis with his saw tooth bayonet. The Marine parried right, knocked the German's rifle out of his hand with a butt stroke; made a diagonal cut down to the neck, and another butt stroke upward to the chin. This latter butt stroke knocked the doomed fellow's head off because he had already been decapitated. Blood spurted like a fountain." Herlihy vomited on the battlefield.

During Minnis's charge, one of his men fell, wounded, close to the river. The Marine scooped him up and carried him two hundred yards to the rear so he could receive immediate medical help. When Minnis finally reported to Herlihy, he told him, "The riverbank is carpeted with German dead and the living are jumping in the river."

Three years after the war, Minnis, who had become a daring Marine aviator, was killed in a crash while testing an airplane at Quantico, Virginia. A bridge spanning the Potomac River was named in his honor.

E nemy bodies clogged the river, some sinking under the weight of their gear, others floating west with the current. Those who made it to the south bank were either killed or captured. The Germans in front of Herlihy's and Dineen's companies gave up crossing there and once back on the north bank swung east to the Jaulgonne Bend and, while the Americans watched—too far away to hit them with automatic rifle fire—went over the river at the place where the French 125th Division ought to have been, but wasn't. The Fifth Grenadiers easily captured the undefended village of Varennes and then started up the slope of Hill 231 toward Moulins, where Captain Tom Reid's F Company was literally holed up in the trenches laid out by McAlexander. The 178th Infantry followed the Fifth Grenadiers over the Marne and up the hill unopposed. If the Moulins Ridge and its apple orchards and dense woods were cleared of the Americans, then it would be easy pickings for the Germans atop Hill 231, overlooking McAlexander's troops, to swing to the right and, in all likelihood, defeat the Third Division by rolling up its right flank, and perhaps then change the outcome of the Second Battle of the Marne and maybe even the course of the war.

Now that McAlexander's flanks were exposed, the enemy was coming at him from three directions.

CHAPTER 18

"THERE THEY ARE! SHOOT THEM! SHOOT THEM!"

The battle had indeed turned into a platoon and company commanders' fight.

Colonel Butts, with hardly any means of communicating with his troops on the front line and thus unable to direct them, feared the worst. Lieutenant Leon Marchand, the French liaison officer, had convinced him Major Walker's First Battalion was beaten, and if that were the case the Germans "would be in front of the firing line along the edge of the Bois d'Aigremont at almost any moment." To Butts, Marchand's assessment made sense. If what they had been hearing was true, that the Germans had broken through Walker's battalion and were headed their way, then Butts had to prepare to meet the enemy before it reached the Bois d'Aigremont. After all, as he had reasoned before the attack, the Bois d'Aigremont was the key point of the battle, and should the kaiser's troops win there, then the Third Division would certainly go down in defeat. All would be lost. And Paris would be imperiled.

Butts had to be certain, however, that his First Battalion had been knocked out of action. He had his adjutant, Captain Sterling Maxwell, send a message to Walker at his command post directing him to report without delay on the situation along his front. He also had Maxwell send messages to the 7th and 38th Infantries, letting them know that he was being heavily shelled, had many casualties and had not yet received any definite news regarding his front-line battalion. He also wanted a report sent back to him about the situation on their fronts.

He finally sent messages to both Brigadier General Crawford and Major General Dickman pleading for reinforcements and even asking the division commander, "Why don't you send airplanes for this fight?"

The only reports Crawford, the frustrated Sixth Brigade commander, had received from Butts "called for help and reinforcements without specifying what had happened to make them necessary."

Crawford believed Butts had enough men to hold the Bois d'Aigremont. "He had a battalion more than he needed to man his trenches," Crawford wrote after the war. "He had plans for action and he had trenches with wire entanglements in front that should have withstood anything short of days of bombardment and heavy succeeding waves of attack."

If Crawford was frustrated with Butts, then Butts was equally frustrated with Walker—all because communications had broken down. Runners were not getting through, and when they did, they arrived hours late.

"I had told [Walker] it was extremely important for him to keep me informed of the development of the situation," Butts bemoaned, "and to report promptly in case of attack."

Frustration cut both ways. Walker, believing he was about to be surrounded, had moved his command post to a ravine south of the Fossoy-Crézancy Road. He got word to Butts, his first message since the start of the bombardment, that there was nothing yet to report and he shouldn't "rely entirely upon me for information." Walker had sent the message at 2:15 a.m. It took almost three hours for it to reach Butts.

Walker, in fact, sent another message to Butts that arrived thirty minutes after the first message. In it, he reported losses in his battalion

were very great, that B and C Companies were total losses and the survivors were now stragglers, wandering to the rear. He also reported,
according to Butts, that because communication within the battalion
had been impossible "the battalion was not under his control." He asked
that the artillery shell the ground just north of the railroad embankment.

In fact, Lieutenant Hays, who'd been riding back and forth between
Butts's command post and the headquarters of the 10th Field Artillery's
Second Battalion and, according to Butts, was "always on the lookout
for targets," asked the colonel if he "wished him to fire on the area south
of Mézy and Ru Chailly."

If there were still soldiers from Walker's battalion in that area, then
they would be hit by friendly fire. Butts was not ready to unleash the
artillery on his own troops even if the Germans had overrun them.
Besides, information was too indefinite to allow Hays to direct fire into
the area. Instead, Butts ordered the young artillery lieutenant to keep
up his normal barrage on the north bank of the Marne. Hays cautioned
him that he'd been firing intermittently since midnight, and if he kept
it up he'd soon run out of ammunition.

As it turned out, B and C Companies, holding the river between the
7th Infantry on the left and the 38th Infantry on the right, had
not yet been overrun—as Walker had warned and Butts had chosen not
to believe. In C Company's Second Platoon, led by First Lieutenant
James H. Gay, Jr., because of the waist-high wheat field that extended
from the ravine where the soldiers were positioned to the river, the men
had a clear line of fire. During the night, although his platoon had been
pinned down by tracer bullets that swept the valley and by mortar
attacks, Gay, who'd earned his commission at the Fort Oglethorpe
training camp seven months earlier, kept sending up Star lights over
the river, illuminating his front so he and his men could spot any of the
enemy trying to cross.

At dawn, his platoon was still in its rifle pits, ready. He sent several runners to his flanks and rear to make sure the Germans hadn't surrounded him. He had no way of knowing because the runners were all killed in the continuing barrage. He tried to keep liaison with First Lieutenant A. C. Eldred and his platoon, positioned behind him. That also failed.

"I knew absolutely nothing of what it was all about," he wrote to Walker two years after the battle, "or what was happening except in my own little sector."

At about four-thirty, one of his men came up to him and said the Germans had gotten over the river and were directly in front of the platoon. Gay then saw them. They were rushing through the wheat field in small squads of three or four or five men. They'd dash forward for ten or fifteen yards and then drop flat, hidden by the wheat.

"Every time these men were visible my troops opened fire and covered the entire wheat field where they had been with a raking fire of bullets and rifle grenades."

Gay's platoon was holding its own. On his left, the platoons of James R. Kingery and Dennis C. Turner were under constant machine-gun fire that covered the low ground by the river. Then a floating pontoon bridge was thrown across the river in front of Turner's men. Germans clambered over the bridge. From a range of 250 yards, Turner directed an effective rifle attack on the bridge. But it did not stop all the Germans from reaching the south bank. Taking advantage of the cover offered by the wheat field, the enemy moved around to Turner's right flank. Other German troops made it over the river on Turner's left and got around behind him, cutting his platoon off from any support.

Kingery's platoon was similarly surrounded. In the fight, Kingery's luck ran out. He took two shots to the abdomen and fell mortally wounded. A sympathetic German soldier, Sergeant Hugo Lamp, watched Kingery drop. There was no time to tend to his wounds in the heat of battle. But afterward, he noticed Kingery being placed on a German stretcher. He was dead. Lamp took his identification card. Kingery was first reported as missing in action. Later, it was reported that he had been a prisoner of war and had died at a German prison camp on August 3. In 1921, Lamp wrote to Kingery's widow, letting her know that her husband had been killed in battle and had not perished in a prison camp, as reported. He told her the Germans always took good care of the wounded, whether friend or foe, and they were always taken to a hospital. As for the date of his death, he added, "For sure, the transport of the dead to the rear took some time so it is possible he was given over to the Earth on 3 August."

Kingery's platoon, now surrounded, and Turner's platoon, likewise surrounded, braced themselves for an attack on all sides, threatening the 30th Infantry's first line of resistance. Turner's platoon was down to eighteen men. Their rifle ammunition was gone. Using hand grenades and whatever bullets they could find on the ground or take from the dead, braving enemy machine gunners, they made a dash through the ring of Germans and broke free to the railroad embankment. But once past the railroad embankment, they continued moving south in a disorganized fashion.

On the 30th Infantry's extreme left flank, the platoon of First Lieutenant Arthur V. Savage was holding on. Some Germans had made it over the Marne carrying a machine gun. They set the gun up on the riverbank and began a deadly fire into Savage's platoon—a covering fire so many more Germans were able to come across unharmed. The lieutenant from Philadelphia and one of Princeton University's great oarsmen knew he had to stop the gun. He led a charge against the Germans, killing eleven of the enemy. But the Americans were quickly surrounded and were all killed.

I n support of B Company, just back of the Ru Chailly Farm, was A Company, led by First Lieutenant Philip J. Sexton. Closest to Savage's platoon was Sexton's Fourth Platoon, commanded by First Lieutenant C. William Ryan, a Kansas lawyer. Early on Ryan had tried to find out from Sexton what his mission was to be. He sent a runner out who came back with no information. Ryan went with him to Sexton's command post. Sexton snapped at him for leaving his post. He ordered him back, saying don't get in touch with anybody on his flanks, that what they were doing on his right or left was of no concern, that he was in the strong point and was "to hold it to the death and under all circumstances."

Meanwhile, Second Lieutenant Harrison E. Barringer, in charge of a trench mortar platoon, felt useless. His mortars had been hit and knocked out of action. A number of his men had been killed. Earlier in the fight he had been in contact with Kingery and Turner. Now, trying to make the most of what he had, he sent Sergeant Charles R. Mather from Chicago down to see how the two lieutenants and their platoons were faring and what he could do to help.

Mather worked his way down to where he thought the two platoons were located. Instead, he saw what he took to be the remnants of Kingery's and Turner's platoons moving back through the woods toward Major Walker's command post, much of their equipment scattered on the ground. He hurried after them, trying to find out where they were going. But he lost them in the woods. He returned to Barringer. With the remainder of his own men, Barringer joined forces with Lieutenant Gay. He informed him that Kingery's and Turner's platoons had left the field.

Gay quickly sent out two runners to check his flanks. One of the runners was gone for a few minutes but came rushing back. Germans, he said, had reached the platoon's right rear. The second runner came scrambling in then. Germans, he said, were in the platoon's left rear. Gay went to the rear of the small ravine his troops were in and saw Germans about three or four hundred yards to his left and rear advancing up a hill toward the First Battalion's support troops.

"From these two facts it looked as though we were cut off in our position and after a conference with my noncommissioned officers it was decided we would remain where we were, hold out against any attacks and await further developments."

To Barringer, Gay asked, "What are you going to do?"

"I'm going to stay, too," Barringer said.

While Barringer, whose Stokes mortars had been destroyed, had hooked up with Gay's rifle platoon, Lieutenant Frederick Winant, Jr., in charge of another trench mortar platoon, attached to First Lieutenant Henry Switzer's C Company, had also lost almost all his guns. The German bombardment had blown all but two out of their pits. From the beginning his mortars had been doing a deadly job, sweeping the north bank of the Marne. He felt they were well protected situated in a gravel pit back of First Lieutenant Harry H. Marsh's platoon in the village of Mézy. Then about three in the morning, the Germans opposite Mézy started pounding the ground near Winant's platoon with *minenwerfers*. Winant realized this was the one weapon that could dislodge his mortars.

"The firing of the minnenwerfer [*sic*] is peculiar," he later described, "in that you can watch the shell at the beginning of its flight and at its finish. It starts off very similar to a skyrocket, is lost sight of during the middle of its flight, is picked up again as it descends with great speed. It comes down a long streak of flame."

Winant watched with great anxiety as the shells from the *minenwerfers* crept toward him, getting closer with each shell. Standing outside the gravel pit, he looked on at the approaching danger. Twice the concussion of the exploding shells knocked him down. Getting up for the second time, his ears ringing, he gave the order to his platoon to withdraw to a crater about one hundred yards to the east. They dismantled the Stokes mortars and were lugging them to the crater when a shell made a direct hit on the pit. It struck a stockpile of ammunition. The explosion and ball of flame were terrific. Bits and pieces of rocks and shrapnel shot out from the pit. Something struck Winant's left hip. The wound was not bad enough to knock him out of the fight.

The platoon stayed in the crater "until things became a bit more reasonable." Winant thought they'd be safer near Mézy's railroad station, where, in the baggage shed, they had stored a supply of ammunition. The shelling continued to follow them, so they moved to the backyard of one of the houses in the village.

"We spent about one half hour here dodging the falling minnenwerfers [*sic*]," he wrote.

From there, the platoon retreated to the railroad embankment, the Third Division's main line of resistance, and took cover under a bridge. Winant noticed right away there were no troops from the 30th Infantry anywhere.

"I became a bit uneasy," he admitted. "I thought perhaps all the infantry allotted to this position had been killed."

He needed to let Lieutenant Switzer know the situation. He picked one of his best men, Private Edward W. Rudolph from Carthage, Missouri, to carry a message to Switzer. Rudolph made it to C Company's command post, dodging machine fire as best he could. Winant, not waiting to hear back from Switzer, moved his platoon back to the train station, where the men retrieved their ammunition from the baggage shed. They next set up their Stokes mortars. The range, however, was too far to reach the river. Rudolph, meanwhile, tried to return to Winant, but on his way back the Germans hit him twice, shattering both his arms. He struggled back to Switzer's command post, where his wounds were dressed. Yet he still wanted to go back to his platoon. When he tried to leave, the men in the command post had to hold him down.

At this time, some men from C Company were drifting back from the river. They said they had no idea where the rest of the company was and that it had taken heavy casualties. Winant thought it best to get his platoon at once to Switzer's command post, where he expected the company would make a stand. They ran into a sergeant and two squads from G Company of the 38th Infantry. Winant told the sergeant he was headed for the command post and would return shortly with word on where they'd defend.

At the command post, Switzer said the original plans still held. The main line of defense would be made along the railroad embankment. It was back to the train station for Winant's men, although this time under heavy machine-gun fire from the enemy. Fortunately, they made it without a casualty. At the train station they met the sergeant and his two squads from the 38th.

"I told him that the 30th was going to defend along the tracks," Winant wrote, "and the sergeant put his men along this line at once connecting us at the station."

Winant placed his men in a trench between the station and the bridge. "This position gave flanking fire down the tracks toward the west, and at the same was well protected."

At first, they saw a single German in Mézy. He was dressed in a blue uniform and they thought he was a French soldier. When they realized their mistake, the German had gotten away. But soon afterward, a large number of Germans marched toward them spread out in open formation across the wheat field. The Stokes mortars proved ineffective, hitting only a few of the enemy because of the open formation. Winant's platoon and the two squads from the 38th then relied on their rifles. They cut the enemy down, and although a few made it to the railroad tracks, the Germans were forced to retreat toward the Marne. Winant ordered a detail to go into the wheat field, where, he noted, "it was generally very efficient in 'mopping up.'"

The Germans were not done yet. They had set up a machine gun in the bushes about two hundred yards to the north and three hundred yards to the east of the railroad embankment. Winant put a sergeant in charge of the platoon while he and a Corporal Nelson and Private Redwald H. Bleasdale from Janesville, Wisconsin, headed along the embankment to take out the machine gun. They carried only the barrel of a Stokes mortar and three shells. Bleasdale had already distinguished himself during the early morning bombardment when he stood by his mortar in the midst of the shelling until his pit was blown up. He withdrew his gun to another position and continued firing on a spot in the woods on the south bank where he figured the Germans were hidden, while the enemy machine guns unrelentingly fired back. To find out how many Germans were in the woods, Bleasdale volunteered to go on a scouting mission. Slipping into the trees, he came across several of the enemy and a captured soldier from his own regiment. He single-handedly killed the Germans and rescued the soldier, bringing him safely back to his own line.

When Winant, Bleasdale and Nelson got close enough to take out the enemy machine gunners, they jumped into action. Nelson figured how far away they were while Winant, using his helmet as a base plate, held the barrel with his hands and knees, called "riding the gun," and Bleasdale dropped the shells down the barrel. The first shell overshot the target. Nelson made an adjustment, elevating the barrel slightly. The shell hit the target. They fired a third shell to make sure. The machine gun had been silenced.

On the way back to the platoon, a German sniper shot both Winant and Nelson. Winant was struck in the side, but the wound was not serious. Nelson's was fatal and he died on the spot. Bleasdale had been spared.

The Germans were then regrouping, readying for another run through the wheat field. Others had gotten inside Mézy and had climbed into the second floors of some of the houses. In the windows they placed snipers who had their sights set on Winant's platoon. At the moment, and to the surprise of Winant and his men, half-a-dozen American soldiers were coming up from Mézy to the railroad track. Winant recognized Lieutenant Marsh, whose platoon had been posted in the village. He also recognized Sergeant William H. Jensen. Winant could not figure out how they had worked their way out of Mézy and slipped through the Germans without getting shot or captured.

With Marsh and his handful of men, Winant felt his platoon was now solidly reinforced, but the snipers were a problem and had to be taken care of. He dispatched Sergeant Jensen at the head of a patrol to go back into Mézy and clean them out. Jensen and the men with him went from house to house and killed the snipers. When they were finished with the grisly business, the sergeant covered his men as they returned to Winant's platoon without suffering a casualty.

About one thousand yards behind Winant and the remains of C Company, and behind the village of Mézy, Major Walker had placed D Company, commanded by Captain Jud Lasseigne, in Cemetery Woods. Lasseigne ordered First Lieutenant Iverson B. Lawton to take the First Platoon, almost fifty men, and move it out of the woods and into a series of shallow trenches that overlooked the wheat fields now filling with Germans. The trenches were in terrible condition and, worse, crammed with dead and wounded soldiers, most likely from B Company. Lawton had the wounded sent to the rear without any medical assistance. He next had the dead thrown out of the trenches and then organized his men as best as he could. They opened fire on the Germans, some of them crawling out into the wheat fields to get better shots at the enemy. In a quick conference between Lawton and his sergeants, they debated whether to make a counterattack in support of the Americans by the river.

"We could see with our field glasses a large number of German infantry in and around the old quarries back of Mézy, and could also see a large number of German infantry along the Railroad from Mézy east and a few scattered detachments along the front and to our right."

They decided a counterattack was not feasible, but believed they could hold on until nightfall. Lawton sent word to Lasseigne about their situation. Lasseigne replied in person, inspecting First Platoon's position. He found the "morale of our troops had revived and everyone was in excellent spirits, but very hungry and sleepy."

Lasseigne ordered Lawton to hold his position at any cost, that he would try to get reinforcements and at nightfall they would counterattack. The captain next went to check on the other platoons in his company.

Then stragglers from Turner's platoon appeared in front of Lawton's platoon, including Turner himself, coming toward them. Turner walked right up to Lawton and stated in a very loud and highly excited voice that an overwhelming number of German infantry were across the

Marne and headed south. He told Lawton to look at his front where he could see large parties of Germans.

"In the smoke and haze," recalled Lawton, "it was hard to discern whether the troops he spoke of were enemy or friendly troops."

Because of Turner's agitated state, Lawton took control. He slipped his pistol from its holster and, using it as a prod, ordered Turner's wounded stragglers to march to the rear and get medical assistance. Lawton was more concerned that the men within earshot of Turner or those who were able to watch his actions might get "demoralized." He ordered Turner to find Lasseigne, who was near Walker's battalion headquarters, and give him a report of the conditions at the river.

When Turner found Lasseigne, he was still "greatly agitated." To Lasseigne he exclaimed, Lasseigne reported, that "there was 5,000 enemy across the river; that they were crossing the Fossoy-Crézancy Road and that the 38th was falling back and that my position was completely surrounded." Lasseigne did not believe a word from Turner. He sent the first lieutenant to the rear. As far as Lasseigne knew, part of B Company was still holding its own and A Company in the rear of B Company was still holding its original position.

An hour after Lasseigne had his confrontation with Turner, his company was hit with enfilading fire. It convinced him that the enemy had taken the hills. He believed then that B and C Companies were either killed or captured, that maybe Turner had been right after all. When C Company's First Lieutenant Joseph P. Guillett got word to him that, in his words, his position was "exposed from all sides and that very shortly the Germans would be in my rear. I had decided it was time for me to fall back."

While Lasseigne was making his decision to withdraw, Lawton had been reassuring his troops, reorganizing his position and sending out runners right and left to find out what was going on with other companies. The runners never returned.

But Garland Green showed up. The young private, although wounded in the arm, had been carrying messages throughout the night—one of the few runners who had so far eluded death or serious injury. He had a verbal message from Lasseigne. He said that Lasseigne was near the village of Crézancy, that he sent his compliments to Lawton, but now, in Lawton's words, he "ordered me to fall back with the entire command through Crézancy in the direction of Courboin." The order surprised Lawton. He questioned Green closely and said he could not fall back except by a written order or "authoritative verbal order." His last orders, he said to Green, were to hold to the very last. When Green repeated the order, he was "very emphatic" and "vouched for Captain Lasseigne's authority in originating these orders." Lawton then accepted the orders.

Acting immediately, he got his men to fall back slowly in a skirmish line through Cemetery Woods. He followed his troops to the rear. Once in the woods, he lined up his platoon in marching order, five paces between each solider, and had a Sergeant Friday lead them while he guarded the back. The platoon marched through the woods and halted between two brick walls on the outskirts of Crézancy.

"I found a great number of troops of all companies of the 1st Battalion of the 30th Infantry straggling in and around Crézancy. I ordered these troops to fall in to my column and to attach themselves to my command, thus recruiting my company up to about 140 men."

For Lawton's platoon there was no place to shelter in Crézancy. He took his men along a path past a farm trying to find a place to take up a strong position. The farm had been leveled by artillery, and the mutilated bodies of two officers and several enlisted men were seen among the rubble. "Great numbers of dead and wounded were all over this territory." Once they were beyond the farm, an officer from the 38th Infantry stopped Lawton. He said that the regimental commander wanted to see him at his command post.

"Upon reporting to Colonel McAlexander," Lawton recalled, "I was required to state why and where I might be straggling with my command." The colonel ordered him to turn around and march his men one hundred yards to the north, into a wheat field, and hold the ground there.

It was now nine o'clock in the morning.

Obeying the order, Lawton got his men headed toward the wheat field. "The morale of my men was very low at this time," he reported. One of his soldiers, trudging in front of him, couldn't stand it any longer and killed himself.

More troops from the 30th Infantry began to filter in from the north. Major Walker reorganized them, ordering Lawton to get his men on the high ground along the Aqueduct Line, where he, Walker, had his new command post. Lawton held this position all morning and deep into the afternoon.

B ack at the Ru Chailly Farm, Ryan's Fourth Platoon, which had been on the left of Lawton's platoon, listened to the fighting at the river's edge between B Company and the enemy. "We could hear Chauchats and rifles firing, the rattle of machine guns," Ryan remembered, "and out of the fog and within a few yards of us before we could see them came men of Co. B."

The soldiers of B Company said the Germans were streaming across on a pontoon bridge. They said Lieutenant Savage had been killed and the company commander, forty-year-old Captain Kay McCallister, had been wounded and was "out of his head" and they were bringing him back. They asked for a stretcher. Ryan had no stretchers because the two Red Cross men assigned to his platoon had fled during the bombardment.

As the fog and smoke began to clear, the men in Ryan's platoon spotted Germans directly in front of them.

"I could see German infantrymen, wearing overcoats," Ryan wrote, "coming straight toward us in approach formation."

Also coming toward them were more stragglers from B Company. According to Ryan they were "cool and walking." He called out to them to join his platoon and fight. Some did; others kept on walking to the rear. He said his platoon was going to hold, that he had a strong position atop the hill. Two of the B Company soldiers who stayed to fight were Forrest E. Ferguson and a Private Baroynski. Both were later wounded.

Ryan dispatched a runner to Lieutenant Sexton to let him know the Germans were on their way.

The enemy came at them at a slow walk, "as steadily," Ryan observed, "as though on a drill ground." The officer leading them held a walking stick and kept swinging it back and forth. "Because of the B Co. men coming across our front and because I judged it would be more effective to hold our fire, we waited until the Germans came as close as the British did at Bunker Hill."

When the enemy was about thirty yards from the American line, Ryan gave the order to fire.

"Don't shoot!" hollered one of Ryan's men. "They are B Company men!"

Ryan shouted back, "They are Germans! Commence firing!"

The automatic rifles thundered to life. When Private Joseph Parsons was unable to see the Germans from the trench, he jumped up on the parapet and fired his heavy Chauchat from his shoulder. The Chauchats rattled like machine guns.

"There was no yelling, swearing or cries of pain," Ryan wrote. "But each man attended quietly with spirit and determination to defeating the enemy. They were fighting without passion or hatred and apparently with complete forgetfulness of their own safety."

The fight was over quickly. The Germans scattered, hiding below the hump of the hill. The Americans then stopped firing because they could no longer see the enemy.

Lieutenant Sexton showed up, waving his arms and screaming, "There they are! Shoot them! Shoot them! Why don't you shoot them?"

"We'd be glad to do so," Ryan shouted back, "if we could see any of them!" He said that his platoon had just driven them off and the only danger now was if the enemy circled around and hit them on the flanks. He suggested to his commander—it was not an order—to stay where he was while he moved several of his men to the platoon's right flank to strengthen it. A runner raced over to Ryan with an order from Sexton. Ryan was to go back into the woods where the rest of A Company was positioned in foxholes and bring back ammunition. Sexton said he planned to stay where he was and fight all day if necessary.

Between the trench and the woods was an open stretch of land. Ryan knew he had to make a dash for the woods. He ordered the runner to come with him. The runner balked, afraid to venture into the open. Ryan drew his pistol, spoke sharply to him and the two soldiers broke for the woods. Safely reaching the woods, they found the company scattered about. There was only one officer with the company, First Lieutenant Paul C. Ward. He gave Ward an update and asked him to put together a detail to carry the ammunition back to the Fourth Platoon. Ward acted fast and efficiently. The ammunition was soon on its way. Ryan then had Ward form a skirmish line in front of the woods. The company was high enough on the hill that it could look down on the Germans.

Ryan returned to his platoon. He saw Lieutenant Sexton going up and down the line, encouraging the men, but taking unnecessary risks by exposing himself to the enemy. He kept shouting, "Keep those guns going! Keep those guns going!"

But there were no Germans to be seen. Ryan climbed up on the parapet and still could not see the enemy.

The Germans tried twice to get a machine gun around to the platoon's right flank. The two machine gunners closed to within a few yards of the Americans, but were shot and killed. A Company clearly had the advantage because of the hill. The Germans withdrew and started to cross to the north side of the Marne. Ryan ordered his men to fire into their backs. Some of them refused and others reluctantly followed the order. Ryan picked up a rifle and a clip and started to shoot at the retreating enemy. Sexton walked up to him, yelled at him to stop and to put the rifle on the ground.

The enemy in front of them had been beaten, and for now A Company's fight was over.

B etween A and D Companies, a much-weakened K Company was holed up in Cemetery Woods, in front of its original position at the edge of the Bois d'Aigremont. Captain John C. Adams had earlier in the morning confided to First Lieutenant Johns Hopkins that he didn't believe a man in his company would get off the hill alive. The Germans were still shelling the whole area, including the woods where Colonel Butts had his command post. The K Company soldiers had moved into the company's strongest position, next to a sergeant and another soldier from the regiment's machine-gun company who was firing his gun at the Germans pouring across the river. The sergeant's hand had been nearly severed at the wrist, the flow of blood being stopped by a tourniquet.

W ith K Company's situation "very perilous" because its flanks were unprotected, Adams needed orders from either Walker or Butts to tell him what to do. Since Butts was closer, he asked for a volunteer to risk his life and go to regimental headquarters. George Frank, the company bugler, came forward immediately. Adams wrote out a note to Butts. Clutching the note, Frank took off.

"Our position on the hill was getting more and more precarious each minute," recalled Hopkins, "and we eagerly awaited Frank's return."

Frank was working his way through shellfire and much gas that had swept over the ground when a shell splinter struck his gas mask, rendering it useless. He kept on running, hoping to make it to regimental headquarters before the gas got to him. Then he stumbled across a mortally wounded soldier, "a poor fellow lying on the ground with a very few minutes left for this world." Frank wanted the soldier's gas mask. In his heart, he knew he couldn't take it while the man still had a breath of life in him. He knelt down beside him and waited for him to die. Later, Frank said, "Gee! That fellow took a Hell of a while to die!"

Frank made it to regimental headquarters and returned safely to

Adams's command post. Butts ordered Adams to take his company to its original line of defense at the edge of the Bois d'Aigremont. Platoon by platoon K Company fell back, and when it was repositioned, it held its line. So far, the Germans had been unable to reach the woods that made up the Bois D'Aigremont.

I t was obvious as the morning wore on that the 30th Infantry had pulled back from the river, gathering its strength at the Bois d'Aigremont, where Butts expected the Germans to attack in full force. It left McAlexander's left flank open and the right flank of Colonel Tom Anderson's 7th Infantry unprotected as well. Major Jesse Gaston, commanding the 7th's Third Battalion, was upset that the 30th Infantry seemed to have disappeared. In a desperate message to Anderson, he complained that his liaison was broken with the 30th Infantry and he had sent out patrols from his platoons on the right to find any part of that regiment and come up empty. Anderson in his report to Dickman, wrote, "It was from that time on for about five hours that this battalion commander kept informing me by telephone and runners that his right was critically menaced by the enemy, who it was later learned had crossed the Marne near Mézy and attempted to turn the 7th Infantry out of position." Major Gaston was angry. "It is not understood," he wrote, "why the regiment occupying the sector on my right withdrew, thus endangering my line and a whole position of defense without at least warning my right flank platoon."

M ajor Walker felt himself in a quandary. It seemed the messages he sent to Colonel Butts had not reached the colonel. The regimental commander needed to know the dire situation facing his First Battalion. Sensing that Butts was impatient for a report, Walker decided to make the twelve-hundred-yard trek to Butts's command post through heavy shellfire on his own, but with one runner accompanying him—just in case. Working their way over to the command post, they made the harrowing trek safely.

Meanwhile, moments before Walker entered the dugout, Butts, a map spread out on a table, was conferring with Hays about whether they should fire artillery on the south bank of the Marne and risk hitting their own men. Butts wanted to wait. To Hays, he said that he "felt certain some definite news would be at hand within the next few minutes."

Almost on cue, Walker and his runner slipped into the dugout, surprising Butts and Hays. Walker brought bad news. He said he had not received any written messages from his five company commanders all morning. He told Hays the information that "I had received indicated that the two front companies were a total loss and that companies A, D and K were disorganized, that many reports had been received to the effect that many of the officers had been killed or wounded."

Butts recounted Walker telling him that "B and C Companies were totally lost, that there was a large number of stragglers between my headquarters and his own from Companies A and B and from the engineer details which had been dismissed by the engineers as soon as the bombardment began. He reported that the losses of all of his companies were very great but that he had practically no success in trying to communicate directly with his company commanders."

The decisive news from Walker, however, was the fact that the Germans were south of the Marne in the S.O.S. barrage line that Colonel McAlexander dreaded because he believed his troops would get it in their backs from the division's own artillery. Relying on Walker, Butts then asked him if there was any danger that some of their men might get hit. Walker said a few might get hit who were near the Ru Chailly Farm, but that they certainly ought to fire the S.O.S. barrage south of the railroad at once. That was enough to convince Butts and to justify what happened next.

Turning to Hays, Butts said, "Go ahead."

CHAPTER 19

FRIENDLY FIRE

Now Lieutenant Hays had to ride back again to Grèves Farm to give his battalion commander the order to shell south of the Marne. The thick woods he had to travel through looked as if it had been swept by a fierce storm. Trees were uprooted, timber strewn everywhere, and the ground churned up with shell holes. Hays could not find a way through the tangled forest. His best chance was to ride over open fields, exposing himself to enemy airplanes. A German aviator hunting easy prey quickly spotted Hays. He bore down on him, the plane's engine loud, the machine-gun bullets that tore up the ground around him louder. Hays spurred his horse back into the woods to wait out the Boche pilot. When he saw his chance, he and his horse bolted into the open again. But the airplane was on him. He ducked back into the woods. He kept up this cat-and-mouse game until bullets ripped into his horse, killing the poor animal. Hays then made it to Grèves Farm on foot.

When he got there, he saw that the American and French batteries were under fire from airplanes and enemy artillery zeroing in on his battalion. Direct hits had knocked out of action one of the French batteries.

Dead bodies lay near most of the battery pits. The first-aid station was jammed with the wounded, and worse, ammunition was running low. Without artillery support the infantry troops in the front line would be at the mercy of the Germans.

Out of the morning haze and smoke from the big guns, the sweat-soaked, powder-caked artillerymen saw from their rear mule-drawn caissons and wagons loaded with ammunition coming across an open field. With German airplanes hovering above them, the drivers cursed the mules into a trot, lashed out at them with their whips while the men riding shotgun leaped from their wagons and snatched the bits and yanked the mules forward. A cheer went up when they reached the ammunition dump and began to unload the shells.

Hays gave Butts's order to Major Easterday to take aim south of the river. The Germans had made it over the Marne and were concentrating their forces on the railroad track. Butts said hit them at the railroad tracks, but to also sweep this bank of the river to prevent fresh troops from crossing. Hays jumped onto a horse and started back to the 30th's headquarters to let Butts know his orders were being carried out. He hadn't been in the saddle too long when the horse was shot out from under him. The fall from the dying animal jarred Hays. But he got up and backtracked to Grèves Farm, got on another horse and worked his way to Butts's command post. The horse did not make it all the way. It was struck and wounded, and Hays had to leave the frightened animal behind.

Inside the command post, he reported to Butts. He informed the colonel that his artillery battalion had just received six hundred rounds of ammunition. He said there were many wounded among the artillery crews and that nearly every battery was under fire. He feared that if the Germans' unrelenting artillery and airplane assault on the 10th Field Artillery's Second Battalion kept up for another hour or so, he "doubted if there could be any artillery left to support [Butts's] regiment."

The colonel then showed him a message that had come up from the field that the shells from the 10th's batteries were falling too short and ripping into his own troops.

Obviously, an adjustment had to be made immediately. Once more Hays was on his way to Grèves Farm. He eventually made several more trips back and forth, losing two more horses—a total of seven. On his last trip to the 30th's headquarters, a shell exploded near him and hot, sharp fragments killed his horse and wounded him severely in both legs. He was carried into Butts's dugout and the wounds were dressed.

"He was borne away," Butts wrote, "laughing as if the whole show was a huge play that he enjoyed to the utmost and that horses being shot under him was a great joke to the Germans. His spirit was the same during all the trying hours of the battle."

For his action, Lieutenant Hays received the Congressional Medal of Honor, the only soldier in the Third Division to receive America's highest honor during the Second Battle of the Marne.

B ut the damage had been done.

Five hundred of Butts's men, fighting desperately on the front line, where they had just halted the enemy from advancing to the railroad embankment, were suddenly hit with the shells from the 10th Field Artillery as well as from French batteries. Although the shelling helped disrupt the enemy, according to General Crawford, "it threw the river line detachments into confusion."

One of the river detachments especially hit was B Company, now led by First Lieutenant Frederick Winant, Jr. At first Winant didn't know where the new round of artillery that was striking his position was coming from. Then he realized it was friendly fire. It was more "disquieting" than the shelling from the Germans. As he recalled, "We signaled back to the hills where our guns were located but apparently without success." He hunted around for "some pyrotechnics, hoping these might be picked up in spite of the daylight." His frantic search led him into the 38th's subsector and there he met up with Captain Jesse Wooldridge for the first time. Fortunately, Wooldridge had the signal flares that Winant needed. The lieutenant was then able to send a message to Butts to "lengthen the range."

The shelling soon afterward ceased. Down to only a few men, Winant and a squad joined forces with Wooldridge's company. Three years after the war, in a letter penned to Major Walker, a still bitter Winant wrote, "I do not know to this day where that fire came from or who was responsible for it."

Another river detachment that came under friendly fire was made up of two platoons from C Company, which had been consolidated into one. Leading the platoon was First Lieutenant James H. Gay, Jr. Earlier that morning, after being cut off from the rest of the Second Battalion and before being hit by its own artillery, C Company had made a courageous stand. Then, during a lull in the fighting, as Gay began to reorganize what was left of his company and try to get some food and coffee to his men, "our own artillery fire came directly on top of my position. The demoralizing effect of this can readily be imagined and in a few minutes more men were killed and wounded from our own fire than we had throughout the whole night from the German fire."

Gay's platoon had no cover, no place to run for protection. He had to make a decision—either follow the orders given him "that there shall be no retirement" or "use my own judgment and initiative by withdrawing and thus preventing complete annihilation of the Platoon."

He decided it was best to retire. He had thirty-five fit men, a number of others wounded by the shelling and having to be helped to the rear, and one German prisoner, a major. He formed his men in column formation and marched them toward the rear, where they ran into a platoon from First Lieutenant Henry C. Switzer's C Company, led by Second Lieutenant A. C. Eldred. They thought it best to head to C Company headquarters. As the two platoons, now numbering close to eighty men, continued falling back, they were still coming under frightening friendly fire. Reaching the railroad track, they placed their men in single file in a ditch that ran alongside the tracks. Gay was in the middle of the file when he heard men up front firing their rifles.

Looking up, he saw seventy to eighty Germans dashing across the tracks, running "away from us like a flock of sheep." His men kept shooting, and "you could see the Germans dropping at the rate of one every two or three steps," until the survivors who made it over the tracks hid in a patch of woods. Gay's men followed them over the tracks and into the woods. When they came upon the Germans, they were huddled in the thickets. Seeing the Americans, they threw down their weapons and surrendered. Gay lined them up and, fearing more Germans were on his right, placed his men on the left side of the prisoners so if there were any enemy out there they'd have to shoot at their own men before hitting any of Gay's soldiers. He moved to the head of the column, and spotted a line of ditches filled with armed Germans. They were as surprised to see the Americans as the Americans were surprised to see them.

With his men leveling their rifles at the Germans, Gay called for them to surrender. They put their rifles on the ground and climbed out of the ditches. Gay now had about 150 prisoners and more than 50 of his own men. He needed to find someone in authority to tell him what to do about the prisoners. Leaving Eldred in charge, he went to Captain Jed Lasseigne's dugout. Lasseigne wasn't there, only a few badly wounded soldiers.

"Since it was manifestly impossible to rush all over the country trying to find someone in authority I returned to the platoon," he recalled. He reasoned it best to march his motley group to regimental headquarters. While on the road he saw his former commanding officer, Lieutenant Switzer. He seemed dazed. Gay offered to turn over command of the two platoons and the prisoners to him. Switzer refused. He marched along with Gay and never issued an order. An hour or so earlier Switzer and several of his men, running out of ammunition and surrounded by Germans, had been captured. Switzer feigned his death and escaped.

From his command post, General Crawford noted that Gay came to the rear with his command, somewhat less than 100 men, bringing away about 150 prisoners he had taken. "These were probably the last of the 30th Infantry front line garrison, except the detachment of Lieutenant Marsh, which remained all day in Mézy holding his post. The other 30th Infantry first line troops had been driven back, captured or destroyed."

The Second Battalion of the 10th Field Artillery and the French batteries not only struck troops in the 30th Infantry, they also struck Colonel McAlexander's 38th Infantry. While he kept tabs on the 10th's First Battalion, making sure they did not fire on his men, he was livid at the action coming from Butts's regiment on his left. He believed that Major Walker's First Battalion, holding the front line, had relied on the "strategy of elasticity" and moved a mile back from the Marne to behind the Fossoy-Crézancy Road.

"The colonel of that regiment called for an S.O.S. barrage on his front," he angrily recalled, "the artillery answered his call and fired indiscriminately along the entire front and into the back of my men who were still holding the Marne. This artillery fire, which started before noon, July 15th, was not stopped until about two o'clock. There were two French heavy six-inch guns far to the rear whose fire could not be stopped, but finally died out about six o'clock."

Captain Eddy Herlihy of H Company noticed that just when the attacks on the battalion's left flank had stopped and German shelling seemed to be winding down, there was a heavy burst of artillery fire west of where the river made a sharp bend to the south. "Fortunately," he reported, "it was not as intense as the fire of our own artillery which began falling from the rear. At one time, our own shells were falling on the rear embankment while German shells were raking the top and front. Up to this time, nothing had shaken the confidence of the men. Losses had been heavy; dead and wounded were far more numerous than effectives; yet morale was high. But when our own artillery opened fire on the survivors, nerves gave way."

He believed that if the Germans had attacked while the Americans were getting hit by their own artillery, then the German attack would have been successful, and who knows what might have happened.

At his battalion command post, Major Rowe and his staff were "silent and helpless witnesses of losses from our own artillery during which came numerous pleas for help from Reid and for mercy from Herlihy and Dineen." Rowe shot off all his signal rockets to keep the artillery from firing on his men. Still the shells fell. The only way to have it stopped was to send a messenger on foot.

After a while the "situation improved." "I have no way of knowing how many of my men of Rowe's battalion were killed or wounded by this fire," McAlexander wrote. "I was frantic with rage at the damned French artillery who held Cruikshank to maintaining that S.O.S. zone on maps and in orders. Coordination? Oh, yes! A coordination of American, French and German artillery to shoot to death as gallant a battalion as ever bore arms in the world's history."

The friendly fire, devastating as it was on the Americans, stopped the Germans from reaching the Bois d'Aigremont. Butts believed that after getting a lot of concentrated artillery fire "the enemy lost all stomach for its planned organized attack. Our scattered platoons in the front area did their part and the artillery did the rest."

Butts, defending the friendly fire years later, wrote that "there had been some mistakes but the accomplishments had so far out-weighed the errors as to obliterate them, and reduce them to no importance."

After the range of the artillery had been lengthened, Butts and his second in command, Lieutenant Colonel Cromwell Stacy, made a personal reconnaissance of their lines along the northern and western edges of the Bois d'Aigremont while under heavy enemy artillery. They concluded that the Germans were not making any progress in their attack. By the afternoon of the 15th, according to Dickman, "it became definitely known that the attack had failed in the 30th Infantry sector."

Butts then requested that the 111th Infantry of the 28th Division, now in support of his regiment, immediately relieve the 30th.

Backing his request, Stacy in his operation report to division head-quarters, sent at noon on the 15th, included the following: "The men are absolutely worn out from being 10 solid hours under shell fire without having a drink of water, and the regiment ought to be relieved. We have been exposed to mustard gas, chlorine and chocolate gas and if a good many of our men don't get their clothes off we are going to have casual-ties from mustard gas. It is absolutely impossible for the men to get food, for all except what was in cans is spoiled from the gas. They are still in the line and they will hold the line, but they ought to be relieved and given a chance to clean up and rest and get something to eat because we have been on the alert for 10 days in addition to this attack last night."

He and Butts had a good reason for the request. Their men had suffered the most casualties of any other regiment in the division during twelve hours of combat. More than twenty-five officers and four-teen hundred men were reported killed, wounded or missing. Robert H. C. Kelton, Dickman's chief of staff, in a letter to Colonel Fox Conner on Pershing's staff, wrote, "Butts's regiment got the worst drubbing, but stopped the attack along its outpost line."

By midnight on the 15th, the 30th Infantry was in the process of being relieved. Major Walker was glad to get his battalion out of the Bois d'Aigremont. It was daylight by the time it began its withdrawal. His surviving men asked to march out, and he led them in single file back toward the woods just east of Courboin. "They were worn out, dirty, hungry and very low in spirits," he recalled. Before they reached Courboin, they were too exhausted to continue on. Walker let them rest for a long time. When they got to Courboin, a truck train picked them up and carried the troops to another village. Here they were given baths, a hot meal and new uniforms. Walker kept his old coat as a souvenir because a chunk of shrapnel had pierced the flap of the jacket, reminding him of a narrow escape.

Outside the village, the battalion slept in the woods. By July 18 it had not yet left the encampment in the woods. Corporal William Fitzgerald put in his diary, "We still make our home in the woods. About one third of the regiment is left, the rest are either killed our wounded. . . . Every one shell shocked, but happy."

CHAPTER 20

"THEIR DEAD MINGLED WITH OURS ALONG THE TRACK"

If Captain Jesse Wooldridge hadn't believed in a Divine Providence that directs all things for the best, then he confessed that he would have lost his mind on July 15. All through the night as shells hammered south of the Marne with a fury that drove soldiers mad, and then into the morning as hordes of the enemy tried to fight their way across the river, and now just before noon as the Germans viciously attacked again at his front and left flank and were streaming over the crest of Hill 231, threatening his regiment's far right flank, the banker from San Francisco had to wonder, fighting in this devil's inferno, what was God's intended plan? How could it be for the best?

All around him men were either dead or writhing in agonizing pain as bullets from machine guns and automatic rifles whined over the battlefield like swarms of angry hornets. German planes took down French planes and then flew up and down the line spraying Major Guy Rowe's Second Battalion. And the Third Division's artillery fell on its own men by the river, coming perilously close to breaking their spirit.

"These bastards are coming at me from the flanks as well as from the front," Wooldridge swore to Captain Eddy Herlihy of H Company when he had the chance.

If that wasn't bad enough, only a single ambulance and a handful of litter bearers had been able to reach the wounded in Wooldridge's company and most certainly in Herlihy's company as well. If not for a civilian noncombatant working for the Young Men's Christian Association and attached to the 38th Infantry, Richard C. Shreve from Rochester, New York, many of the seriously wounded would have died. Using his own automobile, a Model T Ford, Shreve helped evacuate the worst cases to the medical-aid station set up in the village Paroy.

Wooldridge's original company of almost 225 men, holding the ground outside the Mézy train station along the railroad embankment, was down to 52. On his right, he had tried to get Herlihy to lend him some men. In a desperate fight of his own, Herlihy refused, but had his riflemen pour lead from their position on the railroad embankment into the Germans in front of Wooldridge's company. At least Wooldridge's company had earlier in the morning been reinforced by Lieutenant Harry Marsh and thirty riflemen, remnants from C Company of the 30th Infantry, and by twelve more men from the same regiment, all that were left of a Stokes mortar platoon led by Lieutenant Frederick Winant. Marsh and his men had just fought their way out of Mézy. After being surrounded by troops from the Sixth Grenadiers, they had dashed from house to house before hooking up with Wooldridge's company at the station.

"They were a godsend as only a handful of my original command remained," recalled Wooldridge of the men from the 30th Infantry. Wooldridge also sent a message to Major Rowe, pleading for him to move in some support. Although Rowe released a platoon, it never arrived.

Winant's orders from his captain, Henry Switzer, were to stick to the railroad embankment closest to the train station, which was still in the 30th's subsector. He would not leave this position even though Wooldridge wanted him to join forces in a combined front. Marsh, on the other hand, had no such orders and turned his men over to Wooldridge.

The Germans from both the Sixth Grenadiers and the 47th Infantry Regiment still held the advantage, because of their superiority in numbers and their many machine guns, as they made one more charge at the nine-foot-high railroad embankment. The Americans, however, were in a strong position from atop the embankment firing down on the advancing soldiers. In Herlihy's company, First Sergeant Matthew J. Connelly, a veteran of the Spanish American War who had taken over the Second Platoon after the death of its leader, Second Lieutenant Frank Young, walked along the railroad embankment in full view of the Germans, encouraging his men and directing their fire.

"Spanish American War stuff, Matt?" an impressed Herlihy hollered at him.

"Watch it!" Connelly hollered back. To the eight or nine men left in his platoon, he yelled, "Ready, aim, fire."

Herlihy watched as Germans erupted from a grove of trees.

Another shout from Connelly: "Fire at will!"

"Every gray clad man in sight was cut down," a still impressed Herlihy reported.

Whenever the enemy got too close to Wooldridge, he led counterattacks off the embankment, driving the foe back.

At one time, he thought he had a chance to beat back the Germans for good. With about fifteen men, including First Lieutenant Kenneth P. Murray, he set up a skirmish line placing his soldiers with five paces between each other. They hit the enemy's flank halfway between the railroad tracks and the river. But the German resistance was too strong. Two soldiers next to Wooldridge were killed. The right side of the skirmish line faltered. Wooldridge crawled over to "KP" Murray and yelled in his ear, "If we can't keep the right flank up it's no use." At that instant a bullet struck Murray's head. Wooldridge "heard it splash against the inside of his skull." The twenty-one-year-old West Pointer from Mount Vernon, New York, was dead.

The men around Wooldridge were all getting hit. He turned to Private Daniel Weiner and sent him back to the railroad embankment.

Then he worked his way along the line to order the withdrawal of the rest of the men, but everyone had been killed. He and Weiner were the only ones to come out alive. Wooldridge, who would be wounded eight times, once in the chest and once by bayonet, later counted fourteen bullet holes in his blouse.

Back on the embankment, fighting off the Germans and seeing that his battle area was getting smaller, Wooldridge decided to move. He sent twenty riflemen into a stand of trees about 150 yards to his right where they could hit the Germans in a cross fire, and with the rest of his surviving troops he dashed behind a pile of rocks on the south side of Mézy. Near the rocks was a trench dug in the shape of an L. Thinking it would offer better protection, he ordered everyone into the trench. But as they scrambled in, the Americans quickly discovered that it offered the Germans a better angle to strike them with enfilade fire.

"They shot the life out of us with minenwerfers, one-pounders and machine guns in the minute it took us to get into the other arm of the L," Wooldridge wrote.

One of the cooks brought into the fight, described as a "pugnacious" Irishman, groaned, "Orhoor, Captain, we'll never get out of here."

On Wooldridge's right, Herlihy's H Company had finally dislodged the Sixth Grenadiers in front of them because of their blistering rifle fire coming from the embankment, especially from Connelly's platoon, and pushed them back across the river. Herlihy then saw G Company getting raked by the enemy's firepower. He directed his men again to shoot into that company's zone.

Holed up at the Mézy railroad station, Winant and his dozen mortar men, now using rifles, secured Wooldridge's left flank. What finally saved the survivors of Wooldridge's company was the twenty riflemen he had ordered into the woods. They slowed down the Germans. The men in the trench rallied by crawling on their bellies through a gap in the rock pile and, regaining their old position atop the railroad embankment, firing into the advancing Germans with the same deadly accuracy as Herlihy's men had given the enemy.

"It is impossible," Wooldridge wrote, "to express the exhilaration experienced in seeing an attacking body of troops five times your superior in number stop in their advance under your fire, waver slightly, look toward one another and run for shelters, then, rapidly, the whole bunch disintegrate. It is thrilling."

The commander of the Sixth Grenadiers' First Battalion sent an urgent message to 10th Division headquarters: "I cannot hold the position alone. Enemy awaited us fully prepared."

The Germans retreated to the north bank of the Marne. Wooldridge let them go. His men were too tired and too cut up to go after them. But the Germans who could not get away were rounded up—more than two hundred prisoners. The only fighting now was sniping back and forth across the Marne.

Wooldridge's company suffered a casualty rate of well over 50 percent. "We had started with 251 men and five officers," he reported. "I had left fifty-one men and two lieutenants." Next to him, Herlihy's casualties were much lighter except for the Fourth Platoon at the river. In the other three platoons he lost one officer, Frank Young, killed, and another wounded, as well as seven enlisted men killed and fifty-six missing. But in the Fourth Platoon there were seventeen men killed, thirty-one wounded, and four missing.

Surveying the battlefield, Wooldridge recalled, he saw that "Their dead mingled with ours along the track at a ratio of about five to one."

At four-thirty in the afternoon, the Second Battalion was ordered to withdraw from the railroad embankment in order to shorten the 38th's front line. Wooldridge's and Herlihy's companies were to take up positions on the west bank of the Surmelin River, at the Aqueduct Line. Lieutenant Winant, twice wounded and growing faint, decided to withdraw with Wooldridge and report to Major Rowe because he had no way to communicate with his superior officers in the 30th Infantry. He and the few men that he had formed a rear guard formation for the withdrawal.

"The retirement was made in a very orderly manner," Herlihy noted, "although the left flank companies had to fight their way back."

Afterward, Winant tried to locate Major Fred Walker's command post and report to him. But every soldier he met was from the 38th Infantry and could not help him. As he worked his way back into the 30th's subsector, he kept passing out. When he fainted for the last time, he had made it to Walker's command post and fell on top of the dugout roof. He was found the following morning by the battalion mess sergeant.

Winant recovered from his wounds and fought with the regiment in the last major battle of the war. For his action on July 15, he received the American Distinguished Service Cross. Colonel Butts described him as the "ideal subordinate officer. Wounds or strenuous battle conditions never phased [*sic*] him. He was always cool and did just the right thing in every emergency." Wooldridge wrote that Winant "did splendid work in this engagement." Later, at the Battle of Meuse-Argonne, he was shot through both arms. The wounds were severe enough that the Princeton graduate and former volunteer ambulance driver had to retire from the army.

Wooldridge's and Herlihy's companies had halted the Germans at the Marne between Mézy and the Surmelin River. On their left, in the subsector of the 30th Infantry, the Germans had also been stopped and not allowed to take the Bois d'Aigremont.

It was on the far right of the Third Division during the long day of the 15th that, once the fleeing French had left four companies of the 109th and 110th Infantries and Colonel McAlexander's E and F Companies out to dry, the Germans threatened to achieve their goal of completely overrunning the inexperienced Americans and then victoriously sweeping down the Surmelin Valley toward Paris.

CHAPTER 21

//

"WE'VE GOT TO FIGHT, BOYS, SO WE MIGHT AS WELL START IT OURSELVES"

At first light on the morning of July 15, the flamboyant Colonel Billy Mitchell and Donald Brown of the Red Cross, after driving through the night to Mitchell's headquarters at Hautefeuille, where he commanded the First Brigade Air Service, went to the airdrome of the First Pursuit Group. They climbed into one of the airplanes and flew north to where the Allied front lines were and then, seeing no German planes, but only artillery fire, banked east and followed the Marne River. They flew low through light clouds, fog and haze. As their plane neared Jaulgonne, where the banks of the Marne were high and steep, a few German Fokkers came into view. The German pilots failed to see Mitchell's plane. He cunningly avoided them and flew on toward Dormans. Rounding a bend in the river, he and Brown looked down at artillery fire churning up the ground on the south bank. They saw five bridges spanning the Marne, each crammed with Germans marching across in splendid style. Mitchell continued toward Rheims. The battle there was terrible, and the sky was filled with German planes. Mitchell wisely reversed direction and flew west, again following the Marne at five hundred feet. He passed the five bridges still clogged with the enemy and reached Jaulgonne.

"By that time," he wrote in his memoirs, "a terrible combat was taking place on top of the hill just south of the bridges. The opposing troops were almost together. This was the nearest to hand-to-hand combat than anything I had seen so far. I thought they were Americans, and later found it was our 3rd Division."

The hill he and Brown saw was the Moulins Ridge, Hill 231. And it wasn't just the Third Division in deadly combat, but also the desperate troops of four companies of the 109th and 110th Infantries of the 28th Division positioned on the right flank of the 38th Infantry.

The Pennsylvanians were on the other side of the hill, several miles east of Colonel McAlexander's F Company. As dawn broke and the heaviest of the terrifying German artillery bombardment began to ease up, these soldiers discovered something was eerily not right. For the Frosty Sons of Thunder in C Company of the 110th, who would survive the day, what was about to happen to them would forever change their lives as well as the lives of their families and friends back in Somerset County.

The French 125th Division, as noted, had started to slip away in the dark of night as shells rained down from the evil sky. The soldiers in the French 113th Regiment were breaking through the American line and fleeing toward the rear. At first the Americans tried to stop them and reorganize and reform them. The colonel of the 113th made every effort to stop his own men. He had orders from the divisional commander, who himself was in retreat, to "throw [the enemy's] force back across the river." When he failed to rally his men, he mounted his horse and with his staff rode off to the rear, leaving the Americans, who had never been in battle, to fend for themselves. One of the captains from the 125th had made it to the 38th Army Corps headquarters and warned that his division's "principal position [had] broken on the right. The enemy is advancing up the SURMELIN Valley toward Crezancy." He said that the "1st position of resistance in front of the French 113th Inf. is being vigorously attacked and is yielding ground at some points." The colonel of the French 131st Infantry, closest to McAlexander's regiment, he said, "announces that the enemy crossed the Marne . . . and is advancing on the slopes of the Moulins Ruine plateau," thus threatening the 38th's right flank.

Attached to the 131st Infantry was L Company of the 28th Division's 109th Infantry, led by Captain James B. Cousart from Philadelphia, who was acting commander of the regiment's Third Battalion. Captain Edward P. Mackey of Williamsport, Pennsylvania, was in charge of M Company, also attached to the 131st. With the Germans closing in, the two companies were soon in deep trouble. With orders to stand firm, the colonel of the 109th, Millard F. Brown, at thirty-five one of the youngest colonels in the AEF, was reported to have said that his regiment, split up on two fronts, would not be able to hold, and that especially included the two companies with the 131st. Brigadier General Thomas W. Darrah, the 28th Division's 55th Brigade commander, made it clear to Brown that he'd better hold even though the French had fled. "The reputation," Darrah warned him, "not only of the Division, but the American troops depends on our doing our duty."

The French kept on fleeing. One of the platoon captains and his men in B Company had been able to thwart the German advance with rifle fire until the French were gone. Their flanks were then exposed. Captain William Fish, B Company's commanding officer, angrily saw two automatic rifle squads and other French riflemen, numbering about forty men, firing into his First and Second Platoons. He ordered them to stop. As soon as they did, they turned and bolted to the rear.

"Our companies being out flanked fell back making repeated stands until again outflanked," Darrah wrote.

First Lieutenant Martin L. Wheeler from Moscow, Pennsylvania, wounded and refusing medical aid, with his platoon surrounded, looked around for a place for them to escape. A small opening in the woods the Germans had missed offered hope. He ordered his men to drop to their bellies and led them as they crawled through the opening, and as his men made their safe getaway, he stayed behind, holding off the enemy until he was captured.

Meanwhile, the 110th Infantry's C Company's Third Platoon, commanded by First Lieutenant Robert J. Bonner from Philadelphia, was on the river, covering five hundred yards with five automatic rifle squads, when the soldiers in General von Boehn's Seventh Army assaulted his front. The Germans were trying to duplicate what they were doing in front of the Third Division, trying to cross the Marne in boats armed with machine guns and over pontoon bridges, gain a stronghold on the south bank and drive the Americans back. Bonner's men met them face-to-face. Tossing hand grenades and firing their weapons, they blew the boats out of the water and shot many of the enemy. Those Germans who weren't killed outright drowned.

While the Germans regrouped in the woods across the Marne, getting ready for a second assault, the Pennsylvanians in Bonner's automatic rifle pits concentrated their fire on the north bank. Germans toppled over in great numbers. The dead lined the bank or bobbed in the bloody waters of the Marne. Realizing it was not possible to cross, the Germans abandoned their assault in front of C Company.

At that moment, Captain Truxal believed that his company had stopped the Germans; that, in fact, all along the front, from Château-Thierry to the Champagne sector, the Allies, he prayed, had repulsed the enemy. To be on the safe side, to back up his front-line troops and to cover the main road from Dormans to Paris, he brought up in reserve his kitchen personnel. Cook Harry Stevanus, the recently married farmer, switched from baking biscuits to carrying his rifle.

Then Truxal and his troops got a shock that ran down their spines like frigid water. At eight in the morning an enemy soldier had been captured by C Company's rear guard, near the village of Courthiézy. The information Truxal's intelligence staff coaxed out of him revealed that the main German force had easily made it over the river at Dormans at 2 a.m.—six hours earlier—and was now behind the Americans. When the 125th Division had slinked back five or six miles from the river, it had never given orders to the companies of the 28th Division to withdraw. The four companies from the 109th and 110th Infantries and a small contingent of French soldiers that had remained were now stranded, pinned with their backs to the Marne.

The Germans were free to move against C Company. They slipped inside of Courthiézy undetected. Truxal's rear guard was taken by surprise. It was wiped out to the man, everyone killed, captured or wounded.

With the village taken, the Germans pressed on toward the river where the rest of C Company's troops were now trapped, but with no idea what was about to happen to them. The Somerset County men were facing the Marne, not watching their backs, but warily keeping their eyes on the north bank in case the enemy made another assault. They were in rifle pits or crouched behind trenches or other barricades, waiting. Sergeant Robert A. Floto and his Fourth Platoon, which was in a support position along the railroad embankment two hundred yards from the rest of the company, were concentrating on the woods north of the river. They had already withstood one enemy attack. They were ready for a second, if it came.

Behind them a voice, cheerful and drawn-out, cried out "Aha!"

Floto's platoon wheeled around. At least two German platoons were behind them. The two sides exchanged gunfire. "A volley of about twenty-five shots was fired at us by the enemy," said twenty-six-year-old Private Norman L. Zimmerman, a miner back in Somerset. Next to Zimmerman, eighteen-year-old Private First Class Gilbert C. Blades was "hit in the breast and stomach by a number of rifle shots," stated Private Eugene Gibson. "He fell with blood running from his breast." Private Orth Grimm looked aghast at Blades. "His intestines were bulging out, but he was not quite dead." The Americans and Germans then rushed together in "very fierce" hand-to-hand combat, according to Private William S. Sarver.

Zimmerman, Gibson, Grimm and Sarver were wounded and, except for Sarver, captured and hauled off as prisoners of war. Sarver, shot four times in the left leg and right wrist, fell and for the next three days and nights lay helpless on the blood-soaked ground. Blades died next to him, "within arm's reach." German soldiers searched the field, checking the dead and wounded. An officer chanced upon Sarver and dressed his wounded leg and left him there. The wounded Americans were kept under guard. On the beautiful moonlit night of July 18, Sarver escaped. He crawled to a wheelbarrow filled with hand grenades. "I laid the grenades aside and used the wheelbarrow to make my escape. I rested my wounded left leg over the right handle of the vehicle and held up by the other handle with my left hand in that way pushing myself along the road for about a mile." He came to a field where the German soldiers were digging up potatoes and took cover. At night he pushed himself across the field on his back. A French soldier found Sarver and helped him to a dressing station.

After dispatching most of the Fourth Platoon, as they had done to the soldiers in the village of Courthiézy, killing, capturing or wounding the men who could not fight their way out and escape to the rear, the Germans went after the First and Second Platoons. The two platoons, the First commanded by First Lieutenant Samuel Crouse, the oldest soldier in the company, and the Second led by First Lieutenant Wilbur Schell, were between the railroad embankment and the woods that stretched down to the river.

Crouse and Private First Class William Zimmerman, who on this perilous day was celebrating his thirty-ninth birthday, were huddled in a trench in the woods when they heard the firefight between the remnants of the Fourth Platoon and the oncoming Germans. They left the trench and ran up the road along the hill to investigate. They had already gotten word that the Germans were behind them. As they came up the road, they failed to see hidden in the bushes eight Germans and Private Daniel McGuire from New York City, the Germans' prisoner.

"Neither Lt. Crouse or Zimmerman saw us standing there," McGuire later stated. "I called to them but they did not hear. Had the Germans not fired when they did Lt. Crouse and Zimmerman would have continued on past us. The Germans fired when they were within fifteen feet and hit Lt. Crouse in the head, tearing off one side of his skull." Zimmerman was shot through the forehead. Both men were killed instantly.

Using machine guns and flamethrowers, the Germans overwhelmed the First and Second Platoons and, in doing so, wounded and captured a number of men, including Crouse's son, Edgar. While the young Crouse was being led away, he passed by the bloody body of his father.

But two American soldiers not yet killed or captured and causing havoc had to be quickly taken care of—Corporal Herbert P. Jones of Somerset and twenty-year-old Private First Class Lawrence Hartle of Meyersdale. The two had been buried during the bombardment and had just dug themselves out when the enemy was about to overrun their platoon. Seeing the Germans coming toward them, they opened fire. Although heavily outnumbered, they kept the charging Germans at bay for ten minutes. Finally, they were both wounded and the Germans swarmed over them, knocking them unconscious with their rifle butts.

On the right of Jones and Hartle, Captain Truxal defended his flank by ordering a food-rationing party that during the night had brought warm meals to the men and the kitchen force to stay and fight. He placed them along the Dormans-to-Paris road.

One member of the kitchen force was Cook Stevanus. He carried a revolver as well as his rifle. When the Germans closed in from the rear, he had been watching them through field glasses. He picked out an officer. When he shot him, all he saw was the officer's feet fly up in the air. Then, as he later told his grandson, "all hell broke loose." Using his pistol, as Stevanus wrote to his wife, "I brought down 6 Germans with my gun." But the enemy machine gunner got the Meyersdale farmer. Bullets struck his left wrist, tore through his upper arm and below the left knee. His position was then overrun. "When they got me they took my revolver + I was sad as I loved it. It was an old friend."

Stevanus was taken prisoner and held for three days in a German trench. He was eventually freed by French soldiers who then hid him in the cellar of a house until he could be evacuated behind the lines, where he finally received medical treatment. Gangrene had set in by then and he lost his leg above the knee. His arm had been shattered and he never regained full use of it. While he was recuperating in a French hospital, his father died of influenza and a few days later his uncle also passed. After receiving the terrible news, he sent a letter home. "Oh, mother, if I could only have come home to see [our dear dad] before he had to leave us to show him that I was a brave soldier! I know he would have been proud of me."

The remnants of the First and Second Platoons banded together and prepared to fight their way out of the German trap to the rear and to the safety of the Allied lines. They cut through a wheat field and felt they were home free when on both sides of them hidden German machine gunners fired into their midst.

Corporal Samuel Landis, who'd been shot in the back during the bombardment but refused to go to the rear, was hit in the left leg three times. He fell among the dead and wounded of his platoon. To avoid capture he dragged himself into a gulley and then into a shell hole. There he stayed for four days and nights. On the fifth day, weakened by loss of blood and dying of thirst, he crawled into another shell hole, filled with stagnant water. Here the Germans found him. They threw him onto a stretcher and carried him to their own lines, where they placed him on the ground next to Earl Wirik, a twenty-one-year-old corporal from Somerset. Both his legs had been nearly blown off. Landis, Wirik and Private Lyman Driesbaugh of Dalton, Pennsylvania, another prisoner, tried to escape. But Wirik, knowing the end was near, said to Driesbaugh, "I am through, you might as well leave me and try to get out." To Landis, he said, "Sam, I can't live much longer," and he asked the corporal to pray for him. In a letter home, Landis wrote, "Well, mother, that was something I did not have much practice in, but I'm sure I did the best I knew how for him and I think it went to the right place too for he soon was unconscious and I don't think he knew very much about the pain after that." Wirik never regained consciousness and died. After Landis was found by the Allies, his leg had to be cut off.

Mechanic Reuben Rakestraw, the hotel manager and bartender from Humbert, escaped by playing "possum flattened out on the ground and did not dare to move or breathe scarcely. Ants crawled all over me and I did not dare to brush them off." When he had the chance, he slipped into a creek. For the next eighteen hours he remained in the water, swimming when he could, crawling and wading and hiding beneath banks or behind bushes and weeds that hung over the edges of the creek. After a mile he dragged himself out of the creek soaked to the bone. For two-and-a-half days he went without food. To a friend in Humbert, he wrote, "Am still crippling around with rheumatism from it." In a letter to his mother, he stated, "I . . . lost everything but rifle, side arm and gas mask."

Rakestraw fell in with a party of French soldiers and eventually made it to the village of Artonges, where other stragglers from C Company had also made it through enemy lines. "I thought I was the only one left, but ten others reported back ahead of me. Some are prisoners and some in hospital. I only know of three that were killed. I saw them but there were many more." He added, "I was a sight when I reported to brigade headquarters this p.m. [July 18]. I had not slept since Saturday night, and this is Thursday."

One of the soldiers at Artonges was Supply Sergeant Harry Campbell from Rakestraw's hometown. "Harry's all broken up yet, he cried and could not talk when I came in on Thursday."

Rakestraw had faithfully kept a diary every day since the 28th Division left New York, but because he was afraid that he was going to be captured he buried it in a field.

Lieutenant Schell, the Second Platoon's commander, suffered wounds as well and had been taken prisoner.

Nineteen men in Schell's platoon found themselves cut off and, without officers or noncommissioned officers to tell them what to do, seemed helpless until Bugler Walter B. Jones took over. His older brother, Corporal Herbert Jones, was already wounded and probably killed. Walter, a well-known musician back in Somerset and in civilian life a marble cutter, was a twenty-one-year-old undersized soldier with the nickname of "Fat."

He had been with the company since its days on the Texas border. He reorganized the men around him and led the small detachment south toward Condé-en-Brie, where he knew they'd find the rest of the regiment. It was a dangerous journey over the hills and through the woods and open meadows, and numerous times they had to fight their way out of tough spots. One of the men was badly wounded and Jones administered first aid to him, thus saving his life. It took them two days, but because of Jones's leadership all nineteen men made it safely back to the regiment.

While Jones was on his way to Condé-en-Brie, Corporal Alvey Martz, the twenty-five-year-old farmer and father of four, whose religion frowned on military service, rounded up twenty-five survivors of two platoons who were surrounded by the enemy. Taking command, he said to those around them, "We've got to fight, boys, so we might as well start it ourselves."

Yelling with all their might, the Americans charged the Germans, throwing them off. Martz personally shot down three Boche as they made it through an open wheat field and into the protection of the woods. Martz knew somewhere to the south there had to be friendly Allied troops.

In action deserving of the Congressional Medal of Honor, Martz, who grew up hunting in the woods around his remote mountain farm in Glencoe, proved in the thickness of these woods to be a one-man army. Using his pistol, he single-handedly killed fourteen more Germans, hunting some of them down in the woods. He and his small band of men, trying to break through the German trap, came across friendly troops—Sergeant Floto and a handful of survivors from his platoon. Martz turned over his men to Floto. Another American soldier wandered in, "mad all through," according to Martz. He had been with a group of seven men cut off from their platoon. They ran "slap-bang into all the Boche in the world." The Germans rounded them up, except for the soldier who hid and watched as the Germans marched their new prisoners toward their own lines. "I figured I couldn't do anybody any good by firing into the mob, so I came away to look for help," he explained to Martz and Floto.

"I guess we'd better see what we can do for those fellows," Martz said.

All the men now under Floto wanted to go and rescue the prisoners, reported New York *Sun* war correspondent Raymond G. Carroll. Martz said it was a two-man job. He'd go, and he picked Private John J. Mullen from West Philadelphia to accompany him. Mullen, an Irish lad of twenty-three who had lived in the United States for only three years, was a draftee. After basic training at Camp Meade he had been assigned to the 110th Infantry. He carried a watch he'd been given by his parish priest back in West Philadelphia.

With Martz, the hunter, leading the way, the two C Company men then tracked down the six prisoners being conducted to the German lines by two guards. Sneaking up on the guards, Martz whispered to Mullen, "You take the one on the right and I will take the one on the left." They aimed, fired and shot the Germans down. For Martz it was his eighteenth kill. He and Mullen brought the newly freed prisoners back to Floto's ragged platoon.

As they continued through the woods to the rear, the soldiers stumbled upon more stragglers led by Captain Charles L. McLain of F Company. McLain was an observer with the French. From Indiana, Pennsylvania, he took command of the entire group. With the woods swarming with Germans, he ordered the men to hide in the bushes during the rest of the day and travel only at night. McLain had a valuable piece of equipment, a compass. It meant they would not be forced to go wandering around the woods in the dark. He pointed them south to where the main force of the 110th Infantry was still in the village of Condé-en-Brie.

Carroll of the *Sun* later asked Martz, "What happened after you joined Captain McLain?"

"Nothing happened," Martz coolly replied. "He brought us in."

Back on the 15th, when the morning sun came up and the fighting intensified, Captain Truxal had joined his Third Platoon and a unit of French soldiers, including its commander, that had not pulled back with the rest of the 125th Division. With his platoon down to only ten men and trapped against the river, Truxal formed them into a V-shaped defensive pocket. The Americans sought cover wherever they could find it within the pocket—behind trees or stumps or fallen logs— and with their backs to the French, they kept watch on the river in case the Germans tried another crossing. The French, about fifty soldiers in all, faced the south, toward Courthiézy.

Machine-gun fire from the Germans south of the French kept up for almost four hours. Then it stopped. The battleground was deathly quiet. Truxal turned from the river. To his astonishment, the French were surrendering without letting him or his men know. A column of German soldiers was already taking prisoners. Truxal came forward, walking past the Germans to the French officer's command post, his pistol in his hand. The officer had signed a paper stating that he and his men had surrendered. Truxal left the command post certainly in disgust. He looked at his pistol, then unloaded it, broke it down and threw the bullets and pieces into a muddy puddle that sloshed beneath a culvert.

"I took my orders and tore them up, throwing the fragments under the plank," he confessed. "My compass, my map, money, a large penknife with a saw on it, a few other trinkets I hid in my leggings and trouser legs. I had scarcely finished when a German appeared at the mouth of the culvert and ordered me out."

A rosy German report stated how on the morning of July 15 the army of General von Boehn had easily crossed the Marne between Jaulgonne and Dormans and attacked the positions held by elements of the 28th Division, the French 125th Division and, farther east, another French division, as well as Italian troops. "Before daybreak," the report went on, "the assault troops transferred across the river by the pioneers and thereby laid the foundation for the day's success." It described how the infantry "attacked by assault the steep slopes along the S bank of the Marne, and under its protection the bridges were thrown across the river. We fought our way through the obstinately defended wooded country in which the first position of the enemy was located and threw him back to his rear lines."

What was left of C Company had been captured. Captain Truxal and many of his men, nearly all from Somerset County who had not been killed, would spend the rest of the war in German prison camps. The company had now ceased to exist.

Back in Somerset, the first news that their beloved C Company had been in the Marne defensive that stopped the German army appeared in the window of Mullins drugstore on July 18, three days after the battle had started. Local newspapers had placed the *Croix de Guerre* citation for Bugler Walter "Fat" Jones so the townspeople could read it. The citation reported that when there were no officers or noncommissioned officers to give orders, Jones had reorganized a shattered platoon of nineteen men and then led it for two days through the woods and hills to the safety of the rear lines. According to historian Charles Fox, "the entire town became wildly excited. Work stopped as crowds of people flocked to read the citation. As news of the German defeat became public the decision was made to formally celebrate the victory, and the next evening a patriotic meeting was held in the town square, marked by speeches, a parade and the sounding of all the town's church bells and steam whistles."

Then rumors started to reach the county that C Company had taken heavy casualties. On August 8, headlines on the front page of the *Meyersdale Republican* told of the "Blood of Frosty Sons of Thunder."

SOMERSET COUNTY BOYS BADLY CUT UP IN BATTLE

Capt. Truxal and Many Officers and Men Of His Command Reported Missing.

Our "Fighting Tenth" Hard Hit by Huns, but Hit Hard In Return—Company C Bears brunt of Enemy's Fire—Lieutenants Schell and Crouse Reported Killed and Captain Truxal

Missing or Wounded—Many Homes are Mourning Unknown
Fate of Brave Sons.

A column running the length of the front page listed the missing. Topping the list were Captain Truxal, and Lieutenants Schell and Crouse. Also on the list were Sergeant Robert Floto, Corporals John Heitzman, Samuel Landis, William Leckemby, Earl Wirik, Charles Vannear and Edgar Crouse, and Privates Lawrence Hartle, Gilbert Blades and Harry Stevanus.

"Although particulars are meager," the front-page article reported, "the wires have brought sad news to Somerset County during the last few days. Enough had been disclosed to show that the old 'Fighting Tenth' Pennsylvania National Guard Regiment, now known as the 110th Infantry, has suffered severely, but at the same time covered itself with glory in its first clash with the Huns."

The stunned residents of Meyersdale crowded around the newspaper's office, the Thomas and Collins drugstore, the Western Union telegraph office and Leckemby's newsstand and, with hearts pounding, looked for the names of relatives and friends.

According to the weekly newspaper, all kinds of rumors were flying around. A sense of gloom had settled over the entire county. The list of missing soldiers continued to grow. "Sorrow for our boys and sympathy for the relatives of those reported missing was manifested by all, and the hope was fervently expressed that later reports would show they were safe though perhaps prisoners of the enemy."

With more information slowly flowing in, the next issue of the *Republican* reported that the "Frosty Sons Fell While Fighting." But that "Mystery Still Shrouds Fate of Many of Our Boys"

Letters from soldiers who had survived or from nurses in American and French hospitals where the wounded were being carried, from the Red Cross or official communiqués from the War Department finally started to arrive to the worried families of the county.

Frank Stevanus received a telegram from the adjutant general in Washington about his son. "Deeply regret to inform you that Cook Harry L. Stevanus Infantry is officially reported as missing in action."

John P. Kelley, a railroad conductor whose nineteen-year-old son, Charles, had also been reported as missing in action, received an official telegram telling him that his son had been killed. Mrs. Roy Bills, holding out hope, received a similar message that her eldest son, Paul, also reported as missing, had been killed.

A few days after Frank Stevanus got his ominous telegram, a form letter arrived from the Red Cross.

> The American Red Cross sends most sincere sympathy to you in your anxiety, and wishes to assure you that when a man is officially reported as missing, every avenue of information is used in order to trace him.
>
> This search is begun automatically by the Red Cross as soon as a man's name appears on the list of missing. Men who were in the engagement with him are questioned, to find out if possible, from eyewitnesses what may have happened to him. Inquiries are made at the hospitals, and behind the German lines through the International Red Cross to see if he has been taken prisoner.

Finally, on October 15, another telegram was sent to Frank Stevanus from the adjutant general. "Corporal Harry L. Stevanus Infantry previously reported as missing in action since July Fifteenth now reported slightly wounded in action. Department has no further information."

Frank Stevanus died of influenza shortly after receiving the telegram that his son was alive.

Mrs. Marie Fleegle, whose son William Sarver had been shot four times in the leg and once in the arm and had lain on the battlefield for four days and been listed as killed in action, nervously opened a letter sent to her by James Boyd Hubbill of the YMCA headquarters in Paris. "Am writing this," Hubbill wrote, "at the request of Billy who is in the hospital here and is getting along fine. If it were not for a wound he received in the right arm he would be writing himself. If the French in the hospital could understand English he would be the life of the place for he is full of fun and very cheerful."

Marie Fleegle was one of the few mothers in Somerset County who received such wonderful news. Sadly, however, a year after Billy returned to America he was killed in an accident.

More than two hundred men from C Company were on the banks of the Marne on July 14 and 15. Forty-eight were killed or died from wounds, sixty-eight were wounded, and one hundred and twenty-six were taken prisoner. Of the original one hundred and fifty-eight officers and men from Somerset County, the casualties of those who fought in the Second Battle of the Marne were twenty-four killed, forty-eight wounded and sixty-five captured. Only twenty-one escaped death, capture and wounds. It was an extraordinary casualty rate of more than ninety percent—a devastating blow to Somerset County. Certainly no other company in the AEF suffered as much in combat as the frosty sons of thunder.

CHAPTER 22

"THEN I HOLD MY LINES"

While C Company of the 110th Infantry, 28th Division, was getting annihilated, the soldiers of the Fifth Grenadiers, unable to cross the Marne in front of the Third Division's E and H Companies, had moved to Jaulgonne and there, following a rolling barrage, made it over the river near Varennes at 4 a.m. without much trouble because of the rapid withdrawal of the French. There'd been little opposition, only artillery fire from batteries of the Third Division's 10th Field Artillery set inside the abandoned French sector around Janvier Farm on the slopes of Hill 231. Grenadier First Lieutenant Kurt Hesse remembered his men coming upon a trench filled with soldiers. The fight, he wrote, lasted a moment "then we have the upper hand. Thus it generally goes with 'bitter fights at close quarters'; one side is seized with fear of cold steel and runs off." Hesse did not identify the enemy, whether it was French or American.

Moving on, the Grenadiers quickly captured Varennes and then headed up Hill 231 that overlooked the Surmelin Valley and the now unprotected right flank of the Americans. The Grenadiers' new mission, since it had successfully made a crossing, was to turn westward, take the villages of

Moulins and Paroy and move down the road leading to Crézancy and hit the 38th Infantry's Second Battalion with its two companies astride the Surmelin Valley and two companies holding the south bank of the Marne. It was then to hook up with the Sixth Grenadiers and the 398th Regiment of the German 10th Division at the Bois d'Aigremont, where these two regiments should have already taken care of Colonel Butts's First Battalion and put pressure on the remainder of his regiment as well as the regiments on his flanks, the 7th on his left and the 38th on his right.

A little to the east of the Fifth Grenadiers, the German 175th Infantry crossed the Marne also with hardly any opposition, except for the same harassing artillery fire. Like the Grenadiers, the 175th was to head south along Hill 231, and then they were to take the villages of Launay and Connigis and get behind the Americans. "The grim gray line, like an enormous, unclean caterpillar, crept steadily cross the stream" was the way a historian of the 28th Division described the coming Germans. Another German regiment followed the 175th across the Marne and moved to reinforce the Fifth Grenadiers.

One of the Pennsylvania companies standing in the way of this enormous, unclean caterpillar on the eastern side of the hill was L Company of the 109th Infantry. What happened to C Company then happened to L Company. Because the French had withdrawn, they had left the men from eastern Pennsylvania surrounded. Captain James B. Cousart from Philadelphia and several of his men were cut off from the rest of his company. He formed them into a tight circle and bravely held out until forced to surrender. Almost a month later, writing from prison, Cousart said he was "trying hard to forget the fact that I am a prisoner and no more use to my country as a fighting man." Another Philadelphian, Captain William C. Williams, shot three times, refused medical aid and, although bleeding profusely, kept the enemy at bay with automatic rifle fire until his men had made it safely to the rear. Like Williams, First Lieutenant Maurice J. McGuire from Scranton, was also hit and refused evacuation until what was left of his men were safe. Lieutenant James R. Schoch and Sergeant Frank Benjamin, two more Philadelphians, seeing about fifty of their own men about to be overwhelmed by Germans, rushed toward them, firing their weapons as fast as possible. They hurriedly consolidated the men and ordered them to fall back, fighting their way from tree to tree to where they hoped to find a support line. When they finally made it to the 109th's headquarters three miles away, only sixty-seven men were able to report. Lieutenant Schoch saluted his commander and said, "Sir, I have brought back what was left of L Company."

With the French long gone and L Company dispatched, the Germans now set their sights on the Third Division's right flank. Here the fate of the battle would be decided.

I n the 38th Infantry, the men in the companies holding the eastern slope of the Surmelin Valley sensed something was amiss. While they waited in slit trenches in the early morning, they did not know of the retirement of the French troops on their right flank and, noted Captain Parley Parkinson, the regimental adjutant, "in the semi-darkness, smoke and fog . . . did not realize that the greatly superior numbers of advancing troops were those of the enemy until they were almost upon them."

Grenadier Lieutenant Hesse remembered how the low fog that covered the ground, the tall wheat growing in the fields and the patches of woods hid their movement as they approached the 38th's right flank.

The moment the Americans discovered it was Germans coming toward them, Major Guy Rowe immediately scrawled a warning message to Colonel McAlexander and sent it off by pigeon: "The Boche have infiltrated Mézy and the French are falling back on my right. Will you guard my flanks?" McAlexander got back to Rowe, letting him know that he was sending Major Maxon Lough's Third Battalion "to watch your right flank." To Lough, he ordered: "Look to Rowe's right flank." He relayed the urgent information to the commander of the Sixth Brigade, Brigadier General Crawford: "Rowe reports French have given

way on right." Crawford sent the message on to Major General Dickman, alerting him that the "Germans were advancing through woods in
large numbers northeast of Janvier Farm."

Standing in the way of the three enemy regiments were four platoons in Captain Tom Reid's company, one platoon from Captain
Dineen's E Company and a squad from the Ninth Machine Gun Battalion. The 10th Field Artillery battery at Janvier Farm had by now run
out of ammunition and could no longer be counted on. The crew dis-
abled its guns and withdrew. When the bombardment had opened up
at ten minutes past midnight, Reid, as earlier mentioned, dining with
Dineen in the hillside village of Moulins, sent his First and Second Platoons under the command of First Lieutenant Ralph Eberlin of New
York City up Hill 231 east of Moulins to where McAlexander's slit
trenches had been freshly dug. Leading the First Platoon was First
Lieutenant Carl C. Cramer, who had boasted to his family that he was
eager to cut notches in the handle of his pistol for every German he
killed. Like Eberlin, Cramer was from New York City, but had lived in
Kansas City, Missouri, for the past three years. He was a "bright young
fellow," according to YMCA chaplain George Ridout. Sergeant Campbell,
who would later be promoted to second lieutenant, led the Second Platoon. Just before daylight, Major Rowe ordered Reid to get the rest of his
company up to the trenches without delay. In charge of the Third and
Fourth Platoons were Sergeant John Lake and the Ohioan Second Lieutenant Elmer Focke. Once Reid's entire company was in position, it gave
his men command of the railroad line and the main road coming from
the village of Varennes to Crézancy and down off the hill heading toward
where the bulk of E Company had been placed, its men facing north
across the Marne. If any of the Germans came along the road or tried to
cross the railroad tracks, they'd be in Reid's line of fire.

About 750 yards south of Reid's men and still on Hill 231 were B
and D Companies, the only two companies left in Major Harry Keeley's
First Battalion, and three companies of Major Maxon Lough's Third
Battalion. Keeley, nicknamed "Cupid" because of his "cherubic and

youthful countenance," was a West Pointer, among the youngest cadets in the Class of 1911 at barely twenty-one years of age.

The lead companies of the Fifth Grenadiers, making good progress because there were no French forces to stop them, struck at first daylight—not at Reid's troops, but at the right flank of E Company holding the railroad embankment. From atop the northern edge of Hill 231 they shot down on the Americans with machine guns and rifles.

"Everything that can shoot is turned towards the enemy on the right flank," Lieutenant Hesse wrote. "It must be admitted that he is brave. It is not until the fire of machine guns and the desperate shooting of our infantry reaps a most bloody harvest."

An E Company platoon held in reserve then counterattacked, and succeeded in driving the Germans off the crest of the hill. But only briefly. The Germans regrouped and attacked again, threatening the entire right flank of E Company. With more detachments of Grenadiers coming over the hill, Major Rowe's entire Second Battalion was in danger of being cut off from the rest of the regiment.

Meanwhile, as the sun came up and Reid's men had hardly been in the trenches long enough to get fully organized, more Germans appeared, coming along the Varennes-Crézancy road. Lieutenant Eberlin noticed it was a "considerable number of the enemy deployed and advancing from the northeast and westerly along the road and southerly to the hill tops on our right."

Although Reid could hear guns firing off to his left, he "thought they were French as it was hardly light enough to see just who they were and we had received no message of the withdrawal of the French."

By the time it registered with the Americans in F Company that the enemy was upon them, the Germans were close enough to hurl stick grenades into the trenches. Reid's men responded in a second, readjusting to a three-sided defense and then firing into the midst of the foe. For a moment, the Germans were stopped. When more of them came up the road from their encounter with E Company, reinforcing their comrades, they stormed the trenches anew. Against such a strong force the men of the Second Battalion kept up a murderous defense. "The mass of the enemy increased steadily until met by our fire," Eberlin wrote. Once more the Germans faltered. In fact, some of the Germans, only fifteen yards from the Americans, offered to surrender. But then they changed their minds and resumed the offensive.

Reid's men continued to fire into the enemy until the German attack stalled once more. The enemy appeared confused as to what to do next. Eberlin seized the moment. He ordered his men in the First and Second Platoons out of the trenches in a rush and led them in a daring bayonet charge. Sergeant Chester O. Pierce of Carthage, New York, seeing Missourian William H. Vickery, a fellow sergeant, killed, fought with savage fury, slaughtering a number of the enemy. The charge startled the Germans. They were flung back across the Varennes-Crézancy Road in disarray. In the charge, described as "brilliant" by Captain Jesse Wooldridge, Eberlin was seriously wounded. "Carl C. Cramer took up his work," Wooldridge wrote, "meeting the Boche with steel and dispersing them."

The Third and Fourth Platoons covered the charge with rifle fire, and after the fierce clash of bayonets, Cramer was able to get the wounded Eberlin and his men back to the trenches. Eberlin refused to be sent to a dressing station and stayed on to fight.

Even though Reid reported that the Fifth Grenadiers "were all but destroyed and the advance on Moulins and Crézancy broken," Eberlin's charge had been costly.

"Many men were lost in this maneuver," Reid reported, "for the men went too far. However, Lt. Cramer immediately took charge and by skillful leadership got many men back who otherwise might have been killed or captured."

The wounded were taken to an advanced first-aid station while Reid's men in the slit trenches continued to fire into the enemy. One of the wounded, but not evacuated, was Sergeant David McMinn, shot through both legs. He ordered the men in his platoon to carry him back to the line because his legs were broken, and there he grabbed a rifle and fought until a machine-gun bullet killed him.

A lthough Reid's men were destroying the determined Fifth Grena-diers, the fight on Hill 231 was far from over. Enemy airplanes buzzed over the crest of the ridge. Two of them, their machine guns blazing, attacked the trenches. A spotter airplane flew back to the artil-lery batteries and gave them the exact location of Reid's company. Shells began to land on the Americans. A German patrol then appeared on Reid's left flank. It set up a machine-gun squad and blasted away. Another squad got around behind F Company. The trenches were enfi-laded by fire from the machine guns on the extreme right flank. A mor-tar cannon began to lob shells on their position. The barrage from the enemy artillery then increased. And more machine-gun squads were hurrying to reinforce the shattered Fifth Grenadiers, although the squad from the Ninth Machine Battalion slowed them down.

What had happened to the four companies of the 28th Division a few kilometers to the east—cut off, surrounded and eliminated—was, it certainly seemed, about to happen to McAlexander's F Company.

"Fire was heavy upon the line," Reid recounted. "Our position was entirely too exposed and too well located by machine guns in front (2 or 3) and behind (1), also there was a small mortar at the foot of the hill. We had to move but we could not afford to abandon that position, for by doing so we abandoned the companies on the railroad and the Surmelin Valley."

When it couldn't get any worse, incoming fire from Reid's own divi-sion landed on his troops.

"There were times during that long day and night that the men came to the breaking point," he recalled. "With machine guns across the river, on our flanks, behind us and two aeroplanes over us with their own machine guns wide open; the German artillery AND OUR OWN pounding on us, the men were ready to quit." Reid personally went down the line talking to his men, encouraging them to hold the line. But their own artillery almost proved too much.

If the Germans succeeded in taking Hill 231 and then held the high ground, giving them the great opportunity to fire down on Rowe's Second Battalion, the entire division would be in jeopardy. From the day McAlexander's regiment had been assigned this subsector to defend, he had worried that this would happen if the French withdrew. As he had said earlier when setting up his defenses, it would be "like shooting fish in a bathtub for the Germans to be high above us and on my right flank." Reid knew if his company broke and the enemy gained control of the heights, then the rest of the companies in the Second Battalion "would have all been killed or captured." The officers in his company remembered that McAlexander had fought the French command for the right to get at least partial defense of Hill 231 and there was no way they'd let the old colonel down and withdraw. They'd fight to the last, and damn their own artillery.

"Our decision was to go forward, clean out the German mortar and a machine gun and get around the hill under cover," Reid wrote.

The Americans came out of their trenches for a second time, and pressed the attack. Corporal George F. Curry from Capital Heights, Maryland, took out the machine gunners on the right flank. Then, with another soldier feeding the belt of ammunition into the captured gun, he turned it on the advancing Germans. His action made it possible for one of Reid's platoons to take a position it could hold. The mortar was also stopped, and most of its crew killed. Those who got away carried the mortar with them.

Reid led several platoons to the company's left flank, and then, running, they circled around the side of the hill and came up behind their trenches and took out the machine gunners that had been at their back harassing them. Reid put his men in a skirmish line. After knocking out of action two other machine-gun squads, they rushed forward and retook their old position in the trenches. "Here again we did effective work in preventing crossings."

Sergeant Raymond Fisher from Pine Grove, Pennsylvania, kept watch on the railroad track about seven hundred yards away, and whenever German machine gunners tried to get across he shot them. Reid reported that he hit the first three attempting to cross and that alone he stopped a detachment of about fifteen men. A sniper later killed Sergeant Fisher.

But once again the trenches became "unattainable," according to Reid. Airplanes had discovered the Americans were back in the trenches and directed more artillery fire to fall on them. Machine gunners on the east side of the river were violently "searching the top of the hill, and as before their guns worked around our flank and in the rear of us." When the Germans tried to set up their machine guns along the railroad track or in the valley itself, however, Reid's men were able to put them out of action. Still, F Company was forced to evacuate its trenches.

Again, Reid led his men around the hill to a ravine on the east side of Moulins. Here he came across Major Keeley of the First Battalion and his adjutant, First Lieutenant Earle C. Culpepper. Keeley, whose two companies, B and D, were having their own problems with Germans farther to the south, asked Reid what he planned to do. Reid said that even though the top of Hill 231 was infested with machine guns he and his men were going to retake it, that he was going to strengthen his battered company, now down to 125 men, by rounding up clerks, cooks, supply sergeants and Stokes mortar men inside Moulins. Keeley told him that he'd just left Major Rowe's command post. He said that Rowe had asked him to reinforce Reid's right flank with his own two companies and with the companies in Major Lough's Third Battalion. But Keeley admitted he'd not been able to get the reinforcements from Lough's battalion. Two of the battalion's companies, L and M, were trapped behind enemy lines and were having a hard time breaking through.

And Lough, his battalion trying to hold off more Germans, had just gotten a message by wire from McAlexander:

"Rowe is holding like a rock. I will take care of his left flank but you must protect his right. Let's hold 'em. McAlexander."

Lough found McAlexander's message "the best tonic in the world to hear the voice at the other end of the wire assuring me that everything was right."

The only reinforcements Keeley had were his B and D Companies under the command of Captain William F. Freehoff from Vestal Center, New York, "or such of them as he [Freehoff] had assembled." But in the woods he'd lost contact with Freehoff and couldn't find him or his men. Keeley felt he'd better get back to his command post at Paroy and gather up what troops he had there and send them to join Reid and what was left of F Company. Once back at his command post, Keeley felt he'd be better off fighting than waiting around and not know what was going on. He was working his way back to Reid when he located one of Freehoff's platoons, commanded by First Lieutenant Ed C. Bellinger. Taking charge, Keeley ordered the men he had with him and Bellinger's platoon into a skirmish line and, hearing the sound of guns and grenades, headed in that direction. As he neared Reid's position, he at last ran into Freehoff and the remains of B and D Companies. It was pretty much a ragtag outfit, with not many officers and sergeants to lead the troops. Keeley sent Freehoff and his men on toward Reid's right flank, and then returned once again to his command post.

Meanwhile, Reid had split his men into squads and formed them into two sections and placed Lieutenants Focke and Cramer in charge. He collected more ammo from an ammunition dump near Moulins. When he was ready, he once again led his men up and over Hill 231.

"This time we had a pretty skirmish on our right flank with some machine guns, but they were soon out of the fight as our riflemen were doing deadly work," he reported. "We retook the position on the brow of the hill." When the old line had been reestablished, Reid sent out patrols on his flanks while he and a sergeant left the trenches to scout the enemy's position. They soon discovered they'd been cut off from their own men. He and the sergeant had a "lively scuffle getting back," he recalled, downplaying what they'd actually gone through. But what they and the patrols found was German machine-gun squads seemingly advancing everywhere—on the left flank and again behind them.

"We found the woods full of them."

It was now midmorning and Reid's men were utterly exhausted. Realizing that his company had been surrounded and severed from the rest of the Second Battalion, Reid placed his men in a right-angle formation, half of them facing north and the other half facing east. He next brought together all his officers and noncommissioned officers. He said they had two choices. Because they were cut off, they could either battle their way out or try to hold the main road and the east slope of the valley until ordered to withdraw. They decided to hold—but if it got too precarious then they'd fight their way back down the hill.

About this time a runner from Major Rowe's command post worked his way into the trenches and handed a message to Reid. It carried old information, that Major Keeley was organizing two companies on Reid's right, which he knew. But it gave him new orders and a sentence to buck up his troops. "You must close the gap between you and E [Company] at least keep it under close observation for our line must not be pierced."

"You have all covered yourself with glory. Keep it up."

And over on the west flank of the 38th, Wooldridge's and Herlihy's companies were then also covering themselves in glory.

It was a critical time for McAlexander's regiment. He sensed his brigade and division commanders were worried that the Germans were about to overrun his position. He dispatched Lieutenant Colonel Adams by motorcycle to Crawford's command post and then on to division headquarters with the message "I am holding my ground and will hold it." Crawford countered with a tentative order, "Fall back if you think best."

McAlexander answered, "Is it up to my decision?"

"Yes," came the reply.

"Then I hold my lines."

For the next five to six hours, until late in the afternoon, Reid kept his eye on E Company, which was on his immediate left, while his own company held its position "under desultory shell fire and searching machine gun fire." When ammunition ran low, Private First Class James

B. Sircy, a member of one of the automatic rifle squads, dashed through artillery fire to an ammunition dump and returned to the trenches with enough ammo to keep them supplied, buying a little more time.

At about four o'clock, Rowe ordered E Company to retire from the railroad to the Aqueduct Line and for Reid to cover the company's withdrawal. The retirement went off without a hitch. E Company, now under the command of First Lieutenant Howard Ross since Dineen had been put out of action, joined Reid's men in the trenches on Hill 231. The teacher and coach from Blanchester, Ohio, who had enlisted in the National Guard in 1916, turned over his company to Reid. With the additional troops, Reid reorganized his forces.

"We established a good line," he wrote, "and were prepared to hold as long as necessary when orders arrived from Major Rowe to withdraw to the aqueduct line."

When he had a chance, Lieutenant Focke, commanding one of Reid's platoons, wrote to his mother, letting her know he was still among the living: "If you don't hear from me very soon you will know that I was in the thick of it and did my bit. . . . Let me tell you war is Hell but it's a great consolation to live in the fear of God."

At an advanced first-aid station in a farmhouse outside of Paroy on the road to Mézy, scores of wounded soldiers were then evacuated under the tender care of the battalion surgeon, Captain Hoddie Daniels, the doctor from Elkins, West Virginia, who had enlisted in the army in 1917 after his four-year-old son had died. Daniels made sure that as many of the wounded as possible were brought down the hill to a secure location before the Germans moved into Paroy. Meanwhile, the combined companies fought their way down the hill to the Aqueduct Line, the Second Battalion's second line of defense, where it joined up with Freehoff's troops. Freehoff took control of the three companies, placing E Company on the right of his company and Reid's men on the left. While E Company got into its position, a sniper shot Ross in the upper left arm, shattering the bone. Although the wound was severe, the lieutenant refused to leave his company. The arm was not tended to for forty-eight hours and then was almost amputated.

A mile up the hill, the Germans swarmed over the first-aid station. Guards were placed over the wounded as well as the medics who had been left behind.

Down at the Aqueduct Line with the wounded he had helped evacuate, Captain Daniels was not about to desert the others. There were at least forty litter patients still up at his first-aid station. Daniels crawled back up the hill with a few soldiers to rescue them. While he was working his way to the first-aid station, three men at the Aqueduct Line also felt something had to be done to save their own wounded. Sergeant Age W. Swenson; Cook William H. Jones from Fair Haven, Vermont; YMCA secretary Richard Shreve, who had been driving wounded all day to the first-aid station in his own Model T Ford; as well as several unidentified soldiers jumped into trucks, ambulances and the Model T and recklessly drove the mile toward Paroy. As the rescue convoy barreled up the hill, detachments of German machine gunners and snipers tried to stop them, but failed.

Daniels and the men with him, after crawling on their hands and knees in a ditch, jumped up, surprising fourteen Germans. Daniels demanded they surrender. The Germans fired at Daniels. He and his men returned fire, killing eight. Shreve, Jones and Swenson and the men with them, in their vehicles, made it to the first-aid station, where they overpowered the remaining guards. Daniels then supervised the evacuation of his patients. While loading the wounded into the trucks and ambulances, they had to fight off more Germans trying to close in on them. Yet they were able to finish loading the wounded into the vehicles and strapping some of them down. Then they roared down the hill to the Aqueduct Line.

Still on top of Hill 231, but a mile south of the Second Battalion, were the remains of Lough's Third Battalion, L Company, led by Captain Edward F. Smith, General Dickman's aide from Vermont who'd sought a battlefield command and got it from McAlexander, and M Company, in the charge of Spanish American War veteran Captain Robert G. Woodside from Pittsburgh. Woodside had his men dig trenches and then cover them with treetops and branches so that hopefully enemy airplanes wouldn't be able to spot them.

Throughout the morning, stragglers had been coming across the ridge, Americans from the 38th Infantry and from the decimated 109th and 110th Infantries of the 28th Division, and French from the 125th Division who hadn't pulled back with the rest of their men.

"I stopped all the stragglers that came through on their way to the rear," Woodside reported. He separated the Americans from the French and added them to his line. It gave him an additional one hundred men, including the "remnants of one whole platoon from the 28th Division."

Among the stragglers were two French officers. They approached Woodside and told him to withdraw. They explained to him that he could not possibly hold the position he was taking. "I told them we were going to stay there as I felt such a course necessary to protect the portion of our regiment in the valley and on the slopes of the hill behind us."

The fighting continued through the entire afternoon and into the evening. The combined companies, F and E, frustrated the elements of the enemy's 175th Regiment and what was now left of the Fifth Grenadiers. Men from Herlihy's H Company joined Reid's "conglomerate" of Stokes mortar men, signalmen, cooks, mechanics, men from supplies and Reid's company clerk. With the Germans ready to occupy Hill 231, perhaps for good, and thus gain the advantage to take the Surmelin Valley, Reid, afraid the enemy force would soon be too strong to be routed, ordered one more charge, his fourth of the day. Reid had to beat the Germans to the top of the hill. He was also very concerned that his men had no cover whatsoever, not a tree or bush or rock, and enemy planes circling overhead would then be able to pick off the Americans. He divided his patched-together company into squads and sections.

The charge caught the Germans flat-footed. Reid's troops stormed the ridge before the enemy knew what had hit them. "I beat them to it," Reid told McAlexander, "routing numerous machine guns and standing the infantry off with rifle fire."

Lieutenant Hesse of the Fifth Grenadiers, whose regiment had been destroyed, was stunned at the slaughter. "Never have I seen so many dead men, never such frightful battle scenes. The Americans, lying in a grain field in a semi-circle, allowed two companies to approach within thirty to fifty paces and then shot practically all of them down in heaps. This enemy had nerve, we must give him credit for that; but he also displayed a savage roughness. 'The Americans kill everybody!' was the cry of terror of July 15th, which for a long time stuck in the bones of our men."

The Germans failed to take Hill 231, and Reid and the men under him and those in the other battalions fighting by his side saved the Third Division's right flank and—if the Germans were indeed headed for Paris—they all had played a major role in blocking the way.

Fighting on three fronts, McAlexander's 38th Infantry had refused to budge.

Writing for the entire division in a letter to Fox Conner, Chief of Staff Kelton made it clear that the troops under General Dickman's command never left the south bank of the Marne. He noted that although the Sixth Brigade took the brunt of the attack, the Fifth Brigade, led by Brigadier General Fred Sladen, with the 7th Regiment protecting the 30th's left flank and the 4th Regiment sending reinforcements to bolster the 30th, had also made a heroic stand. "We did not drive the Boche back; we killed him by the thousands and those we did not kill we took prisoners. We killed them before they crossed the river, we killed them in the river and we killed them on the south bank as fast as the machine guns and rifles could pump lead into them."

Recalled a devastated General Walther Reinhardt, chief of the general staff of the German 7th Army, "Then and there, the truth came home to us! We simply faced a task beyond our strength!" To him and to his fellow officers, "There could be no doubt anymore that we had not a ghost of chance to force the river successfully."

Then, as soon as darkness covered the battlefield, a crushed General Hugo von Kathen ordered his corps to withdraw behind the Marne.

The 3rd Divison had held its ground.

After the battle, General Dickman was ecstatic, as were all the bloodied and weary men in his division.

When he got the chance, Lieutenant Robinson Murray, in Reid's company, sent off a letter to Dear Peggy Piersol. "I am still perfectly all right, after being right on the nose of the attempted Boche drive and in the front line, too. It was just plain hell while it lasted, but the tide has been turned for the present. We're heading in the right direction." After the war, he and Peggy were married in Paris.

McAlexander penned a letter to his wife on July 20. "The great battle of which you have no doubt read is over. My division played a wonderful part which you will never see in the newspapers. But for the 3rd Division, the Germans would now be on another drive for Paris, but the 8 miles of line assigned to us held like a rock. The French division on our right broke, and the Germans got in our rear, still we refused to go."

When it was over, and McAlexander had spent "the most anxious day" of his life with his regiment fighting on three fronts, he sent another letter to his wife. With more than a touch of braggadocio, he wrote, "Lordy, her army got licked right here on this ground and 'Ulie' done it."

But still there was much more to do.

CHAPTER 23

"WHILE WE ARE YET ALIVE, LET'S GIVE 'EM HELL!"

July 18, 1918. The great switch was on—the "double game" as Marshal Ferdinand Foch had termed it.

For too long the Allies had fought defensively, with their backs against the wall or, in the case of the British in Flanders, against the sea. Throughout most of 1918, the Germans had been on the offensive, gaining chunks of vital territory held by the Allies. Five times since the start of the year they had hurled major attacks against their enemy—the last, of course, *Friedensturm*, Ludendorff's so-called Peace Assault. But now from Soissons to Champagne the combined French and American forces had held. The battered Boche were withdrawing from the south bank, their dead littering the ground and clogging the river by the thousands. From the shaken German High Command, there'd be no more offensive strategies issued. The armies of Crown Prince Wilhelm and Crown Prince Rupprecht were backpedaling toward the protection of the Hindenburg Line, a massive defensive bulwark that stretched from the Swiss Alps to the North Sea. And for every step of the way, the Germans made certain that the Allies paid dearly.

When word that the Germans had been stopped and were in retreat reached Paris, the citizens there went wild. In New York City church bells rang, and crowds gathered in the streets and cheered. Times Square was a madhouse of joy. Stocks on Wall Street roared upward.

The tide of the war had turned.

"The effects of the victory were electrical and far-reaching," General Dickman proclaimed. "With Heine on the run, the American soldier felt more confident than ever. All thought of moving the seat of government from Paris was abandoned. Our war-worn Allies passed from gloom to exultation and confidence in ultimate success. Some of the newer and only partially trained American divisions had undergone a successful test in battle. The Germans had lost the offensive; it was their last attack in the war. The Allied High Command could now undertake the general offensive with confidence."

Marshal Foch concurred. In his memoirs, he wrote, "On July 17th the Germans had been reduced to impotence; on the 18th the guns of the Allies were in turn to make their thunder heard at the time and place which had been fixed upon."

Foch's double game, which had been in the works for some time, meant that while he was devising a plan of defense along the Allies' entire front, he and General Henri Pétain, at the same time, were making preparations for a major offensive that would eventually throw twelve French and twelve American divisions and eight British divisions at the Germans. Their offensive plan was to go into effect as soon as the Germans had been halted—the perfect one-two punch. On the eve of the Second Battle of the Marne, Foch had gone to Pétain's headquarters, where they had "definitely decided that the French counter offensive would be launched as a reply to the German attack."

Two days after the Germans had launched their failed attack, Foch was then convinced the enemy had been "reduced to impotence." Sarcastically, he wrote, "What, indeed, had been the results of this 'Friedensturm' which, it had been so loudly proclaimed, was to bring peace by one victorious rush? Nothing but bitterness and deception, forerunners of defeat." Foch was now ready to counterattack.

At 4:45 on the morning of July 18, General Charles Mangin's Tenth Army, poised on the Aisne River ten miles west of Soissons, and General Jean Marie Degoutte's Sixth Army, waiting on the Marne River east of Château-Thierry, opened Foch's counteroffensive. The Tenth Army was made up of 18 infantry divisions, 3 cavalry divisions, nearly 500 artillery batteries, 41 air squadrons and 375 tanks. Two of the infantry divisions at Mangin's disposal were the First and Second U.S. Divisions comprising the American III Corps. Degouttte's army was now made up of elements of the American Fourth, Twenty-sixth and Twenty-eighth Infantry Divisions. Because the Third Division was then in the process of receiving replacement troops for the men lost during the days of fighting on the banks of the Marne, it had been temporarily shifted to the French Ninth Army. Once it was brought back to its original strength, it would rejoin the Sixth Army and be a part of Foch's counteroffensive. Therefore, it was not to cross the Marne on the 18th. The 38th Army Corps had also been temporarily detached from the Sixth Army and much to the disappointment of its commander, General de Mondesir, had to stay south of the Marne for the time being while it waited for General Dickman's division to be refitted and reequipped.

Major Walker, although his regiment had been relieved, heard the big guns in the early morning and awoke with a start, realizing it was not desultory firing. The noise was too great. To him, it meant one of two things—either the Germans had launched another massive offensive or the Allies were making their great counterattack. He began to worry about the men in his battalion. If the Germans were attacking they were in no condition to be called back into battle. He was much relieved when he found out it was the start of Marshal Foch's offensive.

In the meantime, General Dickman's first order of business was to clear out any Germans still south of the river or lurking in the forests that covered Hill 231. Clearing Hill 231, the Moulins Ridge, in conjunction with the 73rd Division of the French Ninth Army, and pursuing the enemy until they were either all captured or killed or had fled north of the river, went to Colonel McAlexander's 38th Infantry's First and Third Battalions, commanded by Majors Harry Keeley and Maxon Lough.

The Second Battalion, in the meantime, which had taken the brunt of the German attack a few days earlier and was then hit with gas shells when it was holed up in the woods, was held in reserve. One reason: its commander, Major Guy Rowe, had been put out of action, blinded by mustard gas from the German barrage, and was on his way to Base Hospital #18 in Bazoilles-sur-Meuse. Captain Wooldridge said of his commander that he was "at his best in a fight. He was one of the purest types of soldier. A true chip off the 'Old Rock,' McAlexander, with his tenacious audacity, stubbornness of purpose and mighty power of will that no enemy can subdue." Rowe's last message from the field to McAlexander, moments before he was blinded, was sent at 4:30 a.m. It read, "Too much mustard. We will probably have to move. Where do you want me to go front or rear?" Now, while his battalion went into a reserve position, for Rowe, personally, with him losing his sight, that was, indeed, to the rear. He stayed at the base hospital for almost two months, until his sight came back, and did not return to the regiment until September 16, as its operations officer.

Dickman reported that although directly in front of his division the conditions were stable, to the east the "situation still was considered dangerous on account of the German positions." Pursuing what was left of the enemy, driving them off Hill 231 and back across the Marne and thus securing the division's right flank, was a top priority.

With his regiment now on the move, although not yet ordered to cross the Marne, McAlexander felt his blood stirring for the first time since his men had checked the Germans at the Marne. His one fear was that his regiment might be relieved; after all, Colonel Butts's 30th Infantry had been relieved and ordered to the rear. And then Butts had been removed as commander of his regiment—although he later took command of the 7th Infantry and led it across the Marne in pursuit of the enemy.

O ne of the Third Battalion pursuit units was the First Rifle Platoon of K Company, led by Westport, Connecticut, resident Second Lieutenant John Henry Hilldring. Although actual hard hand-to-hand combat south of the Marne had dwindled after the 16th, and had ceased altogether by the 19th, the Germans on the north side of the river continually shelled the American position with artillery and gas, even though a number of their own soldiers were still there. The men in Hilldring's platoon, as they waited for something positive to do, and dodged bursting shells and constantly wore gas masks that itched and rubbed their faces raw, found their spirits slipping. Like McAlexander, they needed action.

On the 20th, the colonel ordered Lough's battalion to finally take up a defensive position along the crest of Hill 231 in the Bois de Conde, a forest so densely covered with trees and leafy bushes, some as high as six feet, that keeping in visual contact with other units was extremely difficult. The battalion was in touch with elements of A Company of the First Battalion on the right at the village of Launay and elements of the 138th French Infantry Regiment on the left at Les Etange Farm. At tenthirty that morning, Lieutenant Hilldring had been summoned to his company's command post, where Captain R. G. Moss informed him that the Germans were withdrawing and that in thirty minutes their battalion was to attack northward toward the Marne through the tanglement of the Bois de Conde.

"The information about the enemy and the order for the attack electrified the platoon," Hilldring noted. "Doubt and uncertainly were dispelled. In the fraction of a minute confidence and high spirits returned and despite hunger and fatigue there appeared at once an eagerness for the attack."

A little after 11 a.m. the First Platoon, along with the other platoons in K Company, as well as the other companies of the battalion, began to thread their way through the forest in columns of twos, with M Company in the lead. The morning was sunny, but it was dark in the woods because of the lush underbrush. The soldiers could see no more than ten feet in any direction.

Captain Moss ordered Hilldring to "March close enough to Company M to see it at all times. Go where it goes. Never mind your compass."

For the first time in weeks no small arms fire could be heard. Even with German artillery still busy dropping shells into the woods east of the battalion, there was a death-like stillness in the Surmelin Valley that reminded the men of the same stillness they had felt on the eve of the 14th. Uneasiness came over them. The men in Hilldring's platoon also sensed the same uneasiness in their greenhorn lieutenant, who'd never led soldiers on a patrol before. It had just dawned on Hilldring that this was its first offensive action of the war for the division and that his platoon had to be ready to fight at a moment's notice.

Struggling through the forest, German artillery shells whistling down around them, every eye nervously searching the underbrush for the enemy amid the explosions, equipment, from bandoleers to canteens, clinking against sweaty bodies, the battalion slogged its way for more than a mile without seeing or hearing a single foe. Reaching a clearing, Hilldring and his men could see the vast Marne Valley from Mézy all the way to Varennes. Then incoming friendly artillery shells from 75-millimeter guns hit them. First German fire and then, again, American fire. And there was no way for the battalion to signal back to their own artillery for them to stop.

"Gloom descended on the battalion," recalled Hilldring.

But the soldiers kept inching forward. The battalion turned west and by late evening started down Hill 231, the scene of desperate fighting only a few days before, to Moulins. Hilldring's men spent the night in and around the village, where the bodies of the dead seemed to be everywhere—Germans and Americans alike. In the morning of the 20th the battalion continued on down the hill and reached the west bank of the Surmelin River, a tired and hungry band of soldiers. The only way to cross the small river was over an unguarded railroad trestle. Not sure if the enemy had their sights on the trestle, Hilldring had his men go over it in squad rushes—just in case. It was midnight when they reached their assigned subsector behind the railroad embankment near Mézy. They set up listening posts on the river and organized themselves for defense instead for offense. And waited for further orders.

Still there was not a single enemy to be seen. All the officers agreed that the Germans had "beat a hasty retreat."

Settling in, the company received its first hot meal in a week. After downing their meal, the soldiers were ordered to bury the dead littering their sector. A second order told the men to prepare for inspection. It meant they had to wash, shave, brush their torn and dusty and in some cases blood-encrusted uniforms as best they could, and clean their rifles and sidearms. The men were certain the inspection meant the regiment was to be relieved. The rumor went through the platoon like a "conflagration," Hilldring wrote. No one tried to stop it.

"The men agreed that the 38th Infantry had been at the front for one month and twenty days without relief, had stood the shock of the Friedensturm and had driven the last German to the other side of the Marne," Hilldring recalled. "Carrying parties came up with fantastic tales of the hordes of fresh troops jammed in the rear areas, under orders to take over the whole sector of the division."

But the inspection had nothing to do with the relief of the regiment. McAlexander had come from his command post to check on his troops. Inspecting them, he was impressed with their "excellence of appearance and apparent state of high morale." To Hilldring, he asked if the men were ready for battle.

"Yes, sir," Hilldring replied. "But they expect to be relieved."

"Do they want to be relieved?"

"Yes, sir."

"Do you think they should be relieved?"

"Yes, sir."

"We shall see," McAlexander said and then walked off.

The colonel's regiment was still waiting for its next order—whether it was to be relieved, hold its position or—as he wanted—cross the river and resume fighting.

The day Lough's Third Battalion had started its pursuit through the Bois de Conde, Keeley's First Battalion had been holed up around the small village of Paroy awaiting its orders. The commander of B Company, Captain William Freehoff, took over the cellar of a farmhouse on the Mézy Road, the same farmhouse that Captain Hoddie Daniels, the Second Battalion surgeon, had used as an advanced first-aid station, the same farmhouse where the West Virginian led a rescue mission to save forty wounded soldiers. The surgeon, who had not gone back in reserve with his battalion, was nearby scouring the woods for any wounded who had been lost in the underbrush and left behind. For two days and a night, before Freehoff and his company showed up, Daniels had stayed at the farmhouse with the men he'd already found and tended to their wounds. During those days, the enemy was still around. They repeatedly attacked the farmhouse. But Daniels and his medical team, including litter bearers, succeeded in fighting them off. A number of times Daniels had to put down his medical utensils and use his pistol. Now, on the 19th, he and several enlisted men with him came out of the woods into the yard of the farmhouse. The captain, who in 1917, after his son died, had left his family and given up his comfortable medical career back in the Appalachian Mountains to join the army, never made it inside the farmhouse. A sniper shot and killed him and the men with him. The death of this heroic, passionate doctor sent a wave of sadness throughout the Second Battalion.

The day before Daniels was killed, Captain Freehoff's company was in a defensive position in and around Paroy when a sentry heard noises in the woods. Not knowing what to do, the spooked sentry opened fire in that direction. The entire company then began to fire. Freehoff yelled at them to stop. His men weren't firing at any hidden Germans, but at a patrol party from the Third Battalion. It angered Freehoff that he had not been told that other soldiers from another battalion might be in his area, unless they had accidently wandered in. Fortunately no one was seriously hurt.

Only on the 20th had the soldiers finally gotten their first full meal and full night's sleep since July 14. During daylight, work details were busy burying the dead.

Captain Wooldridge over in G Company recalled how glorious was the food served to his men. They had been eating nothing but goulash taken from dead German soldiers. "My cooks mixed a combination of corned beef hash and canned tomatoes that was a gastronomic poem." He and his striker had to share the only mess kit between them, Wooldridge eating first and the striker waiting his turn.

The next morning, the 21st, at 9:15, General de Mondesir, itching to rejoin the Sixth Army already fighting across the Marne, received orders to move his 38th Army Corps, now consisting of the Third Division and the French 39th Division, north immediately and rejoin the Sixth Army in vigorous pursuit of the enemy. To General Dickman, the ecstatic de Mondesir said he wanted all his troops to cross the Marne at once, "even if they had to swim." The 38th and 7th Infantries were to assemble around the villages of Crézancy and Fossoy and cross the Marne at Mézy. The 4th Infantry was to cross at Château-Thierry. The 30th was to stay south of the river still in reserve. Once reaching the north bank, the division was to attack in a northeasterly direction the villages of Chartèves, Jaulgonne and Le Charmel.

Wooldridge had just bedded down in his bloodstained, filthy uniform, as he described it, his eyes bloodshot, hair matted and every bone and tissue "screaming for rest," for his first real sleep, when he received an order that all captains in his battalion received: "Report to the Major at once."

At ten-thirty that morning company captains of the First Battalion were summoned to Keeley's command post north of Paroy. The major gave them their new orders. That night or early the following morning, they were told, the 38th Infantry was to advance to Mézy, where it would then begin to cross the Marne. Pontoon bridges were to be thrown across the river by the Sixth Engineers. Keeley said that the Third Battalion would cross first, followed by his battalion. The Second Battalion, now led by acting major Parley Parkinson, who'd replaced the blinded Guy Rowe, would be the last to cross the river. The mission for Keeley's battalion was to capture Chartèves. The Third Battalion's mission was to capture Jaulgonne and continue on to the village of Le Charmel. Freehoff's B Company was selected as the advance guard and would immediately follow the Third Battalion over the Marne.

McAlexander's long-awaited switch from defense to offense was at last under way.

Rumors, however, had resounded throughout the First Battalion as they had through the Third Battalion: the regiment, instead of attacking, was about to be relieved. After all, the 30th Infantry had been relieved as early as July 16. As with the rumors in Hilldring's Third Battalion a lieutenant noted that the 38th "had been on the front for one month and 21 days."

Another rumor that percolated throughout Freehoff's B Company, and it turned out to be true, was that the regiment was going to cross the Marne and, in fact, attack to the northeast.

"This was greeted with many growls and much profanity," recalled First Lieutenant Cleon L. Williams, "for the men felt they were entitled to a little rest and a little food, two things that had been very scarce since July 15." One of Freehoff's soldiers said he had heard that the 38th could not be relieved because it had become known as a regiment of shock troops. "The term 'shock troops' changed everything," Williams noted. "Once more the men were ready and eager to go."

When the order was issued, "The 38th will cross the Marne tonight," according to Lovejoy, it "thrilled and startled everyone."

The battle-torn village of Mézy, still under German artillery bombardment and with enemy snipers and machine gunners hidden among the trees on the Marne's opposite bank, making it a dangerous place, was to be the gathering point for McAlexander's entire regiment. With the battalions marching toward Mézy, two companies from the Sixth Engineers, B and F, rolled into the village on July 21 in trucks loaded with timber, boats and what bridging material they had, and it wasn't much. They hoped to use whatever the Germans had left behind in their retreat over the Marne. As the lead truck, driven by Private Frank K. Neumark, neared the river, it came under machine-gun fire from close range. The men in the truck scattered, finding shelter where they could. Neumark ran back up the road to warn the drivers of the other trucks to stop. He stayed by the roadside to alert the entire convoy. Neumark was standing out in the open, and it didn't take long before an enemy bullet crashed into his skull, killing him.

Sergeant Charles O. McKay jumped from one of the trucks, collected several engineers with rifles and automatic rifles and went toward the river to knock out the machine-gun nest. But the Germans manning the machine gun quit firing. McKay decided the best way to locate the nest was to expose himself, draw fire and have his men riddle it with their own fire. It was a bad idea. He caught a bullet in the lungs. First Lieutenant C. N. Iry, hearing his sergeant had been hit, crawled over to him. He and Private John E. Eberle, one of the riflemen, dressed McKay's wound and together dragged him fifty yards up the road with bullets sweeping past them. They got him to a shelter. For McKay the wound proved mortal.

Iry, a graduate of the Mellon Institute of Industrial Research in Pittsburgh, was then put in charge of a detail to construct a floating bridge. But the German machine guns and artillery firing on the river made the work extremely dangerous. To cover Iry and his engineers, the 38th Infantry's I Company moved into Mézy with one platoon from the Ninth Machine Gun Battalion. They took up positions next to the engineers and were soon peppering the north bank of the Marne with automatic rifle and machine-gun fire.

Throughout the day five-ton trucks, laden with planks and two-by-fours, nails, bolts and coils of rope, rolled into Mézy and up to the banks of the Marne and dumped their loads. Lieutenant Hilldring, with the other men of his Third Battalion who had taken shelter in street gutters, behind walls or cellars of bombed-out houses, remembered watching as "one engineer platoon at a time advanced to the edge of the water in broad daylight under direct fire of enemy machine guns at close range. Here the men laced the pontoons and timbers together until exhaustion and casualties necessitated their relief by another platoon."

Hilldring's battalion was also taking on artillery fire. "Every niche in the small town had a man or two crouching in it." One shell hit the house where the Third Platoon had taken shelter. The wall collapsed, killing nine soldiers. The Second Platoon was also struck. More men were killed, and its commander was trapped under a pile of rubble. "The explosions of large caliber mortar shells made themselves heard above the smaller projectiles and above the clatter of the machine guns along the river. It was a terrifying experience which no man could survive without mental, if not physical, damage."

Amid the bombing and the terror, the engineers had to go on a scavenger hunt, salvaging any German bridging material they could find.

With two engineers already dead and others getting wounded, it was decided to put off construction until dark.

It was also decided to send Sergeant First Class John G. Boyle and his platoon from B Company of the engineers across the river to clear out some of the snipers and machine-gun nests. Boyle and his men found, among the salvaged equipment and other things collected in Mézy, a rowboat painted a brilliant white. As they carried it down to the river, German snipers "immediately got busy and wasted a great deal of ammunition," pointed out one engineer. The boat was launched in a small, protective inlet that had to be crossed before the patrol could begin to row from the south bank to the north bank. After several trips back and forth, with Corporal Howard Claypoole from Vineland, New Jersey, working the oars, the patrol landed safely on the German side. Boyle divided his platoon into small parties, sending them out on both flanks to make a disturbance and hopefully draw the enemy's fire, thus revealing their location. Corporals Dewey M. Sharp and George Gormley volunteered to serve as scouts. They crept ahead of the platoon, peering into the brush for any signs of the snipers. Before the men on the flanks could make their disturbance, Sharp and Gormley found the snipers. They exchanged gunfire, silencing the enemy. The patrol then located other snipers and machine-gun nests and silenced them as well. They returned to the south bank, but had hardly cleared out the entire enemy that was still ready and determined to keep the engineers from bridging the Marne. Even if the pontoon bridges and footbridges were successfully pushed over the swift currents of the river, the Germans had to keep the Americans from gaining a bridgehead on the north bank.

Lieutenant Lovejoy was astonished at the work of the engineers. "In broad daylight," he wrote, "those carpenters and mechanics set in place the pontoon boats and planks while under continuous fire from 77's who also poured down from the heights north of the river to those workers on the Marne. But nothing stopped them. Indeed squads crossed the river in small skiffs, all the while under fire, to take possession of German pontoons and bridge-building equipment which had been left on the north bank when the drive the week before had failed."

Miraculously, at least for the moment, the shells exploding in the river and sending up towers of gushing water failed to hit the bridge as foot by foot it began to span the Marne, held afloat by airtight gasoline drums. But as the engineers placed the bridge closer to the north bank, it was struck by a shell, wrecking the part they were working on and wounding several engineers. The men repaired the damage and continued on.

When the sweat-drenched and river-soaked engineers finally finished their first pontoon bridge, they nailed up a plank on its south ramp. Written on the plank: "Made in Germany."

It was four in the morning of the 22nd, hours behind schedule, when the Third Battalion, after enduring the entire night of mortar bombardment that had set what was left of Mézy ablaze, with flames towering above the crumbled skyline, started across the narrow bridge just as the "final lash was tied and nail driven."

Wooldridge recalled, "So at the first peep of dawn, when the sun began to chase fantastic shadows—somewhere—we went over the pontoon bridge, 'Made in Germany,' but repaired and reinforced by the 6th Engineers, and again came in grips with our old enemies at Jaulgonne."

Crossing the pontoon bridge, the 38th once again took fire from enemy machine guns. Artillery shells landed in the river, churning the water so it looked like a boiling cauldron. Although the regiment suffered casualties, it kept moving over the Marne. One officer observed that the battalion "marched with a dirge-like cadence." Lough's Third Battalion hiked through stands of trees and up the hill toward Les Franquets Farm northeast of Chartèves. At 6 a.m. Keeley's First Battalion came next, led by Captain Freehoff's B Company. The battalion marched along the river road toward Jaulgonne. Rowe's Second Battalion, with him now out of the picture, crossed at eight-thirty. In a support role, the Second followed the First as it moved on Jaulgonne.

A day earlier, on the 21st, east of Mézy near the village of Fossoy, the 7th Infantry had crossed the Marne in boats, while near Château-Thierry the 4th Infantry had clambered over on pontoon bridges. Now, with the 38th on its way north, all the infantry regiments of the Third Division, with the exception of the 30th, which would follow in two days, were finally engaged with the enemy as part of Foch's great counteroffensive.

For the division, its mission was to clear Hill 210, capture Les Franquets Farm near Chartèves and then Jaulgonne and Le Charmel. The road leading to and from these villages was set on a mile-wide strip of open ground in the Argentol Valley. The road was surrounded on both sides by the hilly Forêt de Fere to the west and the equally hilly Forêt de Ris to the east. Each forest was nearly impenetrable and the hills rose to over four hundred feet. According to General Dickman, the hills afforded "a succession of artillery positions commanding the road in the Argentol Valley, all the way down to the Marne." He noted there were "ideal locations for machine guns in the edges of the forests and in small patches of the woods in the clearing itself." The advance on Le Charmel "presented a serious problem, in which it was likely that heavy losses would be incurred."

McAlexander felt that taking Les Franquets Farm, although not easy pickings, should be given to the Third Battalion because, like the Second Battalion, it had had a rough go of it in the Surmelin Valley. The First Battalion he gave the harder task of capturing Jaulgonne.

"I sent Major Harry J. Keeley's battalion forward along the highway to capture Jaulgonne," he later commented. "Lough to go along the ridge to the west of the highway and to attack the Germans known to be at the Franquets Farm, above and westward of Jaulgonne." After taking the farm and cleaning out Chartèves, Lough's men were to climb the steep slopes of Hill 210, which loomed over the village like a mountain, eliminate the enemy atop the hill, advance through the southern edge of Fôret de Fere and, joining Keeley's battalion, march toward Jaulgonne.

McAlexander set up his command post in a sandpit on the Chartèves-Jaulgonne road. Here he could keep tabs on both battalions and, if need be, personally direct his troops while they attacked Les Franquets Farm and Jaulgonne.

"As Keeley rounded the main curve in the road that heads straight into Jaulgonne, he came in plain sight of and within machine gun range of the village defenders, consisting of our old contestants, the 10th Landwehr Division, 372nd, 277th and 378th Infantry Regiments," McAlexander wrote. "He was also in full view of the German artillery at Charmel some distance above Jaulgonne. The Germans cut loose with everything they had."

The artillery shelling cut into Keeley's battalion, causing some casualties. The major immediately sent a runner back to McAlexander's command post. He needed his colonel to come forward to assess the situation. By the time he reached Keeley, McAlexander knew a frontal attack on Jaulgonne would be suicidal: "Remembering my near-capture by Indians while a second lieutenant 28 years before, I personally led my troops off to the left of the road where we were partially screened by trees, shrubbery and some farm buildings. After the assault was well under way I gave my attention to the other battalions of the regiment."

To get a better view of the progress of the battle, the colonel moved into open ground. The German artillery and machine gunners took aim at him. Nearby and to the rear of McAlexander, Wooldridge was crawling with his company to get into a new position, away from the pounding shells. Ahead of him the captain was stunned to see his commander between him and the enemy in what he described as a "shell and bullet swept area as a giant scythe might sweep a cornfield." Wooldridge confessed that he was "fearful of our morale if we lost this cold, deliberate North Star, who guided our destinies." He crawled over to McAlexander amid the endless thunder of exploding shells.

"Colonel," he shouted to him, "don't you know that nothing can live in this place?"

"Well," McAlexander shot back, as if defying fate, "while we are yet alive, let's give 'em hell!"

Wooldridge hollered to him that German *minenwerfers* were pummeling wounded troops in the rear. The fact that they were hitting these defenseless men who were being treated at dressing stations drew McAlexander's ire. It was the same cold-blooded shelling that a year earlier had killed women and children in a Paris church and angered McAlexander so much that he vowed to slaughter every German he could find. He ordered Wooldridge to get a platoon from his company and, in no uncertain terms, "Kill every damned one of them!"

Soon afterward, the *minenwerfers* had been silenced.

From his exposed place, McAlexander watched as Keeley's battalion captured Jaulgonne. The German rear guard had put up a tenacious defense. Approaching the village, the Americans found the terrain that sloped rapidly upward perfect for concealing machine-gun nests. There were clumps of trees and bushes and large boulders. The platoons moved forward in small groups, dashing ahead for short distances, taking cover and then dashing forward for a few more yards.

First Lieutenant Cleon Williams in Captain Freehoff's First Platoon found the only way to advance was "by short rushes of two men at a time."

"By this method," reported Freehoff, "moving up in dead space and taking advantage of all available cover, the company slowly drove the enemy back into Jaulgonne." Meanwhile, other platoons of Keeley's battalion worked their way into the northwest side of the village, routing the enemy. By 7:30 a.m. Jaulgonne had been taken, all except for Germans hidden in cellars and up on rooftops. It took another hour to mop up the streets and clear the buildings.

The next stop was Le Charmel, more than a mile to the northeast.

Capturing the village was not in the cards for Keeley's battalion. It reached the outskirts, but Le Charmel was too heavily fortified. German planes constantly harassed his troops while also bringing down four Allied planes. Captain Shelby Ledford of Sault Saint Marie, Michigan, commander of D Company, tried to dig in under a tree. On his left flank, the Germans hit him with deadly machine-gun fire. He was killed along with five enlisted men. One of his lieutenants was badly wounded, and Captain Claude Shelton of Hubbard, Texas, in charge of the Ninth Machine Gun Battalion's D Company, was hit in the arm by an explosive bullet. For the battalion it was a debacle.

Hearing the cries and groans of the wounded, Captain Freehoff dashed across the road to help. He found that Ledford was dead. He got to Captain Shelton and saw that his arm had been practically blown off. He wrapped a tourniquet around the arm and then rushed back to his company that was pinned down behind a high embankment and couldn't move. "Rifle and machine gun fire was grazing the top of the road bank," Freehoff wrote, "and striking in the road in the rear like raindrops in a puddle of water." He felt the only thing he could do was to charge the enemy. He sent his First Platoon out to his left and another platoon out to his right. Leading the First Platoon, Lieutenant Williams ran through a "culvert and up a dry stream bed until opposite the enemy's left flank. From this position we opened fire."

Freehoff then led a bayonet charge down the road embankment. Recalled Williams, "Our surprise attack from the flank, coupled with the frontal fire delivered from the remainder of the company, forced the enemy back into the wood."

Freehoff's company knocked out several machine-gun nests and took fifteen prisoners. But he lost two officers, both severely wounded. For the moment, the charge halted all enemy fire. It gave A and C Companies a chance to retire without suffering any casualties. Williams's platoon covered the withdrawal of the rest of his company. Keeley ordered his battalion back to Jaulgonne. Capturing Le Charmel was put off for another day.

While Keeley's men had captured Jaulgonne and then stalled in front of Le Charmel, Lough's men were having a harder time at Franquets Farm near Chartèves.

After his men had cleared the crest of Hill 210, they had to fight through the heart of Forêt de Fere to reach Franquets Farm. The enemy had set up machine-gun nests among trees and thickets. Snipers were hidden in the branches of the trees. Light artillery shells fell in the battalion's midst and German planes flew over the treetops, firing machine guns and dropping bombs. The thickness of the forest made it hard for companies to keep in contact with one another. When patrols were sent out to locate other companies, they either got lost or were destroyed. Hilldring described how K Company reached a clearing where a narrow road led toward the farm. The Germans had concealed machine guns at the edge of the woods. The men in his company were "struck in the head or back with bullets from the trees. Either that, or the ground beside them was plowed up with shots coming from overhead. Naturally these tactics played havoc with the morale of Company K."

As usual McAlexander had to see for himself how the fight was going. He walked along the slope of the ridge to the western edge of Jaulgonne and began climbing the hill to where the farm was located. "I moved with great care, knowing that at any instant I might have my life candle snuffed out, but seemingly always lucky I reached the top of the ridge between my own troops and the Germans."

Concealed by bushes, he crept within fifty yards of the German machine-gun nests. He hurriedly surveyed the situation and realized a "frontal attack would be idiotic." The only way to destroy the nests was by artillery fire, and thus far his regiment had had no artillery support. He ordered Lough to remain where he was, on the ridge facing Les Franquets Farm, ease his men back a bit and be ready for a possible German counterattack. McAlexander reckoned he needed more support from other regiments as well as artillery to capture Les Franquets Farm and also Le Charmel. He had Keeley fall back to Jaulgonne and hold the village.

His regiment was now in a waiting game.

McAlexander went back to his command post in the sandpit alongside the road leading into Jaulgonne. He didn't like the location. The Germans at Le Charmel could spot it easily with their binoculars and bring down heavy artillery. He also found out that his operations officer had written an erroneous message to the brigade commander, General Charles Crawford, and was about to send it by runner. McAlexander took the message from the officer, read it and then stuck it in his pocket. The message reported that the regimental commander was nowhere to be found and was most likely killed or wounded and that Major Keeley had rushed on Le Charmel and was surrounded and about to be captured. McAlexander then returned the message to the officer and said that he "would probably appreciate having it back in his own hands."

Shells began to fall close by. The operations officer panicked and desperately started digging a foxhole in the sand. The others in the command post were also nervous. To try and calm their nerves, McAlexander climbed up to the edge of the sandpit and sat there in plain sight. A half hour later, he slid back down into the sandpit unscathed. One of his officers had somehow discovered a chair from some place and carried it into the sandpit so his colonel had a place to sit. As McAlexander dropped into the chair, First Lieutenant Thomas Bresnahan, the Middlebury College graduate, standing next to him, was struck by a shell fragment. It sliced though his steel helmet and cut into his head. Picking the bloody fragment out of his helmet, Bresnahan said he was okay. Then he started to turn very pale. McAlexander had him sent back to the dressing station. Moments later, one of his runners stood at the same spot as had Bresnahan. "Another shell came," an amazed McAlexander wrote, "and as I live and breathe, sent another splinter through the runner's helmet and against his head."

More shells kept coming, exploding over the sandpit and sending fragments flying every which way. One fragment tore into the pelvis of one of the colonel's staff officers. He died screaming. McAlexander had him rolled into a blanket and buried in the sandpit. A wooden cross with the officer's dog tags looped over it marked his shallow grave. In a sharp voice, McAlexander said, "Attention!" The men in the sandpit snapped to attention. Then McAlexander said, "Salute!"

By this time, his operations officer, sobbing like a baby, had lost it. McAlexander had him replaced by his machine-gun company's commanding officer, Captain Sidney Young.

Throughout the 22nd and into the 23rd, the 38th did not move, but held the line awaiting support. It was days of "exasperation," according to McAlexander. Finally, orders came down from division headquarters. On the night of July 23–24, the 30th Infantry, now commanded by Lieutenant Colonel Cromwell Stacy, was to relieve the 38th Infantry. The 38th's part in the Second Battle of the Marne was basically over.

When Stacy's men moved in, McAlexander reluctantly turned over responsibility of his subsector at Chartèves to the 30th. His men, "hungry and badly worn through, no sleep and little food for three days of constant fighting," began their withdrawal back across the Marne to the villages they had earlier defended. The old colonel "relapsed from a very positive state of mind to a negative state."

Walking out into the open, the dejected McAlexander seemed to dare the Germans once again to put him into their sights. As if on cue, a shell came whistling toward him. It hit close by. The concussion of the bursting shell lifted him high in the air, knocking him backward fifteen feet as if shot out of a catapult. He smashed headfirst to the ground, a helpless wreck—unable to think, unable to control his body, his ears aroar. Nearby shrapnel from the same shell killed the regimental gas officer, First Lieutenant William McKinley Wallrich from Shawano, Wisconsin. Somehow McAlexander struggled to his feet. Standing perfectly still, he waited to regain control of his body and for his ears to stop ringing. Captain Young rushed to his dazed commander and put his arms around him. He helped him into a house in Chartèves and found a bunk in the cellar. For the next two days McAlexander stayed on his back, recuperating. He knew he ought to go to a field hospital. But with his second in command, Lieutenant Colonel Frank H. Adams, and his trusted battalion commander, Major Rowe, both wounded and out of action, he believed he'd better stay at his post and lead his regiment.

CHAPTER 24

"THIS IS THE ROCK OF THE MARNE"

After being relieved by the 30th Infantry and before recrossing the Marne, Colonel McAlexander ordered his men to the river to bathe, to wash the grime of war off their bodies. As they neared the river, it became clear there'd be no swimming. The tired, filthy soldiers were turned back when it was reported that on both banks of the river hundreds of the dead, Germans and Americans, were scattered everywhere—some half-submerged in the water. Instead, the men crossed the river over floating pontoon bridges and were billeted in the fields and woods and in what was left of the villages they knew so well: Crézancy, Connigis, Mézy, Moulins and Paroy.

Once his men were settled down, McAlexander wrote up his operations report and then went to deliver it at division headquarters in the village of Chierry that was close to Château-Thierry. Dickman had set up his command post in an elegant home owned by a wealthy couple who were very happy to see that Americans were using their place and not the French, who had a bad reputation of looting the houses they occupied.

Inside headquarters, McAlexander handed his report to Colonel

Kelton. While he and the chief of staff talked, Dickman entered the room. To McAlexander's surprise, Kelton grabbed the colonel by the shoulders and pushed him in front of their boss.

"General Dickman," Kelton said, "this is the Rock of the Marne."

A few days later Kelton, who was not shy about expressing what he thought of his fellow officers, even Dickman, wrote to Pershing's assistant chief of staff, Colonel Fox Conner, to give him his opinion of the division's two infantry brigade commanders and the colonels who reported to them. He was probably sure these opinions would reach the desk of General Pershing.

Fred Sladen of the Fifth Brigade he felt was a fine brigadier and "will make an equally good Division Commander." Crawford was "painfully slow" and had "no control over Butts." As for Butts, he found him "pugnacious."

Turning to McAlexander, he wrote, "Of the four Infantry Colonels in this Division, McAlexander is easily the best in my mind. He was like the rock of the Surmelin Valley as George H. Thomas was of Chickamauga, and the sooner you put the brigadier stars on him the better for the A.E.F. for he will make a dandy brigadier commander, energetic, enthusiastic and level headed and absolutely confident that his regiment can lick any Boche outfit."

Afterward, McAlexander, accompanied by his striker, walked over the battlefield where he and his regiment had so recently fought. They walked along the banks of the now famous river where the companies of Captains Eddy Herlihy and Con Dineen had kept the Germans from crossing and gaining a bridgehead. They walked into the valley of the Surmelin, along the railroad embankment where McAlexander had once dared German snipers to shoot him and then on up Hill 231, where Captain Tom Reid and elements of the First and Third Battalions had made their stand that had saved the right flank of the Third Division. In many places where they walked, the ground, it seemed, was a "carpet of enemy dead." The days had been hot and "wrought ghastly damage" to the fallen Germans. Their decomposing bodies spread a deathly stench over the shell-pocked land. Dried blood clung to the barbed-wire entanglements and torn-up bushes and trees. The muddy banks of the river were still stained red. As the colonel and his striker walked, the images and sounds of the violent battle that had raged only days before—the roar of artillery, the crack of machine guns, the clash of bayonets and the cries of men in a death struggle—certainly had to play through the colonel's mind. He wanted especially to see the place where the Sixth Grenadiers had fled back across the Marne on the morning of the 15th. He and his striker went to that place on the riverbank. Here Captain Wooldridge's company assisted by two platoons from the 30th Infantry, led by Lieutenants Marsh and Winant, had stopped the Grenadiers in a desperate fight, saving McAlexander's left flank.

In the mud by the edge of the Marne, McAlexander came across "an elegant Yaeger blanket" that had been carried by a Sixth Grenadier officer in his retreat from the battlefield. The blanket was clotted in mud and blood. He asked his striker if he wanted it as a souvenir. The striker vehemently refused to take it. McAlexander lifted it out of the mud, wiped off the dirt and folded it up. He carried the blanket to his command post in Crézancy. There he had it washed, and then used it for his own blanket. And for the rest of his life the old colonel carried it with him as a lasting reminder of how his regiment had helped thwart the German march on Paris and earned the honorific "Rock of the Marne."

"DANGER BE DAMNED:
WAR IS ALWAYS DANGEROUS"

O n November 20, nine days after the end of the World War, General John J. Pershing from his headquarters at Chaumont "rushed" a brief report to Secretary of War Newton Baker.

My Dear Secretary:

The 3rd Division was holding the bank of the Marne from the bend east of the mouth of the Surmelin to the west of Mezy, opposite Chateau-Thierry, where a large force of German Infantry sought to force a passage under support of powerful artillery concentrations and under cover of smoke screens. A single regiment of the 3rd wrote one of the most brilliant pages in our military annals on this occasion. It prevented the crossing at certain points on its front, while, on either flank, the Germans who had gained a footing pressed forward. Our men firing in three directions met the German attacks with counter-attacks at

critical points and succeeded in throwing two German divisions
into complete confusion, capturing six hundred prisoners.

I am, Mr. Secretary,
Very Respectfully, John J. Pershing,
General Commander in Chief,
American Expeditionary Forces

His strong words of praise singling out one regiment, comparing it to all the brave regiments in American history, omitted the most important thing—the name of the regiment. The omission broke McAlexander's heart, not because the glory would have been his, but because the men in the 38th Infantry who had fought for their lives on the banks of the Marne and Surmelin Rivers were not recognized for their valor that had stopped the German juggernaut and, in doing so, had certainly helped to turn the tide of the war. The omission hurt Colonel Edmund Butts as well because he believed in all his heart that it was his regiment, the 30th Infantry, that deserved Pershing's praise. He believed, too, that it was his regiment that had earned the nom de guerre "Rock of the Marne" and not McAlexander's outfit.

Pershing tried to put the controversy to rest a few months later, naming the 38th as the regiment he had singled out. But the controversy rolled on.

Martin Green, war correspondent for the New York *Evening World* and one of the most respected reporters in the country, who had once been described by Irwin S. Cobb, another legendary reporter of the time, as an "inventive and most capable veteran," threw himself into the controversy. On August 21, 1919, after the Third Division had returned home, Green expounded on a Page Three article in the *Evening World* that "The Rock of the Marne Was U.S. 30th Infantry, Chateau-Thierry Heroes." He claimed to have arrived at General Dickman's headquarters on the morning on July 16 and been told by the intelligence officer there that the "30th Infantry had stopped the German advance across the Marne; that the 30th had taken the brunt of the attack." The story so impressed him that he cabled the *Evening World*, but because of censorship of the press he was not able to identify the regiment. It wasn't until he was back in New York at the end of the war, when Pershing named the 38th as the "Rock of the Marne," that Green decided to right what he felt was a wrong against Butts and his regiment.

"This article is written in no spirit of disparagement of the 38th Infantry," he penned. "It is simply a demonstration of the fact that what might be called history at the battle front in July, 1918, may be displaced by history at A.E.F. Headquarters in December 1918."

Brigadier General Charles Crawford, who had commanded both regiments, was then quoted in the New York *Sun*: "The regular infantry regiment mentioned in the report of Gen. Pershing after the Second Battle of the Marne . . . was the 38th Infantry."

As late as 1930, Butts tried to make the case that he, not McAlexander, was the true Rock, in his book, *The Keypoint [sic] of the Marne and Its Defense By the 30th Infantry*. McAlexander's regiment was not attacked on three sides, he stated. "I have never been able to understand how the idea was obtained that the west flank of the 38th Infantry was in anyway exposed."

Then, on July 4, 1936, Harold L. Reese, who had been a first lieutenant under Butts and who had received the Distinguished Service Cross during the battle, wrote a two-page letter to Pershing on behalf of the 30th Infantry Association Committee. He complained that the surviving veterans of the regiment had been "discriminated against for they have always felt that they, as a regiment, did even better than the 38th Infantry and are entitled to share in any compliments that the Commander in Chief might have to offer." He requested a statement from Pershing "which will tend to correct the unfavorable impression that the general public has formed of the operations of that regiment at that time."

More than four months later, November 14, Pershing finally answered

Reese's request. He regretted that members of the 30th felt the "heroic stand they made on the Marne on July 15, 1918, has not received the recognition that it highly merits." He then quoted the following from his book, *My Experiences in the World War*:

> *Farther west, the enemy succeeded in crossing the Marne, penetrating in one place as far as five miles. In a determined attempt to force a crossing near Mezy he struck our 3rd Division, which was posted along the river, and the fighting became intense, some units of the 30th and 38th Infantry Regiments which were holding the front lines being attacked from both the front and flanks. The brilliant conduct of these units, however, threw the enemy's effort into confusion and by noon of the next day he had nothing to show in most of the 3rd Division's sector for his careful preparations, except tremendous losses.*

He closed his reply, "Through the above I believe that the heroic conduct of the men of the 30th Regiment has been recorded for all time."

Colonel Butts had two other disappointments to endure. The first was that soon after the 111th Infantry had relieved the 30th Infantry, he was removed as commander of his regiment. Later, he took charge of the 7th Infantry when its commander, Colonel Tom Anderson, suffered shell shock. Butts then led it across the Marne in chase of the retreating enemy.

The other disappointment was that he had been passed over for promotion to brigadier general.

In fact, on July 17, 1918, Major General Dickman had actually recommended that Butts be elevated to that rank. In his letter to the commanding general of the First United States Army Corps, Hunter

Liggett, he wrote how Butts's regiment, in the early morning of July 15, defended its subsector on the Marne River and in the Bois d'Aigremont: "The regiment held its position as directed by orders from higher authorities during the attack by superior German forces. The advanced elements on the immediate bank of the Marne were pushed back, but the woods north of the Crezancy-Fossoy line were held throughout, and by vigorous counter attacks the enemy was driven north of the river. The casualties of this regiment amounted to nearly 50%. The forceful character and optimistic attitude of the Colonel infused an indomitable spirit into the regiment and the tactical conduct of the operations was highly creditable."

Yet the recommendation was abruptly withdrawn when it was learned Butts had apparently gone to Paris without telling Dickman or his immediate superior, Brigadier General Crawford. Not getting the coveted star at the same time Colonel McAlexander got his hurt the West Pointer, and he never got over the snub. If General Liggett, later head of the AEF's First Army, had had a chance to move on Dickman's recommendation when he was corps commander, he would have acted favorably and Butts would have gotten his star. Liggett found Butts to be a "fine soldier and a natural, as well as a trained leader of men." He wrote to him twelve years after the war about Butts's disappointment, saying, "You should be a Major General today, in my opinion, for you richly earned it."

For whatever reason, Butts, who did receive the American Distinguished Service Cross, did not get his promotion to brigadier general until years later. But he did cherish a commendation from General Henri Pétain:

> With the approbation of the Commander-in-Chief,
> American Expeditionary Forces in France, the
> Commander-in-Chief of the French Armies of
> the North and Northeast, cites in order of
> the Army:

The 30th U.S. Infantry

An old regiment of the American Army which,
under the energetic and able command of its
Chief, Colonel E. L. Butts, showed itself
faithful to its traditions in sustaining the
principal shock of the German attack of the
15th July, 1918, on the front of the Corps to
which it was attached. Under a most violent
bombardment which caused heavy losses, it
held in spite of the enemy assault, and
re-established integrally, its position, taking
more than two hundred (200) prisoners.

The Great General Headquarters
(Order No. 10/805 "D")
22 October 1918
PETAIN,
The General Commander-in-Chief

A t the very end of his book, *The Keypoint of the Marne*, Butts bitterly wrote, "The regiment trained in Dancevoir and three nearby
towns, located about 25 miles south of Chaumont. Any veteran of the
30th can go back to this training area today and to be royally greeted
by all inhabitants. Every article down to a tooth brush that the 30th left
behind was carefully cared for and they mourn the fine lads of the 30th
who fell in battle and saw that all personal knickknacks of the fallen
were returned to relatives or friends. Dancevoir named its main street
'Les Etats Unis' after the Marne fight; and if you ask the inhabitants
they all know who saved Paris in July, 1918."

Although he and his regiment were not officially recognized as the
"Rock of the Marne," there were many who thought they should have

been. When Butts died in 1950 at the age of 81, a bronze tablet was placed on the wall of the Presidio chapel in San Francisco.

IN MEMORY OF
BRIGADIER GENERAL EDMUND L. BUTTS
THE ROCK OF THE MARNE
WHO COMMANDED THE 30TH U.S.
INFANTRY AT THE SECOND
BATTLE OF THE MARNE
JULY 18, 1918
BORN AUG.15, 1868 DIED JUNE 6, 1950
PLACED BY HIS WIFE

On one side of a tombstone of white marble in Section A, Lot 10062-B, set in 1936 at Arlington National Cemetery the epitaph simply reads:

ROCK OF THE MARNE
McALEXANDER

On August 16, 1918, McAlexander had been promoted to brigadier general and assigned to command the 180th Infantry Brigade of the Ninetieth Division. He wrote to his wife, "General McAlexander's compliments to Mrs. McAlexander. At last the long expected has arrived and I am wearing stars today instead of my splendid old eagles."

He also wrote to her that he had been recommended for the Congressional Medal of Honor. "I feel sure the Division Commander will approve," he wrote with confidence. "Well, that is going some!!! July 15, the Distinguished Service Cross and on July 22, the Medal of Honor."

But it was not to be. His brigade commander, Crawford, made sure of that. Crawford had recommended him for the Distinguished Service Cross, but when McAlexander's top officers, Lieutenant Colonel Frank

Adams, and Major Guy Rowe, suggested that the Medal of Honor would please McAlexander more, he decided against it because, oddly, he did not think much of America's highest award for valor.

"I considered the Medal of Honor appropriate for action involving only the vulgar courage of a soldier," he reasoned, "while the Distinguished Service Cross implied skill and military accomplishment of a high order and was the more desirable. Besides the scandals that had attended the issuing of Medals of Honor cheapened the decoration."

Major Rowe and Captain Jesse Wooldridge, both in Crawford's brigade, were also recommended for the Medal of Honor. Like McAlexander, they received instead the Distinguished Service Cross, as did Butts and Major Fred Walker. Surprisingly, the only soldier in the entire Third Division to receive the Medal of Honor during the Second Battle of the Marne was Lieutenant George P. Hays of the 10th Field Artillery.

Before turning over command of the 38th Infantry to Lieutenant Colonel Frank H. Adams, McAlexander on August 17 sent the following to his captains:

McAlexander, France August 17, Personal note to My Captains:

I have complimented the regiment in orders, for its glorious work on July 15, 1918, on the banks of the Marne; but from the depths of a heart that knows soldierly affection, soldierly love, soldierly loyalty and soldierly devotion, I wish to commend you, Adams, Rowe, Keeley, Lough, Wooldridge, Reid, Woodside, Smith, Ledford, Freihoff [sic], Herlihy, Moss, Parkinson, Gaskins, Becktold, Morrison, Harrah, Lucas, White and others of all ranks, for your wonderful valor and amazing devotion to your Colonel.

Our countrymen will little know and will soon forget the regiment that held the key point against the last great offensive of the Germans. The tide of the World War was stemmed by our regiment at the point where the valley of the Surmelin joins the

Marne. From that moment German armies have suffered
continuous defeat.
   May the God of Battles be kind to each of my officers and men.

   McAlexander, Colonel

The new brigadier general arrived at his new post as commander of the 180th Infantry Brigade a few weeks before the Battle of St. Mihiel. McAlexander didn't have much time to get to know his officers and men before leading them into combat for the first time. He worried about their morale. He gathered all his officers and spoke to them about their combat duties. He told them what he had told the officers of the 38th Infantry when he took over that regiment. He was going to make his brigade invincible and unconquerable and imbue it with a pride that scoffed at danger, that had a soul of intrepidity and honor that would make defeat impossible. "They may kill us," he said, "but they cannot whip us."

   A newly appointed officer asked, "But, General, isn't that dangerous?"

   "Danger be damned," McAlexander shot back. "War is always dangerous."

ACKNOWLEDGMENTS

The diaries, letters and memoirs of the soldiers as well as the reports from units of the Third U.S. Infantry Division and war diaries of the regiments in the German Seventh Army constitute an essential element in my account of the Rock of the Marne. Two key sources held at the Modern Military Records Branch of the National Archives and Records Administration in College Park, Maryland, are letters from the officers of the 30th Infantry's First Battalion to their commander, Maj. Fred L. Walker, and letters by officers in the Third Division's Sixth Brigade to the Battle Monuments Commission. To this I owe a deep thanks to Mitchell Yockelson at the National Archives.

Special thanks are due my agent, E. J. McCarthy, and my editor at Berkley, Natalee Rosenstein, and her editorial assistant, Robin Barletta. Without E. J.'s input and hard work there'd be no book. Also, Mike Hanlon and Tim Stoy. Mike is editor and publisher at Worldwar.com and posts a terrific daily blog, Roads to the Great War. Tim is the Third Division historian. Both men read my manuscript, offered insightful suggestions, and made sure I got the story right.

Of course, my wife, Sue, tackled a lot of the research and was by my side as we pored over mounds of primary material at the National Archives.

I particularly want to thank the families of the soldiers who provided letters, diaries, memoirs and insights into their fathers, grandfathers, great uncles and cousins. I trust I treated their kin fairly.

Robert B. Ferguson and Judy Morrison Gentry, grandson and great niece of Maj. Guy I. Rowe.

Fred L. Walker, grandson of Maj. Fred L. Walker.

Mary Dee Dineen Klingenberg, daughter of Capt. Cornelius Dineen.

Daniel Herlihy and John D. Herlihy, son and grandson of Capt. Edward Herlihy.

Roger Snyder, nephew of 1st Lt. James Kingery.

Rick C. Fitzgerald, grandson of Cpl. William Fitzgerald.

Rick Neimiller, grandson of Pfc. Lawrence Hartle.

Larry C. Bodes, grandson of Cook Harry Stevanus.

Carson L. Bruening, relative of Pvt. William O. Zimmerman.

In my research, I counted on the following folks to provide key information on a number of the soldiers featured in this book: Joseph-James Ahern, senior archivist, University of Pennsylvania Archives; Stanley Anderson, retired colonel; R. L. Baker, MA (MSgt, USAF Ret.), senior technical information specialist, Military History Institute, Army Heritage Center Foundation, Carlisle, Pennsylvania; Dean Scott Barnicle and Elizabeth Robinson both of Middlebury College; Alex Bartlett, Germantown Pennsylvania Historical Society; Ella Buzzard, Cherokee County Genealogical-Historical Society, Columbus, Kansas; Sharon H. Byrd, Special Collections Outreach librarian, E.H. Little Library, Davidson College; Brad Casselberry, records manager/assistant archivist, University of Wisconsin-Stevens Point; Lin Conley, library technician, and Casey Madrick, United States Military Academy Special Collections & Archives Division; and Col. Robert J. Dalessandro, director, Center of Military History, Fort McNair, Washington, DC.

Also, Mike Dicianna, lead reference student, Oregon State University Special Collections and Archive Research Center; Sandra Dickie, Demopolis Public Library, Demopolis, Alabama; David D'Onofrio, Special Collections librarian, Special Collections & Archives, Nimitz Library, U.S. Naval Academy; Robert Doughty, former head of the West Point History Department; Paul Dzyak, Sports Archivist, Pennsylvania State University; Iris at the Miami County Historical/Genealogy Museum, Paola, Kansas; George and Missy Elder, Emanuel County Historical, Swainsboro, Georgia; Michael Frost, Public Services Manuscripts and Archives, Sterling Memorial Library, Yale University; Mary Jones-Fitts, genealogist from Demopolis, Alabama;

Tammy Flint, coordinator, Advanced Data Services, West Point Association of Graduates, West Point, New York; Carol A. Leadenham, Hoover Institution Archives, Stanford University; William McIntire, Dayton (Ohio) Metro Pubic Library; Walter W. Meeks II, director, Fort Stewart Museum; Fort Stewart, Georgia; Dina Melnichuk, research assistant, Hoover Institution, Stanford University; Ashley Monet, Harvard Research Services, Harvard University; Peter Nelson, college archivist, Amherst College, Amherst, Massachusetts; Amanda Nicholson, Special Collections student assistant, Marietta College, Marietta, Ohio; and Kelly Nolin, archivist and Special Collections librarian, Norwich University, Northfield, Vermont.

And Krista Oldham, College archivist/records manager, Haverford College; Chris Owens, Blanchester (Ohio) Public Library; Rosalba Recchia, Seeley G. Mudd Manuscript Library, Princeton University; Pam Schmidt, deputy county clerk, Shawano, Wisconsin; Lucia M. Shannon, head of Adult Services, Brockton (Massachusetts) Public Library; Lisa Sharik, deputy director, Texas Military Forces Museum, Austin, Texas; Beth Smith at the Ohio Historical Society; Lynn Smith-Bartram, Miami (Ohio) University Archives; Sgt. Charles Spence, volunteer researcher/military curator, and Coleen Chambers, Historical and Genealogical Society of Indiana County, Indiana, Pennsylvania; and Joseph F. Watson, Middlebury College Archives.

I'd also like to thank the folks of Somerset County, Pennsylvania, for their help, especially Charles Fox, author of the excellent book *Company C: Somerset County National Guardsmen and the First World War*, and Robert Stembower, former commander of Company C, for his personal research and suggestions. Others include John W. Brant, retired colonel, for his research of local World War I soldiers; Robert Hainzer, Cynthia Mason, Meyersdale Public Library; Damian J. M. Smith, command historian, Pennsylvania National Guard; Mark D. Ware, executive director, Historical and Genealogical Society of Somerset County; Brian Whipkey, editor, Somerset *Daily American*. I'm sorry for not using all the material received from other folks from Somerset County.

I want to thank Don McKeon who took a chance on my first World War I book, *Duty, Honor, Privilege*. And my sister, Lynn Worth-Smith of Clarksville, Virginia.

SOURCES AND BIBLIOGRAPHY

(Author's Note: A controversy exists about the origin of the nom de guerre "Rock of the Marne" and which officer in the Third Division it should belong to—Colonel Edmund L. Butts, commanding the 30th Infantry, or Colonel Ulysses G. McAlexander, commanding the 38th Infantry. It is generally believed that McAlexander was the "Rock of the Marne." To back up that belief, I've relied on the following sources: McAlexander's own memoir, *The Rock of the Marne*, as well as Major Jesse W. Wooldridge's book, *The Giants of the Marne*, and Clarence E. Lovejoy's book, *The Story of the Thirty-Eighth*. In all three books, Colonel Robert H. C. Kelton, the division's chief of staff during the Second Battle of the Marne, is credited with coming up with the famous nom de guerre that the Third now carries so proudly. To me, the convincing fact is a Kelton letter to Colonel Fox Conner, General Pershing's assistant chief of staff, sent on July 30, 1918. The letter is found among the Fred L. Walker Papers at the Hoover Institute at Stanford University. As I quote in this book, Kelton wrote: "Of the four Infantry Colonels in this Division, McAlexander is easily the best in my mind. He was like the rock of the Surmelin Valley as George H. Thomas was of Chickamauga, and the sooner you put the brigadier stars on him the better for the A.E.F. for he will make a dandy brigadier commander, energetic, enthusiastic and level headed and absolutely confident that his regiment can lick any Boche outfit.")

(On another note: The spelling of Plattsburgh. The city in upstate New York ends with an "h" while, for some reason, the title of the Plattsburg Officers' Training Camp does not.)

ARTICLES

"Alva C. Martz, Famous Hun Killer Brought Up as a Non-Combatant." *Meyersdale Republican*, August 15, 1918.

"Alva Martz Hero of His Regiment." *Meyersdale Republican*, August 29, 1918.

"Alvey Martz Accounted for Eighteen Huns." Clipping from *The Somerset Herald*, nd.

"Americans Defense of Château-Thierry." *The New York Times Current History*, July 1918.

"American Women Killed in Paris; Mrs. Lucy Landon and Mrs. Marie Grinnell Among Shell Victims in Paris Church." *New York Times*, April 2, 1918.

Anderson, Major J. W. "With the Tenth Field Artillery at the Second Battle of the Marne." *Field Artillery Journal*, Vol. XIII, No. 5, September–October, 1923.

Anonymous. "The Rock of the Marne: By an Onlooker," nd. The Guy I. Rowe Family Papers held by Robert Ferguson, Valparaiso, IN.

Associated Press. "Americans Block New German Drive; Teutons Hurled Back Across Marne." *New York Tribune*, July 16, 1918.

"Awful Beyond Description; Further Details of Battle of Conde-en-Brie By Co. C Survivor." *Meyersdale Republican*, August 29, 1918.

Bailey, Herbert. "Germans Wilt Before U.S. Men: Later Reports Show Attack Was Met with Furious Resistance." *New York Sun*, July 17, 1918.

Black, Captain Percy G. "With a Regiment of 75's in the Champagne-Marne, Defensive." *Field Artillery Journal*, November–December 1919.

"Blood of Frosty Boys of Thunder, Somerset County Boys Badly Cut Up in Battle, Capt. Truxal and Many Officers and Men of His Command Reported Missing." *Meyersdale Republican*, August 8, 1918.

Brice, Arthur T., Jr. *The Watch on the Rhine*, official newspaper of the Third Division, Vol. X, No. 5, April 1929.

"Casualty Lists Anxiously Scanned." *Meyersdale Republican*, August 1, 1918.

"Clearing the Marne Woods: Gen. Degoutte's Task." *Times of London*, July 26, 1918.

Cobbey, First Lieutenant Luther W. "Story of the 7th Machine Gun Battalion." Vanderburgh County, IN: The American Local History Network, 2000.

"Company C Boys in Prison Camps." *Meyersdale Republican*, September 5, 1918.

"Company C Given Rousing Send Off." *Somerset Herald*, June 28, 1916.

"Company C Surrounded by Greater Number of Enemy; The French Retreated, Leaving the Americans Unprotected." Clipping from *The Somerset Herald*, nd.

"Corporal Landis Lost Leg in Great Battle." *Meyersdale Republican*, August 15, 1918.

"Disposed of 17 Germans in 36 Hours' Fighting; Alvey C. Martz of Glencoe Is Hero of Thrilling Story of Dauntless Valor in Marne Conflict." *Meyersdale Republican*, August 8, 1918.

Dunn, Lieutenant Colonel Michael W. *World War I: Elastic Defense and the U.S. 3d Division at the Marne River.* CSI Report No. 13, Chapter 12. Combat Studies Institute, U.S. Army Command and General Staff College, Ft. Leavenworth, KS, nd.

Duranty, Walter. "Battle of Baptism Only Rite Yank Novices Needed." *Chicago Daily Tribune,* July 22, 1918.

———. "Marne Valley Shows War in Its Horror." *New York Times,* July 30, 1918.

Edstrom, Ed. "Jeff Depot's New Boss Knows What It Is to Fight Germans." Clipping from the *Louisville Courier-Journal,* nd. The Guy I. Rowe Family Papers held by Robert Ferguson, Valparaiso, IN.

"Edward Fairchild Smith" biography, *History of the Class of 1915, Yale College,* Vol. III, 1952.

"Eight Somerset Soldiers Made Supreme Sacrifice; Eighty-Five Men of Co. C Included in Casualty List." Clipping from *The Somerset Herald,* nd.

"Enemy Again Attack: American Troops in Action." *Times of London,* July 16, 1918.

"Fighting Tenth Got Hell While It Lasted." *Meyersdale Republican,* August 15, 1918.

"Financial Markets: War News Cheers Financial Community and Stocks Advance Further." *New York Times,* July 17, 1918.

Forrest, Wilbur S. "German Dead in Heaps Tell Marne's Cost." *New York Tribune,* July 17, 1918.

Fox, Charles. "Company C and the Great War (Parts 1–4)." *Laurel Messenger.* Historical and Genealogical Society of Somerset County, PA, August and November 2004, February and May 2005.

"Frosty Sons Fell While Fighting Superior Force of Foes, Mystery Still Shrouds Fate of Many of Our Boys, Frosty Sons Pitted Against Kaiser's Pet Prussian Guards." *Meyersdale Republican,* August 15, 1918.

"German Drive Checked: Series of Local Battles." *Times of London,* July 18, 1918.

"Germans Reach Marne in 10-Mile Advance; Paris 45 Miles Away." *New York Tribune,* June 1, 1918.

"Germans Held at Marne, Push Westward; French Retake Town; Americans Coming Up." *New York Tribune,* June 2, 1918.

Grasty, Charles H. "Our Men Broke German Wedge, Marne Battleground Made Forever Sacred to Us by Our Soldiers' Valor." *New York Times,* August 26, 1918.

Heavey, Captain W. F. "German Crossing of the Marne River." *Military Engineer,* Vol. XVIII, No. 99, May–June 1926.

Henning, Arthur Sears. "Capital Wild With Joy Over Yank Victory." *Chicago Daily Tribune,* July 16, 1918.

Hesse, Lieutenant Kurt, Fifth Grenadiers. "The Drama of the Marne." *Field Artillery Journal,* March–April 1921.

Hilldring, Captain John H. "Four Days of Infantry Combat, Part I." *Infantry Journal*, May–June 1932.

———. "Four Days of Infantry Combat, Part II." *Infantry Journal*, July–August 1932.

Hopkins, Captain Johns. "A Point of View in the Thirtieth Infantry." *Field Artillery Journal*, September–October, 1923.

James, Edwin L. "Americans Prove Bravery; Valor, Initiative and Endurance Shown in Their Marne Battles." *New York Times*, July 1, 1918.

———. "Yankees Turn Kaiser's Dream to Nightmare." *Chicago Daily Tribune*, July 17, 1918.

———. "Abandon Chateau-Thierry, Crossing of Marne by the Allies Forces Germans Out of the City." *New York Times*, July 22, 1918.

Kelton, Colonel Robert H. C. "American Operations in France." Address to the annual meeting of the Maryland Bar Association, 1919.

———. "History of the Third Division, Regulars in France." *New York Times*, April 13, 1919.

———. "Marne Division Before the Armistice." *New York Times*, June 22, 1919.

———. "The Miracle of Chateau-Thierry." *Century Magazine*, Vol. 98, No. 1, May 1919. In this article, Kelton repeats his statement that Colonel McAlexander was the "Rock of the Surmelin Valley."

Lanza, Colonel Conrad H. "The Turn of the Worm: The Allies in the Second Marne Campaign." *Field Artillery Journal*, July–August 1936.

———. "Five Decisive Days." *Field Artillery Journal*, January–February 1937.

———. "Bridgeheads of the Marne." *Field Artillery Journal*, May–June 1937.

———. "The German XXIII Reserve Corps Crosses the Marne." *Field Artillery Journal*, July–August 1937.

———. "The German XXIII Reserve Corps Crosses the Marne." *Field Artillery Journal*, September–October 1937.

Lavine, Sigmund A. "Six Valiant Brockton Veterans Get Together Decade After Enlistments." *Boston Sunday Post,* March 31, 1929.

"Letters from The Boys 'Over There.'" *Meyersdale Republican*, July 4, 1918.

"Lieutenants Crouse and Schell Gave Their Lives; Captain Truxal Wounded Now in a Hospital; Thirty-Three Are Missing." Clipping from *The Somerset Herald*, nd.

"Marne Retreat: Allies Sweeping On." *Times of London*, July 29, 1918.

"Mary Withers at Front." *Kansas City Star*, June 11, 1918.

"May Have Made the Supreme Sacrifice." *Meyersdale Republican*, August 8, 1918.

Mencken, H. L. "Ludendorff." *The Atlantic Monthly*, June 1917.

Mendenhall, Major John R. "The Fist in the Dyke." *Coast Artillery Journal*, January–February 1936.

Minturn, Captain Joseph A. "Sketching Chateau-Thierry." Vanderburgh County, IN: The American Local History Network, 2000.

"Mother's Good Boy Killed in Battle." *Meyersdale Republican*, August 29, 1918.

Muller, Colonel J. P. "The German Artillery at the Chemin des Dames in 1918." *Field Artillery Journal*, March–April 1922.

Neiberg, Michael S. "The Evolution of Strategic Thinking in World War I: A Case Study of the Second Battle of the Marne." *Journal of Military and Strategic Studies*, Volume 13, Issue 4, Summer 2011.

N. F. M. "Ulysses Grant McAlexander." 68th Annual Report of the Association of Graduates of the United States Military Academy at West Point, New York, June 11, 1937.

"Probably Suffering from Shell Shock." *Meyersdale Republican*, September 26, 1918.

Richardson, J. M. "Flying the Dawn Patrol." *Friends Journal*, Vol. 37, No. 2, Summer 2014.

"Saw the French Retreat: Americans Went in Singing Miss Mary Withers Writes." *Kansas City Star*, July 7, 1918.

Seldes, George H. "Between Battles with Our Fighting Men in France." *Atlanta Constitution*, October 6, 1918.

"Shell Hits Paris as City Worships." *New York Times*, April 1, 1918.

"She Nursed Our Wounded at Chateau-Thierry, Graphic Letters Just Received from Mrs. Herbert G. Squiers Tell How Gloriously Americans Fought and How They Joked About Their Injuries." *New York Times*, July 28, 1918.

Simonds, Frank H. "The Second Battle of the Marne." *New York Tribune*, July 21, 1918.

"Somerset Boy Cited for Bravery on Battle Field." Clipping from *The Somerset Herald*, nd.

"The Terrible Hun Killed and Abused War Prisoners; Boys of Co. C Victims." Clipping from *The Somerset Herald*, nd.

"Tribute to Women Killed by Supergun: Mrs. Landon and Daughters Murdered in Paris Church by Germans, Honored Here." *New York Times*, April 15, 1918.

"Two Hundred Missing, Killed and Wounded, Old Company C Has Ceased to Exist—160 of Its members Prisoners of War, 25 Dead and 15 in Hospitals Is Latest Report." *Meyersdale Republican*, September 12, 1918.

Wheeler-Bennett, John W. "Ludendorff: The Soldier and the Politician." *Virginia Quarterly Review*, Spring 1928.

Williams, First Lieutenant Cleon L. "Operations of 1st Plat., Co. B, 38th Infantry." *Infantry Journal*, September–October, 1933.

Wilson, Carolyn. "Marne People Again Fleeing Before Huns." *Chicago Daily Tribune*, June 3, 1918.

Wooldridge, Major J. W. "The Same Fight as Seen by a Company of the Thirty-Eighth Infantry." *Field Artillery Journal*, September–October, 1923.

———."The Rock of the Marne." *International Military Digest*, nd. The article describes Colonel Kelton telling General Dickman that Colonel McAlexander is "The Rock of the Marne."

"Wounded Somerset Boy Tells of Battle." *Meyersdale Republican*, August 8, 1918.

Zabecki, David T. "Railroads: Strategic Necessity & Strategic Vulnerability. The German 1918 Offensives—A Case Study." *Relevance: Quarterly Journal of the Great War Society*, Vol. 20, No. 4, Fall 2011.

DIARIES, MONOGRAPHS, NOTES, REMARKS, STATEMENTS

Adams, F. H. Undated memorandum. Special Collections and Archives Research Center, Oregon State University, Corvallis, OR.

Anderson, Col. T. M. Statement concerning the Seventh Infantry Regiment, July 17, 1918. *The German Offensive of July 15, 1918.*

Bechtold, Captain Jacob E., I Company, 38th Infantry Regiment. Extracts from monograph "3d Division (US) on the Marne, May 3-July 1918," at the Advanced Infantry Course, Fort Benning, GA, nd.

Butts, Colonel Edmund L. "Notes from Colonel E. L. Butts." Nd. 3rd Division Historical Files, Record Group 129-AEF, National Archives and Record Administration (NARA), College Park, MD.

Combined statements of First Sergeant Frederick G. Brown and Oscar H. Wilcox, C Company, 30th Infantry Regiment, nd. 3rd Division Historical Files, Record Group 120-AEF, NARA.

Combined statements of Privates Louis Silverglat, Dennis Mangino, Isadore Heinhimer and Robert Lueze, 30th Infantry Regiment, nd. 3rd Division Historical Files, Record Group 120-AEF, NARA.

Conner, Colonel Fox, Assistant Chief of Staff, A.E.F. Headquarters. General memorandum to Maj. Gen. Joseph T. Dickman, May 29, 1918. *United States Army in the World War, 1917-1919. Military Operations of the American Expeditionary Forces*, Vol. 4. Washington, DC: Center of Military History, United States Army, 1989.

Dickman, Major General Joseph T. "Remarks at a conference after the Marne campaign," August 1, 1918. 3rd Division Historical Files, Record Group 129-AEF, NARA.

Dickman, Major General Joseph T. Field Order No. 1, May 30, 1918, *United States Army in the World War, 1917-1919. Military Operations of the American Expeditionary Forces*, Vol. 4. Washington, DC: Center of Military History, United States Army, 1989.

Duncan, Brigaier General G. B. Memorandum to Commanding General, 1st Division, A.E.F., December 16, 1917. Special Collections and Archives Research Center, Oregon State University, Corvallis, OR.

Fitzgerald, Corporal William J. 30th Infantry Regiment, War Diary, April 2 to December 25, 1918. Held by Rick C. Fitzgerald, Ponte Vedra Beach, FL.

Frank, Sergeant Philip (P. F.) Lund. *World War I Diary of Sgt. Philip Frank (P. F.) Lund, Company A, 6th Engineers, A.E.F.* Edited by Vickie Lund Pryor. Washington, DC: Library of Congress.

Herlihy, Captain Edward G., H Company, 38th Infantry Regiment. Monograph: "Professional Competition Is Rugged." Herlihy Family Papers, Daniel E. Herlihy, Madison, MS.

Herlihy, Captain Edward G. Diary, June 7, 9, 14, 17, 18, 23, 30 and July 12, 1918. Herlihy Family Papers, Daniel E. Herlihy, Madison, MS.

James, Major Harold W. Lecture delivered at the Infantry School Course, Military History Institute, Carlisle, PA.

REPORTS AND ORDERS

Bolling, Captain A. R. "Operations of the 3d Platoon, Company 'I', 4th Infantry 3d Division in the Champagne-Marne Defensive and Aisne-Marne Offensive, July 5–24, 1918." Advanced Course, 1933–1934, The Infantry School, Fort Benning, GA.

"Campaign of 1918: Americans at Second Battle of the Marne." The General Service Schools, 1921–1922. Fred L. Walker Papers, Hoover Institute, Stanford University, Stanford, CA.

Crawford, Brigadier General Charles, commander, Sixth Brigade, Third Division. "Preliminary Report of Battle of July 15, 1918," submitted July 23, 1918. 3rd Division Historical Files, Record Group 120-AEF, NARA.

Davidson, Lieutenant Colonel F. L. "Action of the 7th Machine Gun Battalion at Chateau-Thierry," dated June 17, 1918. 3rd Division Historical Files, Record Group 120-AEF, NARA.

Drollinger, Major Ziba L. "Operations of the Machine Gun Units of the Sixth Brigade Near Chateau-Thierry, July 1–21, 1918." Advanced Course, 1927–1928, The Infantry School, Fort Benning, GA.

Drollinger, Major Ziba L. "Report on Action of Machine Guns of the Ninth Machine Gun Battalion During the German Offensive, July 19, 1918." 3rd Division Historical Files, Record Group 120-AEF, NARA.

Freehoff, Captain William F., B Company, 38th Infantry Regiment. Extracts from "OPERATIONS of Company B 38th Infantry Along the Marne River." Advanced Course, 1926–1927, The Infantry School, Fort Benning, GA.

Freehoff, Captain William F. "Report of Operations of Company 'B', Thirty-Eighth Infantry, July 15–16, 1918." Fred L. Walker Papers, Hoover Institute, Stanford University, Stanford, CA.

French XXXVIII Army Corps. "General Operations Order No. 135. Distribution of Elements of 3d Div." *United States Army in the World War, 1917–1919. Military Operations of the American Expeditionary Forces*, Vol. 4.

Herlihy, Captain Edward G. "The 2d Battalion, 38th Infantry, 3d Division at the Marne, May 31–July 20, 1918." Company Officers' Course, 1925, The Infantry School, Fort Benning, GA.

Hilldring, Captain John H. "Operations of the 1st Platoon, 38th infantry, 3rd Div. in the Aisne-Marne Offensive, July 20–July 23, 1918, Personal Narrative of a Platoon Commander." Advanced Course, 1931–1932, The Infantry School, 4th Section, Fort Benning, GA.

Hitt, Lieutenant Colonel Parker. "GHQ Operation Report, June 1, 1918." *United States Army in the World War, 1917–1919. Military Operations of the American Expeditionary Forces*, Vol. 4. Center of Military History, United States Army, Washington, DC, 1989.

Keeley, Major H. J. "Report of Operations of the First Battalion, July 17–22, 1918." 3rd Division Historical Files, Record Group 120-AEF, NARA.

Kelton, Colonel Robert H. C., Chief of Staff, Third Division. "Report of Operations 3d Division, July 14 to August 1, 1918," submitted August 5, 1918. 3rd Division Historical Files, Record Group 120-AEF, NARA.

Lough, Major Maxon. "Report of Operations, Third Battalion, 38th Infantry, July 17–21, 1918." 3rd Division Historical Files, Record Group 120-AEF, NARA.

Marchand, General Jean-Baptiste. Report of "The Two Battles of Chateau-Thierry," June 3, 1918, Headquarters, 10th Colonial Infantry Division. 3rd Division Historical Files, Record Group 120-AEF, NARA.

Mason, First Lieutenant R. S. "Supplementary Report of Examination of Prisoners Taken July 15th, 1918." 3rd Division Historical Files, Record Group 120-AEF, NARA.

Mendenhall, Major John R. "Operations of the 7th Machine Gun Battalion in the Vicinity of Chateau-Thierry, France, May 31–June 4, 1918." The Infantry School, 1929–1930, 4th Section, Fort Benning, GA.

Minoker, Second Lieutenant Joseph B. "Report of Operations of Company E, 38th Infantry." 3rd Division Historical Files, Record Group 120-AEF, NARA.

Moss, Captain R. G. "Report of Operations of Company K, 38th Infantry." 3rd Division Historical Files, Record Group 120-AEF, NARA.

Parkinson, Major P. D., regimental adjutant, 38th Infantry. "The 38th Infantry at the Marne, May 31 to July 20, 1918." Advanced Officers' Course, 1924–1925, The Infantry School, Fort Benning, GA.

Pershing, General John J. Extract from Pershing's report to Secretary of the War Newton Baker, November 20, 1918. 3rd Division Historical Files, Record Group 120-AEF, NARA.

Reid, Captain T. C. "Report of Operations of Company F, 38th Infantry, July 15–16, 1918." 3rd Division Historical Files, Record Group 120-AEF, NARA.

"Report of Examination of a German Prisoner, June 22, 1918." Fred L. Walker Papers, Hoover Institute.

Reports by various patrols north of the Marne leading up to July 15, 1918, filed by Captain H. J. Keeley, First Battalion, 38th Infantry Regiment. 3rd Division Historical Files, Record Group 120-AEF, NARA.

"Resume of the Operations of the Third Division, U.S., from May 29 to July 31, 1918." 3rd Division Historical Files, Record Group 120-AEF, NARA.

Short, Major Walter C. "The A. E. F. in the World War: The Champagne-Marne Defensive, July 15–18, 1918." Army General Services School, Fort Leavenworth, KS, nd. Military History Institute, Carlisle, PA.

Stewart, Major J. W., Corps of Engineers. "Operations and Casualty Reports, 6th Engineers, July 15–21, Inclusive. August 1, 1918." 3rd Division Historical Files, Record Group 120-AEF, NARA.

Swanton, Captain Donovan M. Extracts from "The Machine Gun Company, 30th Infantry in the Champagne-Marne Defensive." Military History Institute, Carlisle, PA, 1926–1927.

Tenth German Division. Extract: "From the Diary of the 10th Infantry Division, July 15–18, 1918." Headquarters, American Forces in Germany, Intelligence Section, General Staff, July 22, 1921. Translated from the original. 3rd Division Historical Files, Record Group 120-AEF, NARA.

"The 30th Infantry at the Marne," an unsigned and undated report. 3rd Division Historical Files, Record Group 120-AEF, NARA.

Wooldridge, Captain J. W. "Report of Operations of Company G, 38th Infantry, July 15–21, 1918." 3rd Division Historical Files, Record Group 120-AEF, NARA.

Young, Captain Sidney H., Machine Gun Company, 38th Infantry Regiment. "Report of Action July 21st–25th," submitted July 30, 1918. 3rd Division Historical Files, Record Group 120-AEF, NARA.

LETTERS

Barringer, Second Lieutenant Harrison E., Headquarters Company, 30th Infantry Regiment, to Captain Turner M. Chambliss, May 13 and 19, 1921. 3rd Division Historical Files, Record Group 120-AEF, NARA.

Blakley, First Lieutenant Edward A., Supply Officer, First Battalion, 30th Infantry Regiment, to Major Fred L. Walker, September 10, 1921. 3rd Division Historical Files, Record Group 120-AEF, NARA.

Cochrane, Craig P., to his mother, July 9, 1918. Archives and Special Collections, Amherst College, Amherst, MA.

Conley, Captain L. F., to Capt. Edward G. Herlihy, July 16, 1919. Herlihy Family Papers, Daniel E. Herlihy, Madison, MS.

Denig, Major Robert L., First Battalion, 30th Infantry Regiment, to the American Battle Monuments Commission, December 6, 1925 or 26 (year blanked out). 3rd Division, American Battle Monuments, Record Group 117-ABMC, National Archives and Records Administration (NARA), College, Park, MD.

Dickman, Major General Joseph T., Commander Third Division, to his wife, July 16, July 20, August 22, October 11, October 18 and December 12, 1918. University of Notre Dame Special Collections and Archives, South Bend, IN.

Dickman, Major General Joseph T., to Clem Dickman, his brother, August 5, October 18 and November 12, 1918. University of Notre Dame Special Collections and Archives, South Bend, IN.

Eberlin, First Lieutenant Ralph, F Company, 38th Infantry, to the American Battle Monuments Commission, February 14 and March 7, 1930. 3rd Division, American Battle Monuments Commission, Record Group 117-ABMC, NARA.

Gay, First Lieutenant James H., Jr., to Major Fred L. Walker, November 15, 1920. 3rd Division Historical Files, Record Group 120-AEF, NARA.

Henderson, Second Lieutenant George H., Headquarters Staff, 30th Infantry Regiment, to Major Fred L. Walker, September 19, 1920. 3rd Division Historical Files, Record Group 120-AEF, NARA.

Hopkins, First Lieutenant Johns, G Company, 30th Infantry Regiment, to Major Fred L. Walker, 1921. Complete date is not furnished. 3rd Division Historical Files, Record Group 120-AEF, NARA.

Hopkins, First Lieutenant Johns, to Captain Turner M. Chambliss, April 26, 1921. 3rd Division Historical Files, Record Group 120-AEF, NARA.

Focke, Elmer J., letters to his family, May 8 and June 7, 1918. Focke Papers, Dayton, Ohio, Public Library.

Herlihy, Edward G., to the American Battle Monuments Commission, April 18, 1930. 3rd Division, American Battle Monuments Commission, Record Group 117-ABMC, NARA.

Keeley, Major H. J., to the American Battle Monuments Commission, Washington, DC, May 14, 1925. 3rd Division, American Battle Monuments Commission, Record Group 117-ABMC, NARA.

Kelton, Colonel Robert H. C., Chief of Staff, Third Division, to Colonel Fox Conner, Assistant Chief of Staff, A.E.F., July 17, 18, 20 and 30, 1918. Fred L. Walker Papers, Hoover Institute, Stanford University, Stanford, CA.

Lasseigne, Captain Francis M., D Company, 30th Infantry Regiment, to Major Fred L. Walker, June 11, 1921. 3rd Division Historical Files, Record Group 120-AEF, NARA.

Lawton, First Lieutenant Iverson B., C Company, 30th Infantry Regiment, to Major Fred L. Walker, November 10, 1920. 3rd Division Historical Files, Record Group 120-AEF, NARA.

Murray, First Lieutenant Robinson, F Company, 38th Infantry Regiment, to Margaret "Peggy" Wessell Piersol, a Red Cross nurse working in Paris, June 10, June 22, June 25 and July 21, 1918. Anne Murray Morgan Papers, 1890–1996, Radcliffe College Archives, Schlesinger Library, Radcliffe Institute, Harvard University, Cambridge, MA.

Paschal, Major Paul C., Third Battalion, 30th Infantry, to Major Fred L. Walker, nd. 3rd Division Historical Files, Record Group 120-AEF, NARA.

Pershing, General John J., to Harold L. Reese, 30th Infantry Association, November 14, 1936. 3rd Division Historical Files, Record Group 120-AEF, NARA.

Plough, Second Lieutenant Paul H., to his brother, Harold, December 8, 1918. Archives and Special Collections, Amherst College, Amherst, MA.

Rakestraw, Reuben, letters published in *The Somerset Standard*, August 29, 1918, and *The Meyersdale Republican*, August 15, 1918.

Reese, First Lieutenant Harold L., to the American Battle Monuments Commission, December 6 and 16, 1926. 3rd Division, American Battle Monuments Commission, Record Group 117-ABMC, NARA.

Reese, Harold L., 30th Infantry Association, to General John J. Pershing, July 4, 1936. 3rd Division Historical Files, Record Group 120-AEF, NARA.

Rowe, Major Guy I., to his sister, July 6, 1918. Personal Papers, Rowe Family, Robert Ferguson, Valparaiso, IN.

Rowe, Major Guy I., to General Ulysses G. McAlexander, April 8, 1919. Personal Papers, Rowe Family, Robert Ferguson, Valparaiso, IN. The Library of Congress also holds a copy.

Ryan, Captain C. William, A Company, 30th Infantry Regiment, to Major Fred L. Walker, October 15, 1920. 3rd Division Historical Files, Record Group 120-AEF, NARA.

Smith, Edward F., to the American Battle Monuments Commission, February 23, 1925. 3rd Division, American Battle Monuments Commission, Record Group 117-ABMC, NARA.

Stevanus, Cook Harry, C Company, 110th Infantry Regiment, 28th Division, numerous letters held by Larry Bodes, grandson, Somerset County, PA.

Swanton, Captain Donovan, Machine Gun Company, 30th Infantry Regiment, to the American Battle Monuments Commission, January 20, 1925. 3rd Division, American Battle Monuments Commission, Record Group 117-ABMC, NARA.

Walker, Major Fred L., First Battalion, 30th Infantry Regiment, "Data regarding 30th infantry in Second Battle of the Marne," to Chief, Historical, General

Staff, September 12, 1921. 3rd Division Historical Files, Record Group 120-AEF, NARA.

Winant, First Lieutenant Frederick, Jr., Headquarters Company, 30th Infantry Regiment, to Major T. M. Chambliss, May 27, 1921. 3rd Division Historical Files, Record Group 120-AEF, NARA.

Winant, First Lieutenant Frederick, Jr., to Major Fred L. Walker, July 11, 1921. 3rd Division Historical Files, Record Group 120-AEF, NARA.

Winant, First Lieutenant Frederick, Jr., to the American Battle Monuments Commission, March 20, 1925. 3rd Division, American Battle Monuments Commission, Record Group 117-ABMC, NARA.

Wooldridge, Major Jesse W., to General Ulysses G. McAlexander, nd. *The Rock of the Marne*, undated, unpublished memoir by McAlexander. McAlexander Papers, Oregon State University, Corvallis, OR.

Wooldridge, Major Jesse W., letter written July 28, 1918, and a sworn statement by Sergeant Barney F. Salner, March 19, 1920. Jesse W. Wooldridge Papers, Hoover Institute, Stanford University, Stanford, CA.

Zimmerman, Private William O., to his sister, July 3, 1918. From the family papers held by Carson L. Bruening of Meyersdale, PA.

BOOKS

American Battle Monuments Commission. *American Armies and Battlefields in Europe: A History Guide and Reference Book*. Washington, DC: United States Printing Office, 1938.

——. *28th Division: Summary of Operations in the World War*. Washington, DC: United States Government Printing Office, 1944.

Americans in the Great War: Volume 1 The Second Battle of the Marne. Michelin Illustrated Guides to the Battlefields (1914–1918). Clermont-Ferrand, France, 1920.

Anderson, Major Thomas B. *The History of the 110th Infantry*. Pittsburgh, PA: The Association of the 110th Infantry, 1920.

Anonymous. *History of the Sixth Engineers*. New York: The Knickerbocker Press, 1920.

Asprey, Robert B. *The German High Command at War: Hindenburg and Ludendorff Conduct World War I*. New York: Quill William Morrow, 1991.

Bullard, Robert Lee. *Personalities and Reminiscences of the War*. Garden City, NY: Doubleday, Page & Company, 1925.

Butts, Colonel Edmund L. *The Keypoint of the Marne and Its Defense by the 30th Infantry*. Menasha, WI: George Banta Publishing Company, 1930.

Campaign of 1918: Americans at Second Battle of the Marne. Fort Leavenworth, KS: The General Service Schools, 1922.

Cecil, Lamar. *Wilhelm II, Volume II: Emperor and Exile, 1900–1941.* Chapel Hill, NC: The University of North Carolina Press, 1996.

Cleaves, Freeman. *Rock of Chickamauga: The Life of General George H. Thomas.* Norman, OK: University of Oklahoma Press, 1949.

Cobb, Irwin S. *Exit Laughing.* New York: Bobbs-Merrill Company, 1941.

Cochrane, Rexmond C. *Gas Warfare in World War I: The 3rd Division at Chateau-Thierry, July 1918.* U.S. Army Chemical Corps Historical Studies. Washington, DC: U.S. Army Chemical Corps Historical Office, 1959.

Commandini, Adele (Editor). *I Saw Them Die: Diary and Recollections of Shirley Millard.* New York: Harcourt, Brace and Company, 1936.

Coode, Stephen L. (Dissertation). *The American Expeditionary Forces in World War I: The Rock of the Marne.* Johnson City, TN: East Tennessee State University, 2008.

Coulter, Henry W. *History of the 110th Infantry of the 28th Division, U.S.A., 1917–1919.* Greenburg, PA: The Association of the 110th Infantry, 1920.

Cousart, Captain James B. *Odds & Ends.* Captain Cousart's journal posted on the Internet by his grandson, Eugene M. Cousart, Jr.

Crawford, Charles. *Six Months with the 6th Brigade.* Kansas City, MO: E. B. Barnett, Publisher, 1928.

Dallas, Gregor. *At the Heart of the Tiger: Clemenceau and His World, 1841–1929.* New York: Carroll & Graf Publishers, 1993.

——. *1918: War and Peace.* New York: Overlook Press, 2000.

Dickman, Joseph T. *The Great Crusade: A Narrative of the World War.* New York: D. Appleton and Company, 1927.

Dupuy, R. Ernest, and Trevor Dupuy. *The Encyclopedia of Military History: From 3500 B.C. to the present,* Second Revised Edition. New York: Harper & Row Publishers, 1986.

Eisenhower, John S. D. *Yanks: The Epic Story of the American Army in World War I.* New York: The Free Press, 2001.

Farwell, Byron. *Over There: The United States in the Great War, 1917–1918.* New York: W. W. Norton & Company, 1999.

Focke, Elmer. *My Memories of the War,* a self-published book. Focke Family Papers, Dayton, Ohio, Public Library.

Fox, Charles. *Company C: Somerset County National Guardsmen and the First World War.* Somerset, PA: Historical & Genealogical Society of Somerset County, Inc., 2005.

Gibbons, Floyd. *"And They Thought We Wouldn't Fight."* New York: George H. Doran Company, 1918.

Gorlitz, Walter. *The Kaiser and His Court*, American Edition. New York: Harcourt, Brace & World, Inc., 1964.

Harbord, James G. *The American Army in France: 1917–1918*. Boston: Little Brown and Company, 1936.

Harris, Stephen L. *Harlem's Hell Fighters: The Africa-American 369th Infantry in World War I*. Dulles, VA: Brassey's, Inc., 2003.

Hart, Captain B. H. Liddell. *The Real War, 1914–1918*. Boston: Little, Brown, and Company, 1931.

Haythornthwaite, Philip J. *The World War One Source Book*. London: Arms and Armour Press, 1992.

History of the Sacramento Valley, California, Vol. III, J.W. Wooldridge, Sacramento, CA, 1931.

History of the Third Division, United States Army, in the World War, For the Period December 1, 1917 to January 1, 1919. Andernach-on-the Rhine: Published by the Third Division, 1919.

Hogg, Ian V. *Dictionary of World War I*. Lincolnwood, IL: NTC Publishing Group, 1994.

Infantry in Battle. Washington, DC: The Infantry Journal Incorporated, 1939.

Intelligence Section of the General Staff of the American Expeditionary Forces. *Histories of Two Hundred and Fifty-One Divisions of the German Army Which Participated in the War (1914–1918)*. Chaumont, France, 1919.

Johnson, Douglas V. II, and Rolfe L. Hillman, Jr. *Soissons 1918*. College Station, TX: Texas A & M University Press, 1999.

Kelton, Colonel Robert H. C. "The Champagne-Marne Operation, July 15–17," Chapter XI of *The Medical Department of the United States Army in the World War, Volume III, Field Operations*. Washington, DC: Government Printing Office, 1925.

Lovejoy, C. E. *The Story of the Thirty-Eighth*. Coblenz, Germany: Görres- Druckerei, 1919.

Ludendorff, General. *My War Experiences, 1914–1918, Volume II*. London: Hutchinson & Co., 1919.

——. *The General Staff and Its Problems, Volume II*. New York: E. P. Dutton and Company, 1920.

Ludendorff, Margarethe. *My Married Life with Ludendorff*, translated by Raglan Somerset. London: Hutchinson & Co., 1929.

Lutz, Ralph Haswell (Editor). *The Causes of the German Collapse in 1918*. Hoover War Library Publications, No. 4. Stanford University Press, California, 1934.

McAlexander, Ulysses G. *The Rock of the Marne*. Unpublished manuscript, nd. Special Collections and Archives Research Center, Oregon State University, Corvallis, OR.

——. *History of the Thirteenth United States Infantry*, Regimental Press, Thirteenth Infantry, Frank D. Dunn, 1905. Special Collections and Archives Research Center, Oregon State University, Corvallis, OR.

McEntee, Girard Lindsley. *Military History of the World War: A Complete Account of the Campaigns On All Fronts Accompanied by 456 Maps and Diagrams.* New York: Charles Scribner's Sons, 1937.

McManus, John C. *American Courage, American Carnage: 7th Infantry Chronicles, The 7th Infantry Regiment's Combat Experience, 1812 Through World War II.* New York: Tom Doherty Associates Book, 2009.

Mitchell, Brigadier General William. *Memoirs of World War 1.* New York: Random House, 1960.

Mott, Colonel T. Bentley (Translator). *The Memoirs of Marshal Foch.* Garden City, NY: Doubleday, Doran and Company, Inc., 1931.

Neiberg, Michael S. *The Second Battle of the Marne.* Bloomington and Indianapolis: Indiana University Press, 2008.

O'Connor, Richard. *Thomas: Rock of Chickamauga.* New York: Prentice-Hall, Inc., 1948.

Palmer, Frederick. *Bliss, Peacemaker: The Life and Letters of General Tasker Bliss.* New York: Dodd, Mead & Company, 1934.

——. Newton D. Baker: *America at War.* New York: Dodd, Mead & Company, 1931.

Pennsylvania in the World War: An Illustrated History of the Twenty-Eighth Division, Vols. I and II. Pittsburgh and Chicago: States Publications Society, 1921.

Pershing, General John J. *My Experiences in the First World War.* New York: De Capo Press, 1995.

Proctor, H. G. *The Iron Division, National Guard of Pennsylvania, in the World War.* Philadelphia: The John C. Winston Company, 1918.

Ridout, George W. *The Cross and Flag: World War I Experiences.* Louisville, KY: Pentecostal Publishing Co., 1919.

Roosevelt, Theodore. *Rank and File: True Stories of the Great War.* New York: Charles Scribner's Sons, 1928.

Ryan, Stephen. *Pétain the Soldier.* New York: A. S. Barnes and Company, 1969.

Stallings Laurence. *The Doughboys: The Story of the AEF, 1917–1918.* New York: Harper & Row, 1963.

Stevenson, David. *Cataclysm: The First World War as Political Tragedy.* New York: Basic Books, 2004.

Stump, Al. *Cobb. The Life and Times of the Meanest Man Who Ever Played Baseball.* Chapel Hill, NC: Algonquin Books, 1994.

Survey of World War Veterans of Somerset County, Pennsylvania. Somerset County, PA: Commissioners of Somerset County, nd.

Sweeney, Edwin R. (Editor). *Making Peace with Cochise: The 1872 Journal of Captain Joseph Alton Sladen*. Norman, OK: University of Oklahoma Press, 1997.

Terraine, John. *Douglas Haig, The Educated Soldier*. London: Hutchinson & Co., 1963.

Third Division Citations. Andernach on the Rhine, Carl Reinartz printer, 1919.

Toland, John. *No Man's Land 1918: The Last Year of the Great War*. New York: Konecky & Konecky, 1980.

Thomas, Captain Shipley. *The History of the A. E. F.* Nashville, TN: The Battery Press, 2000.

28th Division Summary of Operations in the World War. Washington, DC: American Battle Monuments Commission, 1944.

United States Army in the World War, 1917–1919. Vol. 3: Training and Use of American Units with the British and French. Washington, DC: Center of Military History, United States Army, 1989.

United States Army in the World War, 1917–1919. Vol. 4: Military Operations of the American Expeditionary Forces. Washington, DC: Center of Military History, United States Army, 1989.

United States Army in the World War, 1917–1919. Vol. 5: Military Operations of the American Expeditionary Forces. Washington, DC: Center of Military History, United States Army, 1989.

United States Army in the World War, 1917–1919. Vol. 15: Reports of the Commander-in-Chief, Staff Sections and Services. Washington, DC: Center of Military History, United States Army, 1991.

U.S. General Services Schools. *The German Offensive of July 15, 1918*. Fort Leavenworth, KS: The General Services Schools Press, 1923.

Viereck, George Sylvester (Editor). *As They Saw Us: Foch, Ludendorff and Other Leaders Write Our War History*. Garden City, NY: Doubleday, Doran and Company, 1929.

Walker, Major Fred L. *Notes of Fred L. Walker (Capt.—Maj.—Lt. Col.) of His Experiences in World War I*. Unpublished memoir, nd, held by Fred Walker, Herndon, VA, and the Fred L. Walker Papers, Hoover Institute, Stanford University, Stanford, CA.

Wilhelm, Crown Prince of Germany. *The Memoirs of the Crown Prince of Germany*. London: Thornton Butterworth Ltd., 1922.

Winter, Denis. *Haig's Command: A Reassessment*. London: Viking, 1991.

Wooldridge, Jesse W. *The Giants of the Marne: A Story of McAlexander and His Regiment*. Salt Lake City: Seagull, 1923.

——. *The Rock of the Marne: A Chronological Story of the 38th Regiment, U.S. Infantry*. Privately printed, 1920.

Yockelson, Mitchell A. *Borrowed Soldiers: Americans Under British Command, 1918*. Norman, OK: University of Oklahoma Press, 2008.

INDEX